MIGHTY LITTLE MAN

MY STORY, HIS STORY, OUR STORY

To Sam,
Purrs & headbutts,
Jonny Payne

— *By* —

Jonathon Scott Payne

ISBN: 1493634046
ISBN 13: 9781493634040
Library of Congress Control Number: 2014908716
CreateSpace Independent Publishing Platform
North Charleston, South Carolina

DISCLAIMER: GI Joe®, Johnny West®, Barbie®, Star Trek®, Coca-Cola®, and M&M's®, are registered trademarks of Hasbro, Inc.; Toytrackerz, LLC; Mattel, Inc.; Paramount Pictures Corporation; The Coca Cola Company Corporation; and Mars, Inc.; respectively. Harley-Davidson® and Catisfaction Cat Clinic® are registered trademarks of H-D U.S.A, LLC, and Catisfaction Cat Clinic, Inc., respectively. Bugs Bunny® is a registered trademark of Warner Bros, Entertainment, Inc. Hemi®, Cuda®, and Barracuda® are registered trademarks of Chrysler Group, LLC. No intellectual ownership of these companies or their products or services is intended or implied.

Front cover image by Jonathon Scott Payne.
Copyright © 2013 Jonathon Scott Payne.

For an unnamed kitten ...

CONTENTS

PROLOGUE

Some people think I'm smart. There are those in my own family who think I must be the "champion" of everything I've ever attempted. The truth is I have them all fooled. I am neither the smartest nor the best at anything at all. If I were to describe myself in only two words, I would have to say I'm simply, "determinedly persistent."

Nothing has ever been easy for me, regardless of what my friends and family think. I have approached all my personal goals, interests, and needs the same way every time, and that is by simple, bull-headed persistence. When I set my mind to accomplish something, or even if I become genuinely interested in something, I pursue it with my whole heart—it becomes my passion.

One passion began at a young age when I decided I wanted to be a military man. I wanted to follow in my step-grandfather's footsteps and become a paratrooper, but I also wanted to fly for the United States Air Force. Another was when I decided it was time to restore my very first car. By the time I got around to it, it was a rust-bucket. But it was my baby, so in my mind no effort was too great. In each case, I went all-out in my pursuits, and I knew even then that I was passionate about them all.

I once heard someone say, "Don't ever let anyone tell you, 'you can't.' You may not be *allowed*, but never accept *can't*."

In addition to that profound statement, I also learned an extremely valuable lesson somewhere along the way: if a goal is worth pursuing, it's worth doing whatever it takes to make it a reality. These two things most definitely served me well in the pursuit of my passions.

As I grew older, however, I realized I had another passion. This one wasn't as obvious, even to me. In fact, it would not be until I was in my fifties and in the middle of one of the most heart-wrenching events of my life that I would realize it even existed. Perhaps it was my persistent approach to other things that prepared me to face what was to come and allow the passion to reveal itself to me. I may never really know why I feel the way I do. But what is clear is that this is likely the strongest of all my passions. Even at times when I wasn't aware of it, it was there throughout my career in the military, the restoration of my car, and all the ups and downs of my life.

I have a passion for animals, especially family pets, and most specifically—cats.

For most of my life, there has been at least one cat in the house. One of the very first pictures taken of me was with Fluffy, a calico who was the matriarchal house cat. I was only an infant, not yet walking, and that picture of Fluffy as she stood dutifully right next to me, as though *she* were the true object of the photograph, reveals the beginning of a lifetime with my furry, little friends.

Jonny and Fluffy; 1961.

Some people seem surprised to learn I am a cat person since men are stereotypically seen as dog people. But I *am* a cat person. I'm also an engineer with a military career behind me. I'm southern born and bred. I'm a Harley-Davidson riding, gun loving, pickup truck driving, muscle car building, GI Joe collecting nut. I can be eerily calm under pressure—well, externally at least. I can be very outspoken, almost to a fault, especially regarding things devoid of common sense. I'd like to think I would not hesitate to pull the trigger in defense of my family or my country. With luck, I'll never have to find out.

But as tough as all that may seem, another truth about me is that I turn into the biggest of babies when it comes to my cats. I *love* my cats. Well, I love all animals really.

I suppose I'd have to hold my mother responsible for that. Mama is a huge cat and animal lover and she always had pets in our home. I'm like her in many ways, especially with animals. Mama is all of four-foot nine-inches tall and a whopping ninety pounds soaking wet, but don't cross her. She can become ferocious in the blink of an eye. When it comes to animals, she's like a mother bear protecting her cub, and the size of her opponent makes no difference whatsoever. Remember, dynamite comes in small packages.

As a result of growing up in my mother's house, baby-talking is usually the way I communicate with animals, especially cats. But even through the baby-talk, I think cats understand exactly what I'm saying, even if they sometimes act as though they don't. And every cat person knows their cats most definitely talk to *them*. A simple meow can mean anything from, "*I'm hungry*," to, "*Pet me now*." It's a matter of being able to listen and *feel* what they want—and most importantly—obey.

I've "owned" dozens of cats; or rather, they owned me. Several hung around for only a short time—sometimes weeks or even months. Others were with me for their lifetime. Though I loved them all, there was occasionally one who reached into my heart more than the others did. But even among the special ones, there is one special cat who stands out.

His name is Little Man.

It's very hard to specify just what it is that makes us all so attached to our pets. Losing a pet can be one of the most painful things in life. I often ask myself, why?

I suppose it's because, as caretakers for our pets, we provide for all of their needs, and when we are sick, they cuddle up to us and give us love and warmth. We are essentially all they have. We invest the time, money, and extraordinary effort to ensure their well-being, and in return, we share an incredible bond that not even death can break. As many of us know, sometimes all it takes is one look from our pets to make our hearts melt.

Little Man and I share a bond like that.

No book about Little Man and me would be complete without an understanding of who we were prior to his life-threatening incident, and certainly not without discussing his predecessors. After all, it's those whom we meet and know that contribute to who we are today, and animals are no exception. They most certainly contribute too, in their own unique ways.

This is my story.

This is Little Man's story.

This is our story.

CHAPTER 1 –

MY CHILDHOOD "PETS"

I think my mother knew very early on that I was going to be an animal lover like her. When I was still too young for kindergarten, she took me to see the movie *Old Yeller*. I watched intently, but never uttered a sound. When Old Yeller died at the end, my mother was in tears. I was like a stone.

During the drive to my grandparents' house after the movie, she asked, "Jonny, did you like the movie?"

I didn't answer.

There was silence in the car during the rest of the trip. When we finally arrived, I jumped out of the car, ran into the house, confronted Pop and Wanna, my names for my step-grandfather and grandmother, and screamed with tears streaming down my face, "THEY KILLED MY DOG!"

I was hooked. But I came by it honestly—from both sides of my family.

When my mother was eight years old, she befriended a kitten. Pets weren't allowed in the apartment complex where she lived, so the landlord told her she couldn't keep it. In response, she went on a hunger strike. She put several blankets on the ground outside, and she sat with that kitten constantly. Finally, she won. That kitten grew to become Fluffy, the cat in the photograph with me as a child.

Right about that same time, the man who would become my father had a dog he shared with his brother. One day as the dog was out running around the neighborhood, someone called animal control to come pick it up. My future grandmother, Maw Maw, as she is known today, got wind of it and ran out, found the dog, and brought it into the house just as the animal control men came to the front porch.

Maw Maw reached into the house and pulled out a shotgun. She rested it against the side of the house right next to the front door, stared those men down, and said, "Y'all aren't takin' my dog."

They didn't.

Although there were several others, the earliest recollection I have of family pets would have to be of Sugar, a black cat who sucked on the tip of her tail to the point she wore the hair right off, and Duchess, a monster of a German shepherd. There was also Chu Chu, a snotty-nosed little Chinese Pug. I don't remember what happened to Sugar or Chu Chu, and for the longest time I thought we had to give Duchess away because she gave the garbage collector such a bad time. In actuality, Duchess got out of our fenced back yard and was hit by a car. That occurred when I was in the first grade, but I was fifty years old before Mama told me the truth. Guess I'm still just her "oldest baby boy" and in need of her protection.

My parents divorced when I was very young, and it wasn't until after she married my stepfather and we moved out into the country into a little, two-bedroom farmhouse on seven acres that the really interesting things happened. The place was small but very quiet and comfortable with a huge twin-oak tree in the center of the yard. That tree looked like something out of a painting. It even had a tire swing. I loved climbing in that tree.

There were two pastures, a large one and a smaller one. The smaller one had a little red barn about fifty yards from the tree line along the edge of our property. My stepfather was a lineman for the power company, and one day he strung a cable from the bottom of the barn all the way across the smaller pasture to a tree about twenty feet up. He took a hollow pipe about a foot long, spread some grease on the inside of it, tied a rope to it, rigged up a catch to hold it up in the tree, and then turned my brother and me loose. We had a blast. Sliding down that cable was hilariously fun, especially after a big rain since the ground was soft and muddy. However, I don't think Mama was very fond of those times since she had to wash all our muddy clothes.

Across the old country road from our house was an elderly couple who owned eighty acres. Their two-story house was made entirely of rock and had fifty-two windows. They lived upstairs. The downstairs was full of antiques. At the corner of their immaculate yard was a small tree that was just the perfect size for my GI Joe action figures. I had a great time posing my soldiers around that tree. My gosh, I do miss those times.

As for our animals, there was Cindy, the roughest, toughest, meanest little Chihuahua in the entire world. She was born with a crooked jaw that caused her tongue to stick out the side of her mouth, and she had to be bottle fed at birth. She weighed about five pounds at her heaviest, had the most irritating bark ever heard, and was convinced she was actually a Great Dane. I've witnessed Cindy chase grown men onto the nearest piece of furniture in their efforts to get away from that little terror of a dog. And she loved to chase the cows. The cows would run at first, then turn around and chase her right back. I think she did that on purpose. It was just her way of having fun and controlling everyone and everything around her.

In addition to Cindy, we had four cows, a few chickens, one goat, two unbroken horses, two ducks, a Beagle that was allergic to grass, and a squirrel that lived in a tree in our yard.

That Beagle sneezed her way through life. If she wasn't within eyeshot, she could always be found by just quietly listening. All it took was a quiet moment on the back porch. In no time we would hear a sneeze and look in the direction of the sound and see the tall grass in the pasture rustling…there she was.

Of course, Mama being the way she was, every animal was spoiled rotten. Pretty Boy was a multicolored fighting rooster with a big, sharp spur on the back of each leg. Every evening, Mama would go outside, pick up Pretty Boy, and set him on a tree branch to spend the night. Then every morning she would step outside, take him from the tree branch, and set him back on the ground. Good grief.

And I can't forget about the kiddie pool Mama bought—for the ducks.

One morning at about three o'clock, we were awakened by my stepfather yelling, "Everybody up! The cows broke through the fence! Let's go round 'em up!"

It was a cloudy, stormy night, and he had come home late after repairing some downed power lines. It was pitch-black outside. Streetlights in our area were nonexistent.

I grabbed some clothes, dressed, and headed out. I thought I could hear a cow or two down the little country road from our house, but could barely see my hand in front of my face. If I looked hard enough, I could see the edge of the ditch running along the side of the road. I started a slow jog in the direction of the noise.

BAM!

I ran right into one of those cows, bounced off, and fell straight to the ground.

"Found one!" I yelled.

That cow turned to look at me as if to say, "*Hey! Watch where you're going, will ya?*"

I pushed and prodded her back into the pasture.

Then there was Ol' 77. Ol' 77 was an Angus bull my stepfather purchased to fatten and sell to the butcher for meat. Mama spent countless hours at the fence, feeding, petting, and talking to Ol' 77. 77 was the number on the yellow ear tag stapled to his ear.

After we had him for a couple of years, it was time to take Ol' 77 to the auction. After he was sold, his ear tag was removed and he was placed in a pen with several hundred other cows and bulls. Mama couldn't stand the thought of Ol' 77 being butchered, but she knew there wasn't a thing she could do about it. She couldn't leave without telling him goodbye, but how to find him?

She walked over to the pen holding all the sold cows, climbed up on the highest post, and with tears streaming down her face, yelled at the top of her lungs, "OL' 77!"

He came a-running, just like he had for the last couple of years, and Mama got to say her tearful goodbyes.

After Ol' 77 was gone, we had two cows bred to a bull to grow our little herd again. As a grade-schooler about ten years old, I thought it was cool the day I witnessed the birth of two calves. A couple of weeks after they were born, my younger brother Jeff and I went out in the pasture, got down on our hands and knees, and played with the calves like they were dogs. We playfully head-butted and tackled and petted them. Boy-howdy, was that a mistake. They grew into full-sized animals, but still wanted to play with us like they had when they were little. I owe my life to a little creek running along the pasture right next to a barbed-wire fence separating the pasture from our yard. Many times I could go out in the pasture, but only if I carried a broom handle to fight off those cows, and when that didn't work I'd have to jump over the creek and hang on to the fence until they tired of waiting for me to play some more.

One day my stepfather and his crew were clearing trees to make room for some power poles. As one tree fell, he noticed a squirrel's nest on one of the branches. As he approached it, he could see a little, baby squirrel that began to run away. He caught it by throwing his hard hat over it. He placed it in a little cage and brought it home. Of course, Mama was thrilled, and before anyone could prevent it, she reached right in that cage and had her finger bitten by that little squirrel. We named him Hickernut.

Hickernut was fairly tame in no time. It wasn't long before he grew tired of his cage, so we decided to just turn him loose in the yard. He made himself right at home in the trees next to the house. We soon discovered he loved M&M's. Many times, he would come on the front porch and try to bury his M&M's in Mama's flower pots, forcing her to chase him off with a broom.

I credit Hickernut with helping me develop the patience sometimes needed in dealing with animals. Some of my fondest memories are of Hickernut. I used to grab a few M&M's and head out the door, stand at the bottom of one of those trees and call out, "Hickernut," and there he would come, climbing down head-first toward me and my candy. I'd place my fist against the tree trunk, and then put an M&M on my shoulder. Hickernut would sniff at my fist for a while, but soon he would realize his treat was on my shoulder. Without hesitation, he would crawl right down my arm, sit on my shoulder, and enjoy his treat. Sometimes, if I was careful enough, he even let me gently pet him. What an experience that was!

The only animal I had yet to pet during those days was the goat. Eventually, I was able to practice enough patience to make him comfortable enough for me to get close. But not until I learned a valuable lesson.

I was trying to get close enough to pet him one day, but he kept running away from me. We had a pile of old boards stacked next to one side of our many fences, and the goat ran over the top of them and stopped on the other side. I followed, but stopped short of getting closer when I reached the top of the pile. I stood there for a moment or two and waited to see his next move before he finally ran off. I started after him, but tripped because something snagged my shoe. I stumbled backward and felt a nail go between the toes of my right foot. As I pulled my shoe off the nail, I saw blood. Then the pain started.

A trip to the doctor for a tetanus shot revealed not one hole in my foot, but two. Apparently, when I stopped at the top of that pile of lumber, I was standing there with a nail in my foot and never knew it. Then when I tried to move, the nail came out of my foot and reentered when I fell backward. When I thought the nail went between my toes it actually went between my foot bones. Ouch! I never did anything like that again. Eventually I was able to pet the goat on occasion, but that quickly ended because that goat just didn't like being touched.

One lazy, summer afternoon, we decided we were going to ride Princess, our mare. We grabbed an old saddle out of the barn, threw it on her back, and cinched it up—but the girth was nowhere near tight enough. I climbed up and walked her about ten feet when the saddle slid off and hung directly under her belly as I tried to hang on for dear life. I promptly dropped to the ground and crawled away in a hurry. I wasn't about to make that mistake again.

Jeff decided it was his turn, so we rounded up Princess again, tightened the girth, and up he went on her back. She was going to have none of that. She started bucking, and in two shakes Jeff was flying through the air. He landed with a thump, jumped up, and ran toward the gate with Princess chasing him right on his heels. We found another home for her soon afterward.

Our other horse, Dan, was one of the most beautiful animals I've ever seen. He was solid black with a long, flowing mane and loved to run back and forth in the large pasture. Since he had never been broken, he could be petted only from the other side of the fence. He was marvelous to watch, but not much fun otherwise, so he was sold, too.

It wasn't long before the queen arrived, and her name was LuLu. LuLu was a blue point Siamese cat, and she was beautiful. I don't remember where we got her, but she was definitely Mama's cat. When Mama became pregnant with my brother Jason, she couldn't bend over to pick up LuLu. She would just grab her by the tail and lift her right off the floor and into her arms. It took some getting used to, but soon LuLu would rub up against Mama with her tail stretched straight up into the air expecting to be picked up. She was spoiled rotten in no time.

LuLu disappeared more than once for a week or so to give birth. We never kept any of her kittens, but made sure to find good homes for them. She made a little den under the house one time, and my mother, who by that time was nine months pregnant, did not hesitate to crawl under the house to make sure she was all right.

Once, however, LuLu disappeared for weeks. To this day, I can remember asking, "Mama, what happened to LuLu?"

Tearfully, Mama replied, "She's just gone, honey. I'm not sure we'll ever see her again."

That was that … or so I thought.

Shortly thereafter, on a particularly stormy night after a trip to the grocery store, I was bringing grocery bags into the house through the front door.

Suddenly, Mama screamed from the kitchen, "LuLu!"

I dropped the bags on the floor, ran to the kitchen, and saw LuLu sitting on the kitchen floor just inside the back door looking like nothing at all had ever happened. But here's the kicker: she was bone dry! To this day, Mama swears LuLu was abducted by aliens. How else could she be gone for weeks and then return, bone dry, in the middle of a heavy rainstorm?

One night during another storm, several tornadoes came through our area. We didn't know about them at the time since it was long before there were any kind of warning systems or announcements by the weathermen on the radio or on the three stations we got on the television. As my mother washed dishes, lightning came in through the window, struck the dishwater, and knocked her right off her feet. The plugs for the washer and dryer next to the kitchen were blown out of the wall. Mama snatched up LuLu, my brothers, and me, and we all headed to my grandparents' house. Had we not left, we would have been stranded with no way to get out for groceries or anything else. Trees were down all over the road, and power was out for days. It was a full week before we could return home. Of course, we had another round of searching for the cows when we finally arrived back at the house. Oh boy.

Mama's marriage to my stepfather lasted eight years. After the divorce, the four of us—Mama, Jeff, Jason, and I—moved into an apartment in town. All the animals were gone except for LuLu. LuLu was there to stay.

☙ ☙ ☙

While we had LuLu, Pop and Wanna had Bitzy. Bitzy was the granddaughter of Fluffy. She was solid black with a small tuft of white fur on her chest. She was also the runt of the litter; hence the name. Like Mama and me, Pop loved cats. In fact, he spoiled Bitzy to no end. She got to sample just about everything Pop ever cooked, and Pop could *cook*. Soon, Bitzy was not a little bitty thing like she was when she was named. She was fat and sassy and about as happy as any cat could be.

She also had some peculiar habits. She used to dive-bomb Pop and Wanna from the windowsill every morning in her efforts to wake them. When that didn't work, she discovered she could push the snooze button on their alarm clock and make the alarm sound at will. I have no idea why that old alarm clock worked that way, but it did.

Bitzy was a pistol.

☙ ☙ ☙

It wasn't long before Mama, Jeff, Jason, LuLu, and I found a nice little house, close to school, in a quiet, little neighborhood. Things seemed to be going well, but soon there were financial troubles. It was also the time of one of the most disturbing and heart-wrenching events of my young life.

Jeff had found a kitten. It was just weeks old, a female with wispy, gray fur. She was a sweetheart. We had her for only about a week when she got out of the house for several hours before Jeff found her. She had been brutally

8

attacked by a dog and was barely alive. She didn't look that bad at first, but soon her injuries became evident. It broke my heart. We carried her to my mother.

Mama looked her over. With tears in her eyes, she said, "I don't know what to do. We don't have the money to take her to the vet, and the car needs gas anyway."

Jeff and I replied in unison, "But we have to do *something*!"

Another look at that kitten revealed she was bleeding from both ears and her nose and mouth, and she couldn't stand up. She also had very labored breathing, and cried at the slightest touch. She was dying, obviously from internal injuries.

My mother thought for a moment, dried up her tears, and said, "All right boys. I need you to be very grown-up about this. I'm going to need you to do something."

I was only about fourteen years old, but I thought I knew what was coming. This was *Old Yeller* all over again, only this time it was real.

Mama asked my brother, "Jeff, don't you have a friend down the road who has a .22 rifle?"

Oh God, no.

"Yes, Ma'am," he answered.

"I need you both to go ask him for it. We're going to have to put this little kitten down. She's suffering, and we need to do the right thing."

Jeff and I looked at each other, and without a word, we turned and walked out of the house. Jeff carried the kitten. We both knew there were no words for what we felt.

Jeff is three years younger than I am. His friend was about fifteen or sixteen, and a good kid. We explained what had happened and what we needed to do, so he asked his father for the rifle. One look at us with that kitten was enough to get my brother's friend to volunteer to go with us to do what had to be done. He volunteered to be the one to pull the trigger. He knew it would have been extremely painful for either Jeff or for me. We were all teary-eyed.

There were some woods behind our row of houses, and we carried that sweet, little thing, the rifle, and a shovel about one hundred yards into the woods to a little clearing.

Jeff placed the kitten on the ground, and she cried softly with a gurgled sound. More blood came out. Although she was the one dying, I was sure I felt worse.

I said, "I can't stand to see her like this. Please don't miss, and make it so it only takes one shot."

Suddenly, the kitten stood up. She took a few steps toward us, shook her head a little, and steadied herself in a sitting position.

What? I thought. *Maybe she's okay. Maybe we can...*

A shot rang out. Although the aim was true, the bullet did not do the job. We watched in abject horror as the kitten jerked and writhed for several seconds. Although I don't think she was conscious, her little body autonomously kicked at her head with her hind legs in a slow but steady, repetitive motion, and all the while she was completely silent. She never made another sound.

But she, or rather her body, didn't stop kicking.

"You're going to have to shoot her again!" Jeff said.

"I only brought one bullet! I'll have to go home and get another one," his friend replied.

"Run," was all I could say.

It took only about five minutes for him to return with more ammunition, but it was the longest five minutes of my life. To our amazement, the kitten was still kicking at her head. As quickly as he could, Jeff's friend put another round into his single-shot rifle, took careful aim, held his breath, and pulled the trigger. Finally, the kitten was at peace.

We dug a little hole, placed her gently into it, covered her with dirt, and placed a few rocks on top of the dirt. We thanked Jeff's friend and he took the rifle and shovel and walked away.

Jeff and I just stood there for a minute or two. We didn't speak. There were simply no words for what we felt. He turned to go back to our house, but I couldn't move. Jeff waited for me. I stared down at that little grave and wished there had been something—*anything*—I could have done to prevent what happened. I felt horrible. I didn't know what to do. I didn't know what to say. Finally, we walked home together in silence.

When we got back to the house, Jeff went straight to his room. He was obviously deeply affected, especially being the one to find her in the beginning and then again after the attack. But he never really showed much emotion. I went to Mama. I did not tell her what happened, and no words were spoken. We just held each other for a minute or so. Then I went straight to LuLu as she napped on top of the couch, buried my face in her fur, and just breathed in her scent. She lifted her head and kissed me on the cheek.

LuLu.

I thanked God for LuLu. She knew, and she helped me get through that painful time. I have never spoken of that horrible day since.

The kitten never even had a name.

I grew up an awful lot that day. Something happened to me, and it's something I cannot possibly put into words. That kitten died decades ago, but the pain is still there. Her short life gave me a better understanding of the preciousness of all of God's creatures. It's not that I didn't appreciate them before, it's just that now I have a much more profound sense of their worth. Even today, I can remember standing over that little grave as though it were yesterday, and I thank God for giving us such precious little critters, even if He takes them away after what seems to us like too little time spent with them. But more than that, the feeling of helplessness I felt all those years ago when we had to put that kitten down has given me something that has stayed with me unto this day: the drive and determination to never let anything like that ever happen again.

CHAPTER 2 –
HIGH SCHOOL AND COLLEGE

When I turned sixteen, my father gave me a car for my birthday. It wasn't new, but it was cool nonetheless. It had been involved in an accident and slid into a tree. The driver's side headlight was crumpled, and it had a dent in the roof from a limb that fell from the tree. Mechanically it was fairly sound, but it needed some work. My father repainted it before he gave it to me. I vowed to one day "fix it up." Believe it or not, I still have it to this day. It's a 1972 'Cuda 340. She's bad, and she's my baby. I drove her all through high school. Love that hot-rod!

During my junior year in high school, a stray cat just decided one day that our house was his home. We named him Tommy. He was hilariously funny, and loved to chase the balls on the old pool table we had in the basement. He was still a young cat, so he could get his head almost all the way down the holes in the pool table. He did that quite often until he got his head caught between two balls as they were rolling down the track underneath the table to one end where they were collected for reuse. I remember his head popping back up out of that hole. He stood there with a funny look on his face, shook his head a little to reset his gyros, then jumped down. He didn't get back up on the pool table much after that … poor Tommy.

🐾   🐾   🐾

Although my grandmother on my father's side remarried when I was only seven years old, it was not until I was in high school that I learned about my step-grandfather's past: he was a paratrooper during World War II and fought in the Battle of the Bulge. I was in awe of him. I decided I wanted to go to Jump School and earn my jump wings, just as he had.

A little later, I decided I wanted to be an Air Force officer. Since there was no way either of my divorced parents could pay for my schooling, I had to find another way. My grades were good, so I felt I had a fair shot at a scholarship. I started to research the possibilities and wound up in my school counselor's office. That was where I learned about the United States Air Force Academy. My mind was made up and I started the process. It literally takes "an act of Congress" to gain admission to a service academy. Candidates must receive at least one nomination from the President, a Congressman, or a Senator to be eligible for consideration by the selection board. I accidentally ran into our Congressman while he was on a reelection campaign on the grounds where I worked after school as a draftsman, and a few weeks later I had a nomination. The next step was an interview with an officer.

The night the officer arrived at our house, we let him in and sat down to talk. We talked about everything about the Academy: how hard it would be, the quality of the education, the opportunities that were there, and the fact that I would graduate as a second lieutenant in the Air Force. I was excited about the possibilities.

Then we heard a knock at the door.

One of our neighbors saw Tommy get hit by a car and came to the door to let us know. The officer walked outside with us. Tommy was there on the side of the road. He was dead. There was no blood or anything, so fortunately for Tommy, it must have happened quickly. The officer scooped Tommy up, handed him to me, and the next day I buried him in the backyard. I said a little prayer and my goodbyes. Again, LuLu comforted me.

By the time I graduated from high school I received and accepted an appointment to the Academy. It's a beautiful place in Colorado Springs, Colorado. The mountains really are purple at certain times of the morning. The air is cool and clean, but the winter winds can knock people right off their feet. I liked it. It was a welcome change to the stifling heat and humidity of the Deep South in Alabama.

Before I finished the basic training course during my first six weeks at the Academy, I received the news that my grandmother, Wanna, died. Mama intentionally withheld the news from me until after the funeral because she knew I wouldn't be able to attend and didn't want me struggling with trying to figure out how to leave in the middle of training. Pop was alone. Then about a year and a half or so later, he remarried and gained a wife and two stepchildren. I was happy for him.

I was always very close to Wanna and Pop. Even though he was actually my step-grandfather, Pop married Wanna when my mother was only seven years old. Mama always told me that when she went into labor with me years later, it was Pop who had labor pains. He even had to be wheeled around the hospital in a wheel chair. My brothers and I had a remarkable childhood, and we owe much of our happiness to Wanna and Pop. Since my mother and father divorced when I was very young, Pop was more like a father than a step-grandfather. His influence is what led me to become an engineer.

During the Christmas break of my sophomore year at the Academy, I became disheartened. Mama was doing her best, but ever since Wanna died, she began to struggle with financial troubles. Things were so bad we were forced to cancel Christmas—we had no gifts, no decorations, nothing. In addition to my concerns with Mama's finances, I was doing okay academically; not great, but I was getting by. Also, I soon came to realize that those military things I wanted to do, such as realize my dream of learning to parachute, fly single-engine aircraft, and soar, would likely be unavailable to me because I was as blind as a bat and had to wear Coke-bottle glasses, or so they seemed to me, and therefore didn't qualify. Those types of things were normally reserved for people who were going to become pilots.

Shortly after arriving back at the Academy after the break, I made one telephone call to the drafting company where Pop worked. I had worked there too during high school, and when I left to attend the Academy, they told me I could come back anytime. They had a program where draftsmen could work for one semester, then alternate and go to college for one semester, repeatedly, and all tuition was paid by the company. It seemed like the answer to all our problems. I asked if the offer to work there still stood. It did, so I picked up the phone and called Mama.

Before I left home to attend the Academy, we heard stories about other cadets' parents. Some of them reportedly told their children that if they ever left the Academy, before graduation, they were not to bother to come home.

Not Mama. She made sure to tell me before I left that I was always welcome to come back home, for any reason. In fact, she told me exactly what she would say: *How fast can you get here?*

When she answered the phone, I said, "Mama, I think I need to come home."

Sure enough, she said, "How fast can you get here?"

A week later, I was home. By that time, Jeff had his own family and Jason lived with his father, my former stepfather, so it was just the two of us. Well, the two of us and LuLu.

I started work just days after I returned. Times were hard. I remember sitting at the kitchen table with Mama, combining both our paychecks and paying bills, but not having enough left over to pay half the power bill. It seemed all either of us did was work.

Any spare time I had was spent at Pop's playing pool with his new stepdaughter, Caroline, a cute sixteen-year-old, and petting Bitzy, of course. As soon as Caroline and I met, we became instantly competitive with each other. Soon, however, we were good friends. We rode around in the 'Cuda, went to a rodeo, tried some country and western dancing, and I even jumped in Pop's van one day with his whole family for an impromptu weekend trip to the beach —all on a whim—where Caroline made me put baby oil all over my body. That resulted in the worst sunburn I've ever had.

Work continued of course, but with hard work, Mama and I were able to catch everything up in surprisingly little time. Though I was looking forward to going to school the following fall, I still wanted to be an Air Force officer. I talked things over with Mama.

"Mama, I still want to go into the Air Force and be an officer, even if I can't fly. But if I do that, I most likely won't be able to work while I'm in school. Can we pull that off?"

She said, "Honey, I think we can make do. You do what you need to do for you."

Then she said something very profound, and it's something that has stayed with me unto this day.

She said, "Jonny, sometimes life grants an opportunity, and many times it will be a once-in-a-lifetime thing. When that happens, the best thing to do is just grab hold with both hands, and even with your teeth, if necessary, and don't let go."

So, I contacted the nearest Air Force Reserve Officer Training Corps, or AFROTC, and asked about the possibility of a scholarship. That's when I got a neat surprise. The Academy had already sent my name to them with a recommendation that I be asked to compete for a scholarship. They were simply waiting for my call! I started the application process, and within two months I was enrolled as a junior in an AFROTC program. My career was back on track.

Just before starting class again, I decided to do a little work on the 'Cuda. Pop had a large garage in the house he shared with Caroline and her mother, so Jeff, his wife, and I went over there to get the job done. We were going to add exhaust headers to the 'Cuda.

One weekend as we were under the car, I crawled out to check the time while Jeff remained to continue his work on an exhaust pipe. I discovered it was time for Jeff's wife to go home.

Jeff said, "I'm in a good spot and I don't want to stop. Go ahead and take her home for me and I should have this done when you get back."

I left and returned about thirty minutes later to find pieces of the exhaust pipe all over the place. The job was nowhere near completed, and Jeff was sitting in the 'Cuda listening to the radio.

I said, "I thought you said you were gonna have this done when I got back."

He replied, "I cut my finger."

"Let me see."

All I could see was a short gash about a half-inch long right across the top of his knuckle. There was hardly any blood at all. It looked more like a scratch than a cut.

"You call that a cut?" I said.

Jeff said, "Oh yeah? Check this out."

He moved his finger. I could see all the way through the joint—even in-between the bones.

I shook my head and sighed, "Let's call Mama."

Mama took Jeff to three different emergency rooms before she could get the proper care for his finger.

The first two doctors wanted to amputate it.

Shortly after I started school again, there was no more spare time for anything, not even a game of pool with Caroline, and I saw Pop and his family only rarely even though I spoke with him on the phone almost daily. But in no time Mama and I had another addition to the family to keep us occupied. A big, black and white cat decided we belonged to him and kept hanging around the house. He got into something he shouldn't have, and Mama threw a towel at him to scare him away. It landed right around his neck like he was using it to dry off after a good, hard workout at the gym, so we named him Butch.

Butch was something else. He was big and beautiful and, of course, spoiled in no time. Believe it or not, he helped me get through physics in college. I would sit at the kitchen table, spread all my laboratory data around in preparation to write my lab reports, and Butch would jump up on the table and plop down right in the middle of all my papers. I would literally have to lift his leg or his tail to see some of the information for my report, and Butch would just lie there. Moving him was out of the question. After all, he was helping.

The fact that Butch "helped" me with school was particularly strange since Butch was dumber than dirt. Butch would often get lost, but not outside. He would get lost in the hallway. There were only two directions from which to choose, and yet he would just wander around and bump into the wall.

He had a very distinctive meow that sounded just like, *Maaaaammmmahh!*

That's right, Butch could say, "Mama."

He would call for her when he got lost. Poor Butch. I've seen brighter doorknobs.

During a birthday party for my brother Jason's seventh birthday, Butch jumped up on the table and promptly caught his tail on fire from the candles on the cake.

Everybody screamed, "Mama, Butch's tail is on fire!"

She simply turned and said, "Well, put it out!"

We patted him down in an effort to put out the fire. Butch never ran or anything. As we stood there, out of breath, thanking God the house didn't go up in flames, Butch just lay there on the table, looked at his tail, gave a little sigh, licked his paw, and wiped his face. Then he yawned. He never seemed to understand what all the fuss was about. He sat on the table the whole time we were eating the birthday cake.

Although he was usually very stoic, there was one time when he got into trouble with me. Looking back, I think now that it may have been my fault, but at the time, I felt his actions were very inappropriate. I had to discipline him.

I've always been very affectionate with my cats, and Butch was no exception. To this day, I like to pick cats up and cradle them on their backs in my arms, then snuggle them face to face. They always seem to like it. But one day, Butch decided he wasn't in the mood.

I had taken a break from studying, picked him up, cradled him on his back, and started to snuggle him with my face when he hit me right between the eyes with his paw. His claw stuck in my forehead with the curved part of the claw underneath my skin. I had to take his paw in my hand and gently wiggle his claw loose from my head. I calmly put him back down on the couch, walked to the bathroom to inspect my injury, and saw a thick glop of blood running slowly down between my eyes. There was never any pain.

After I cleaned myself up, I went back toward the couch.

"Butch!" I yelled.

He took off. I caught him and held him up where I could see him face to face, and said, "Don't you *ever* do that again!"

He knew he was in trouble since I'd never before raised my voice like that to him. He looked down with a look of shame, and my heart melted. I'm such a softie. I hugged him tight and stroked his fur, and he purred right back. We were buddies again.

One of the coolest things about Butch was that he was very protective of LuLu. One day while Butch was under the bottom step of the deck leading from the back door to the yard, LuLu flew over the fence with an angry tomcat right on her heels. She ran up the steps to the deck right over Butch's head, through the doggie-, um, kitty-door, and into the house. Butch, timing his move perfectly, crawled out from under the step and stood right in the path of that tomcat. He never made a sound. He just stood there with his incredible bulk and waited for that tomcat to sign his own death warrant. The tomcat froze in mid-step, too terrified to move. I watched the whole thing from the kitchen window.

I called out to my mother, "Mama! You gotta come see this!"

She came running, saw what was happening, went out on the deck and started yelling, "Shoo! SHOOOO!"

But that tomcat was too terrified to move lest he antagonize the monstrosity of Butch staring him down.

Finally, Mama got two pots from the kitchen, carried them out onto the deck, and started banging them together. The tomcat took off, terrified. Butch hardly moved. He just sighed, turned around slowly, and resumed his watch under the steps. Butch was awesome—dumb, but awesome.

One Saturday morning, Butch was the subject of a most unusual "experiment."

Mama and I awoke to find the house looking like a crime scene. There was blood all over the place, and it was smeared in several places as though a struggle had taken place. We weren't sure what to think at first, but then realized it must be from one of the cats. We immediately rounded up each one. Finally, we found Butch.

He had a huge gash on one of his hind legs, apparently from an attempt to jump over a chain link fence. It was obvious he had lost a lot of blood, and he didn't look well at all. I had some papers to complete for school, so I remained behind to clean up the mess while Mama took Butch to the nearest veterinary emergency center.

After an examination, the doctor on duty realized Butch's life was in danger because he had lost so much blood. He needed a blood transfusion immediately, or he would die. Unfortunately, there was a very limited quantity of cats' blood available. They used all they had, but it was not enough. In a last-ditch effort to save him, the veterinarian gave Butch human blood.

I don't know for certain what Butch was given. I don't know if it was blood plasma, whole blood, platelets, or from where it came. It doesn't seem biologically possible for a cat to receive human blood. But whatever it was, Butch lived. I have asked Mama several times over the years if all of that is really true. Every time her answer is the same: "Yes. It's true."

Butch simply up and disappeared one day, never to be seen again. We think someone saw him and picked him up. He was, after all, a big, beautiful cat. I still miss him, and my mother and I still talk about him to this day. Yes, Butch was another special one. I was reminded of him a couple of years ago when Mama gave me her favorite book of all time, titled *The Silent Miaow*. As I opened that book for the first time in over thirty years, out fell some pictures of… Butch! They were pictures I took of him decades earlier. Oh, the memories!

Butch.

Not long after Butch disappeared, Mama and I were in the car on the way back from somewhere, and she spotted a sign. Someone was selling kittens for ten dollars each.

"Let's stop and have a look," she said.

"Mama, we need another cat like we need a hole in the head," I replied.

She stopped anyway, and got out to look around.

I told her, "Oh, go ahead, but I'm staying in the car."

About five minutes later, she appeared at the passenger's side window with a calico kitten in her arms and said, "Oh, isn't she …"

"No," was all I said.

She reached through the open window of the car and placed that kitten right in my lap. I made no attempt to hold it or anything, but I did look down. That was a mistake. The next thing I knew that kitten was curled up under my chin purring like crazy and I was reaching in my wallet for the ten dollars. What a weakling.

We named the kitten Katie, and like all the rest, she was rotten in no time.

Another stray, a mostly white male with a large black spot on one side, decided we were his. His name was obvious. We called him Spot.

Spot went everywhere I went. He slept with me, followed me all over the house, and even went into the bathroom with me. He loved to jump up on the toilet seat and watch me get ready for work or school.

Late one night, I awoke and got up to go to the bathroom. Spot jumped off the bed and ran in front of me to his usual place on the toilet. The room was pitch-black. After all, it was the middle of the night.

All of a sudden, I heard, *SPUUULLAAAAAASH!*

Spot had tried to jump up on the toilet seat, but the lid was up. I laughed so loud I woke Mama. She came in the bathroom, took one look, shook her head, and went back to bed.

CHAPTER 3 –
IN THE AIR FORCE

By the time I graduated from college and became an officer, I was married to Joy, a fellow cadet whom I met in the AFROTC program at Samford University who was working on her pharmacy degree. Before long, our first son was born, and since Joy wanted to name him after me, but wanted nothing to do with the name Junior, we named him Jonathon II. My first military assignment took us to Florida at Eglin Air Force Base. That was good since it meant we wouldn't be that far from home.

Not long after that, my mother married a man she had known since I was an infant and moved to Mississippi. Of course, LuLu was still there, too.

I was sure I was going to enjoy my time in the Air Force even if I couldn't be a flyer. But after being on active duty for only a week, another officer I didn't know walked into our unit wearing a flight suit and a strange set of wings on his chest. The wings didn't look like the pilot or navigator wings I had seen many times.

Intrigued, I asked a co-worker, "Who was that, and what does he do?"

When I was told he was a flight test engineer and graduate of the USAF Test Pilot School, and also that it was possible for me to apply and actually fly jets one day as a non-rated officer, I was excited to say the least.

A day later, I was summoned to the colonel's office for an introduction. The colonel, as commander of our unit, had a policy in which he would personally meet one-on-one with each new officer.

He asked a little about me personally, and then asked, "What is it you would like to accomplish in the United States Air Force?"

From what I had learned only the day before, I knew the answer to that question and said, "Sir, in the short term there are two things I'd like to do."

"And what might those be?" he asked.

"I want to go to Jump School at Fort Benning, and I want to be a flight test engineer and attend the Test Pilot School at Edwards."

He laughed and said, "Well, I can't help you with Jump School since we really have no need for you to attend that training, but I'll tell you what. If you can figure out a way to go at no expense to the government, and convince the Army to give you a slot, I'll sign your orders."

"Thank you, Sir."

"But as for TPS, I'm a graduate myself, so I'm very familiar with the process. My secretary can show you which forms you need to fill out to begin."

"Thank you again, Sir. I really appreciate that."

"Good luck, and welcome to the Armament Laboratory."

When I got back to my office, one of the other lieutenants working there asked me what I said to the colonel.

"I told him I want to go to Jump School and TPS," I said.

The lieutenant laughed and said, "Jump School? You can't do that."

I just looked at him without saying a word and thought to myself, *'Can't?' We'll just see about that...*

I hit the ground running and ready to do whatever it took to accomplish my goals. I immediately began trying to figure out how to attend both schools. I soon learned only a dozen or so engineers out of several hundred applicants are selected each year to attend the Test Pilot School, so the odds were against me. What I needed to do was make myself more competitive. Jump School was looking even less likely as it was an Army school, and like the colonel said, there was really no need for me to go. But I wanted to do it nonetheless. It was a chance I never really had while at the Air Force Academy, and I thought this would make up for a previously missed opportunity.

Eight months later, and to everyone's surprise, I managed to get a much sought-after slot at the United States Army Infantry School's Airborne Course, a three-week long, grueling course in which I would make five jumps in the final week to earn my jump wings. I thought again about my step-grandfather, and I couldn't wait to attend.

He never talked about what happened "over there" during the war. All I knew was what my grandmother told me: as he exited the aircraft during a combat jump, shrapnel tore through his parachute and cut a huge gash across his belly. Because of the holes in his parachute, he came down extremely hard. Upon impact with the ground, he jammed the knuckle of the middle finger of his left hand into the center of his hand. To this day, there remains a huge knot on the back of his hand, and he can't completely straighten his middle finger.

During the course of my training, I took the advice of several others with whom I worked. We all knew this course was not going to be easy, so as an incentive, if I ever got to the point where I thought I couldn't go on, I carried some miniature jump wings in my pocket to look at in the privacy of my room as an aid to give me the confidence to continue. I looked at them every day even though I never once considered quitting. I also had them with me for all five jumps I made during the course. Interestingly enough, only about two-thirds of the class made it through, and I was one of them.

What surprised me the most during that training was my lack of fear. I remember standing up, hooking up, and shuffling to the door for my first jump. I had tried so hard for so long to get there that no force on earth was powerful enough to keep me from jumping out of that door. As an officer, I was assigned as stick leader, and as such I was always the first in my stick (line of jumpers) to jump.

The hardest jump for me to make was not the first, the second, or even the third. It was the fourth. That was because I knew if I got hurt on the fourth jump, just one jump shy of completing the training, everything would be for nothing. As far as I was concerned, all I had to do was make it through the fourth jump. Then, if anything went wrong on the fifth and final jump, they could pin my wings on my carcass—but at least I would be, "Airborne!"

When I graduated from Jump School, I bought another full-sized set of jump wings and had them chrome plated as a gift for my step-grandfather. When I gave them to him, he had the most remarkable thing to say. My other accomplishments—graduating from college and becoming an officer—didn't instill much pride or excitement in him.

But when I gave him those jump wings and showed him my own that I had earned, he simply said, "Well, now you've done something."

That was all he needed to say. From that day forward, I have called him, "Airborne." My grandmother says he likes that.

🐾   🐾   🐾

After Jump School, life moved on. Since I knew Mama would never, ever, ever, let me have LuLu, we started looking for a cat of our own. It wasn't long before we found a female tabby, and we named her Cheeta because she was *fast*.

Cheeta loved to run all through the house. She would literally rebound off the walls with all four feet while taking corners at seemingly supersonic speeds. Her favorite game involved a superball, one of those hard rubber balls with incredible bouncing characteristics. Cheeta would stand and look at me with her back about two feet from a wall, and it was my job to toss the superball over her head so that it bounced off the floor, into the wall, and back over her head. Then she would jump after it and try to catch it in mid-air. She seemed to like it best if I placed the bounces just out of her reach.

Cheeta was another one of those cats who liked to "help" me study. In order to make myself more competitive for selection to attend the Test Pilot School, I decided to pursue a master's degree. I usually carried my books in a hard leather briefcase that I set on top of a metal file cabinet at home. Cheeta loved to curl up in that briefcase or right on top of my papers for hours while I studied. She was rotten.

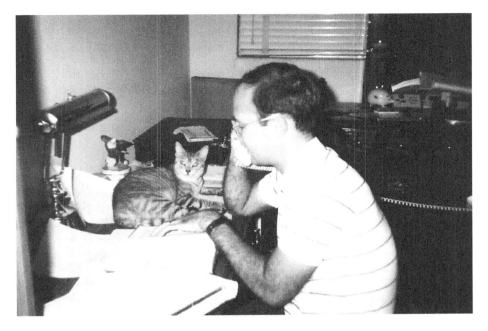

Cheeta "helping" me study.

It wasn't long before I became certain that earning a master's degree was not going to be enough, so I decided to get a private pilot's license to make myself even more competitive. I took out a bank loan and began taking flying lessons. I'll never forget the day of my first solo.

I flew solo, or completely alone, on a Saturday, a few weeks after beginning the flying lessons. But only two days earlier, on Thursday, I still could not land the airplane, no matter how hard I tried. Then, On Friday, everything just "clicked." By Saturday morning, I was landing with ease.

After several practice takeoffs and landings, my instructor suddenly told me to taxi over to a taxiway to the side of the runway and stop. When the aircraft came to a stop, he jumped out and said, "Solo!"

I knew I wasn't supposed to fly solo without his signature in my logbook, so I yelled over the roar of the still running engine, "What about my logbook?"

"I signed it yesterday!" he yelled in response.

I never saw him do that.

I took off. For a student pilot's first solo, he is required to complete three "stop-and-go's." This means the student must take off, land, come to a complete stop on the runway, and then take off again—three times.

On my third approach to landing, I looked to my right at the empty seat, then back toward the approaching runway and said aloud, "TPS, here I come!"

That was the day the movie *Top Gun* opened in theaters, which, of course, we went to see. Talk about pumped!

Not too long after that, I had my "check flight" and earned my private pilot's certificate.

While all this was happening, I completed Squadron Officer School, or SOS, by correspondence, the first of several professional military education courses required of Air Force officers. All three—the master's degree, SOS, and flying lessons—were done at the same time, and I also worked full-time during the day as a mechanical engineer for the Air Force. Needless to say, I was one busy guy, and exhaustion had a whole new meaning for me. I could never do anything like that again. But I still wasn't selected to TPS after three attempts, even after volunteering and traveling to TPS to brief the students and authoring some of the study materials. It didn't look like this was something I was going to pull off.

Before long, it was time for a new assignment, so I decided to do something completely different: become a missile launch officer in Montana. My new job in the Air Force required four months of training in California before I reported to Montana, and the apartment we landed for the temporary stay did not allow cats. We gave Cheeta to Mama. The decision to do so was not a difficult one since by that time, we had another addition to the family, a son we named Brandon, and Cheeta had scratched his face once as he crawled on the floor. So, Cheeta went to Mama's in Mississippi. We also needed a new car. I was still driving the 'Cuda, but it didn't have seat belts in the back seat and most certainly wasn't a family car. We bought a used car from another military member, and the 'Cuda went to Maw Maw's house in Alabama.

About six months later, we headed out to California and stopped in Mississippi for a visit. Mama had more cats then, but LuLu was still there. She was about eighteen years old. She looked much older and was very frail, and she had some teeth missing. Interestingly enough, at feeding time, Mama's other cats rightfully deferred to LuLu. She was always left alone to eat first.

One afternoon, I went into my mother's living room, sat in an old recliner, and LuLu came over to me and jumped right in my lap. She snuggled down between my leg and the arm of the recliner, and just sat there and purred while I petted her. That was the last memory I have of LuLu.

Not long after that visit, I was in Montana and got a call from Mama.

"Jonny, I just wanted to tell you, LuLu is gone."

"What do you mean, gone? Where did she go?" I asked.

She said, "She just knew it was her time, honey. She walked out of here the other day and I haven't seen her since."

LuLu was the last of all those animals we had in my youth, and she lived to the ripe old age of nineteen. I'll always remember how content she looked while napping and the feeling of her at the foot of the bed as I slept. I took many pictures of her during her lifetime. She was a special one. I miss her still.

Montana winters are cold and snowy, the perfect weather for a cat to pile up and nap in our laps, but we didn't have a cat. We found a lady in town who, through the kindness of her heart, was known for picking up strays, nursing them to health, having them spayed or neutered, then finding good homes for each and every one. She never charged a cent. God bless her soul.

When we went to pick up our new cat, her rescuer had a little talk with us. The cat we were after was a domestic, longhaired female, solid gray, with gorgeous green eyes, and had been attacked by a dog. I immediately had visions of the little, gray kitten from my youth, and like Cheeta, I decided this cat was going to be strictly an indoor cat. The poor thing was afraid of her own shadow and extremely timid. She had patches of fur missing, but she was beautiful nonetheless. One frightened look from those eyes and I was hooked. We took her home.

It was weeks before she would come out from under the furniture during daylight hours. Her fur eventually grew back, but she was still tiny and frail. After trying various names, nothing seemed to fit. Eventually, we simply called her, "Kitty."

Kitty was never a lap cat. She loved to be petted and to sleep on the foot of the bed, but rarely liked to be held. She did have a very touching habit, however. Whenever she wanted attention, she would walk up to me and ever so gently reach out with her paw and lightly touch me on the arm or leg. Sometimes I would *see* her do this rather than *feel* it since her touch was so gentle. I was in love.

We both loved Kitty, but Joy had her heart set on getting a dog. She wanted a Shetland sheepdog, or "Sheltie." In an effort to make that dream come true for her, we found a breeder less than one hundred miles from home and made arrangements for a visit. The breeder introduced us to a pregnant female and promised us one of the puppies. We were about to purchase a thoroughbred Sheltie, a *Lassie* in miniature. We were excited.

About eight weeks later, we got the call to come pick up our new puppy. She was a pretty, little fur ball with tons of energy. We couldn't wait to spoil her. At the time, one of our favorite movies was *The Princess Bride*, so when the breeder asked what name to include on her registration papers, we named her Princess Buttercup Boo. We just called her, "Buttercup."

In no time at all Kitty and Buttercup were fast friends. Many times when Buttercup wanted to play, she would paw at Kitty's side while she napped. Sometimes, Kitty would wake up and play, but at other times, she would just ignore Buttercup. That's when one of us would step in and play.

After three years in Montana as a missile launch officer, I decided to try one more time to get into TPS and was finally given the opportunity of a lifetime.

On my fourth attempt, I was selected to attend TPS at Edwards Air Force Base in California. I was finally going to fly for the Air Force, even if only as a back-seater. Sometimes I think I was selected only because the selection committee was tired of dealing with me and wanted to shut me up. Whatever the reason, I felt I was ready. It seemed my persistence had finally paid off.

CHAPTER 4 –
FLYING!

I began the course of study at TPS in January 1992. I was assigned to Class 92A with ten pilots, five other engineers, and one navigator. I was also very lucky. There is a requirement for engineers to start the course with no more than eight years of active duty. I started the course seven years and fifty-one weeks after first hearing about the possibility of attending. My eighth anniversary on active duty was the very next day. Talk about luck.

As if I wasn't already excited that I was actually going to fly military aircraft, it wasn't long after we all arrived and checked in that we got word the space shuttle was going to land right there at Edwards. Since we had access to the flight line, we all headed out there to witness the landing. I grabbed a camcorder for the occasion.

We found an old, rickety wooden tower about fifty yards from the edge of the runway. It looked like it had been there since the early days of flight testing, but we didn't care. We wanted to see a real, live, space shuttle up close. So up we went.

Within minutes of climbing the tower, the double sonic boom shattered the chitchat. Soon we could see the shuttle gliding toward the runway. At this point in its landing, no engines are running. It's just a glider. What surprised me was the sound emanating from the shuttle anyway. It sounded like a train coming right at us as it pushed the air out of the way and neared its touchdown point.

I filmed the whole thing. I didn't know at the time, but a photographer from a local newspaper was also out there taking pictures. The next day, on the front page of the paper, there was a picture of all of us on top of that old tower with the space shuttle, still airborne, right in front of us. Awesome.

A day or so later, one of the instructors, a flight test engineer and graduate of the school, called a meeting for all the engineers in our class. The topic was to be something of concern to all new fliers—airsickness.

Airsickness occurs when the signal to the brain from the eyes does not match the signal to the brain from the ears. In other words, when the eyes make a person think the motion he *sees* is a certain way, but the ears tell him things *feel* differently from what they appear, the result can easily lead to airsickness, a very uneasy, queasy feeling. Throwing up is not uncommon. Typically, the tendency subsides once the flier becomes accustomed to the environment of high-performance flight.

I'll never forget what the instructor told us that day. He said, "All right. There are three kinds of people. There are those who *have* thrown up in an airplane, there are those who *will* throw up in an airplane, and there are those who lie about it."

He then told us his own hilarious story about the first time he flew a high-performance aircraft at TPS—and threw up everywhere. I decided the best thing for me to do was to carry along one of those gallon-sized storage bags on every flight, just in case.

Just days later, I was scheduled for my first flight. It was in a T-38, a very sleek, high-performance trainer with tandem seating, which meant I was in the back seat behind the pilot. I was unbelievably pumped. I still couldn't believe I was actually going to pull this off and fly for the Air Force, something I had dreamed about since I was in high school.

When the day finally came, I strapped on my parachute and walked out to the jet with my instructor pilot, another graduate of the school. He made sure I was all strapped in properly, then he climbed into the front seat. After firing up the engines, we taxied to the end of the runway and stopped at Last Chance.

That's where some members of the ground crew have one last chance to look over the airplane to make sure everything is fine.

Within minutes, we were screaming down the runway. I felt the pilot pull the nose up and the wheels leave the ground. We were airborne, and I was in a jet!

The flight was a familiarization flight intended to introduce non-pilot students to the airborne environment. We pulled "G's," which means we turned the aircraft in such a way that the acceleration of gravity (that's where the "G" comes from) increased and made everything feel heavier. For example, at two G's everything "weighs" twice as much as it does at one G. One G is what we feel just walking around on the ground.

We did rolls, and since I was already a private pilot, the pilot let me take the controls for a time before taking them back and continuing with the flight. We performed what would become my favorite maneuver, the loop. That's where the pilot pulls up on the nose from straight-and-level flight and makes the aircraft fly in a complete circle. At the top of the loop, the aircraft is flying in the opposite direction, but upside down, or inverted. As the pilot continues the maneuver, the airplane completes the circle and winds up right where it started heading in the original direction.

I was having the time of my life—until I started feeling not-so-very-good.

The last thing we were scheduled to do on that flight was a supersonic run where we would break the sound barrier.

I'm going to fly supersonic? No way, I thought. Yet, that's just what I was about to do.

When we got to the appropriate altitude, the pilot said, "Throttles coming up, heading for Mach 1."

I felt a little punch from the engines as we accelerated toward Mach 1, the speed of sound. Within seconds, the needle on the Mach meter edged its way past '1.0' and the pilot said, "We are now supersonic."

I threw up. I threw up breakfast. I threw up supper from the night before. The only thing left was a candy bar from the third grade.

That came up, too.

I felt miserable.

There's no way I'm ever going to get used to this, I thought.

The pilot, however, took in all in stride and said, "Hey. Don't worry about it. I threw up my first time, too."

Even so, I was bummed. After trying so hard for so many years to make my desire to fly for the Air Force a reality, I was feeling a little under-confident to say the least.

A few days later, it was time for my second flight. This one would be in an old F-4 Phantom II, and it would turn out to be my one and only flight in that aircraft type since they were being phased out of the inventory. I should have been excited, but all I could think about was the possibility of throwing up again.

Once in the airplane, I tried to focus on the job at hand. We taxied out of the parking area, and as before, we stopped at Last Chance and waited for our turn to proceed. I had my head down as I studied the note cards strapped to my knee. This flight would include another supersonic run—only faster this time—up to Mach 1.5!

As I was going through the plan for the flight with my head still down, I suddenly looked up. Right in front of the nose of our aircraft, just feet away and about to take the active runway, was a Boeing 747 with none other than the space shuttle strapped on its back. I never saw it taxi. It just appeared out of nowhere.

The view of the shuttle from the cockpit of that F-4 was inspirational.

All right, Jonny, you can do this.

I didn't throw up again.

Even though completely unexpected, the most incredible thing about TPS wasn't the flying—it was the friends. I made some of the best friends any man could hope to find anywhere. Some went on to command their own military units. One achieved general officer rank. Four became astronauts at NASA.

Me? I wrote a book about a cat.

And I am honored beyond belief just to be in the same class photo with those guys.

One of my friends was Mike Bloomfield, our class leader and the highest ranking member of the class. Before being selected to attend TPS, he was an

Eagle driver: an F-15 fighter pilot. His call sign was simply, "Bloomer." Bloomer is a big, teddy bear kind of guy as long as he's not pushed too far—like I did one day.

We were all in our classroom still getting acquainted and walking around waiting for the next lecture when the jokes and ribbing started—normal stuff for a gaggle of pilots and engineers. Even though we all picked on each other as the mood determined, it was apparently my turn as the target, and Bloomer was picking on me.

That's when I made a major faux pas, a big one, and was about to learn a valuable lesson.

I reached over to Bloomer and ripped the Fighter Weapon School Graduate patch off the sleeve of his flight suit. The unmistakable sound of the Velcro ripping off echoed around the room, and everything came to a screeching halt. There was not a sound in the place, and nobody dared move. All eyes were on me.

Uh-oh, I thought.

Someone on the other side of the room said, "Dude is dead where he stands."

Before I could turn back to face Bloomer, he had me in a tremendously powerful headlock. I could barely breathe, let alone move. So I did the only thing left to do.

I squeaked, "Okay. So, do you give up, or do I have to get rough?"

Bloomer was obviously caught off guard that a little pip-squeak like me would dare say such a thing. He simply laughed and let me go. I very gingerly reached up and replaced his patch, patting it down so that it was nice and snug and exactly where it should be on his shoulder, and then gave him a big, toothy grin.

We've been friends ever since.

Another friend I made at TPS was Rick "CJ" Sturckow. CJ sat immediately to my left in the classroom and was the epitome of a Marine fighter pilot. He flew the F/A-18. My first flight at TPS with a fellow student was with CJ in a T-38. During that flight, he demonstrated, using an old, abandoned bus in the California desert as a target, how he used to kill tanks in the first Gulf War.

CJ (on the left) and me before our first flight together; 1992.

Landing was a special treat when flying with CJ. He had a saying that went something like, "There is no price too high to pay for looking good around the field."

During every break to the downwind leg of the landing pattern, CJ would practically bounce my head off the canopy as he jerked the aircraft into the turn to downwind. I'm sure we looked way cool doing it.

Every evening before an academic test, another classmate and I would meet at CJ's house to study. We all lived on the same street in base housing, so that made it easy. We did study, but in a big way it was really just another excuse to chat and chill out from the super-stressful curriculum.

CJ did a very nice thing for me once. One morning on the way to class, I had trouble with my pickup truck. I was just driving along when suddenly I could barely turn the steering wheel. The truck limped into the parking lot. I shut off the engine, slammed the door, dragged myself to my desk, and plopped down in utter frustration. I did NOT have time for problems like that.

CJ took one look at me and asked, "What's wrong, Spayney?"

"Spayney" is what a handful of my TPS classmates call me to this day. It's nothing more than a combination of my middle initial and last name. At the time, however, my call sign was Curly. That's because I'm as bald as a bowling ball. Go figure.

I told him about the truck.

He just said, "Gimme the keys."

I tossed them at him and he left. About an hour later, CJ sat down at his desk next to me and handed me the keys to my truck along with one rusty bolt. As I recall, not a word was spoken. He simply handed them off and then walked away to work on whatever was on his plate at the time. I found out later that all but one of the bolts to the crankshaft pulley had fallen off my truck and the pulley was barely hanging on. The belt was useless at that point, and that was why I couldn't steer. CJ had bought new bolts, replaced the old ones, and readjusted the belt. My truck was as good as new and I didn't have to do a thing.

Another friend at TPS was Rex Walheim, a flight test engineer like me. He sat immediately to my right during class. We became fast friends right from the start. We have a little code we express to each other. It is simply, "Tango. Quebec. Lima. Acknowledge."

That means, "Total Quality Lunch."

TPS was undoubtedly the busiest time of my life. By the time the eleven month course was over, I was absolutely exhausted. But I had made some incredible friends and had flown over thirty types of military and civilian aircraft. Luckily for me, during every phase and even for my final project, I was able to fly the "cool" jets instead of the "heavies." I was the envy of all the engineers in my class and became well known for performing a loop. If I flew in an airplane capable of performing a loop, I looped it.

In fact, Rex used to tell me before every flight, "Don't forget to loop it."

After graduation, I hung around "the schoolhouse" as an instructor in the performance branch while I waited for the slot in my follow-on assignment to be vacated, and Rex went to one of the test units there at Edwards. He called one day and passed the code, so we met at the Officer's Club for an outdoor lunch. Our table overlooked the flight line, and that was the day the F-22, still under development, crashed on the runway. Fortunately, it wasn't a catastrophe, and the pilot was unhurt following his pancaked landing. It's all just part of the process of figuring out and correcting any problems before fighter pilots take these airplanes into combat.

Not long after graduation, I looked forward to my follow-on assignment as a flight test engineer—in Canada. Just days before leaving California I was handed a file to keep for my personal records. It contained the applications I had sent in over the years in my multiple attempts to achieve selection to the course, as well as copies of transcripts and letters of referral.

On one piece of paper, a person on the selection board had circled some information describing how well I had done as a missile launch officer. As I looked at that piece of paper, I remembered what the colonel said to us years earlier just as we were about to begin our training to become missile combat crew commanders. I'll never forget it.

He said, "You will never again, not for the rest of your life, be better trained, more knowledgeable, or more proficient at anything than the job in which you are about to undertake."

He was right. We were all very good at what we did. When "nukes" were involved, Strategic Air Command demanded, expected, and accepted nothing less.

I realized it was that experience combined with everything else I had done to make myself more competitive that got me into TPS. It certainly wasn't that I was better than other candidates were. It was simply that I had done something to set myself apart, even if it had nothing to do with flight test engineering. Fortunately for me, it worked.

I also realized one other thing: sometimes when we think God is telling us, "No," what He's actually saying is, "Not yet."

CHAPTER 5 –
O CANADA!

In the summer of 1993, my little family and I headed north out of California. We drove in separate vehicles. I was in the pickup truck with Brandon and Kitty while Joy was in the car with Jonathon and Buttercup. We communicated via handheld citizens' band radios. It was going to be a long trip.

We stopped in Las Vegas for two nights before heading farther north. It was so hot the glue on some of the boxes in the back of the truck disintegrated, and the boxes could no longer hold their contents. Just a few days later, we went back through Montana and decided to take Going-to-the-Sun Road through Glacier National Park, one of our favorite places we visited while we were in Montana the first time. When we crossed the Great Divide, we stopped at the top of the mountain at a little visitor center, and minutes later the snow started. It was hard to believe that just days earlier we were sweltering in one hundred and ten degree heat, but now we were freezing.

We crossed the border into Canada on Canada Day, July the 1st, their equivalent to our 4th of July. Because of the relationship between Canada and the United States at the time, there was no need for a passport. Since it was a holiday, the border was minimally manned and we were simply waived on through.

I reported to Canadian Forces Base Cold Lake in Alberta, Canada, the next day. Since I had already been up there a few months before on a house-hunting trip, we already knew where we would live. I got a kick out of the fact that rent was paid "to Her Majesty the Queen of the Commonwealth." The house was on base and had a fenced backyard, which was great for Buttercup, and even had a separate garage. Beyond the fence was an open, grassy area about the size of an acre with trees lining the far side. Buttercup had a blast. She absolutely loved running around out there, as long as we were nearby.

Even though Buttercup was one of the sweetest dogs ever, there were a couple of things she didn't like at all—birds—especially if they flew through *her* yard or landed on the fence, and airplanes, if they dared to fly overhead. Many times during my assignment in Canada, I could see Buttercup in our yard from the cockpit of an airplane as I flew over our house on the approach to landing. Of course, she had no idea she was barking at her Daddy.

I met my supervisor on my first day on the job. He was a very nice Canadian officer, a major, with a thick, French-Canadian accent. We introduced ourselves, but communication was difficult. I could barely understand his accent, and he was lost with my Southern English accent. He would ask me a question, and I would try to answer, but we weren't getting very far. Soon, another officer walked by, noticed what was happening, and stopped to translate. So there we were, three military officers from totally different parts of the world trying to communicate—and all three of us were speaking English.

A few weeks later, Brandon started the first grade. The same day he started school I got a call from a Canadian immigrations officer. We talked about how both the Canadians and I were happy I was there and that I was looking forward to my duties.

Then he asked, "Don't you have a child in school?"

I answered, "Yes, I do. As a matter of fact, he started today."

Then came the shock.

The immigrations officer informed me I had not taken the proper steps to immigrate my son into Canada. I was confused because I was never told or instructed to do that. He further stated I was to remove my son from school immediately and that the Immigrations Office would consider the matter and determine if my son would be allowed to remain in Canada.

Naturally, I took immediate steps to get to the nearest Immigrations Office to straighten things out. My commander, a colonel in the Canadian military, got involved and the matter was solved by the end of the day. I still had to go to Immigrations and get our proper papers, which I did, and it was also determined that the border guards had dropped the ball by not informing me of the need to fill out immigration paperwork.

Even though I was there by invitation of the Canadian government, which was pointed out in a not-so-friendly way by my senior leadership to the Immigrations Office when this whole thing blew up, I still had to take the proper action. I was happy to do so and understood the need completely.

Other than that one little fiasco, my time as an Exchange Officer in Canada was the best assignment of my military career. It wasn't long before I met my new best friend, Maurice, a French Canadian who attended "that other" test pilot school: the United States Naval Test Pilot School at Patuxent River Naval Air Station in Maryland. Soon the ribbing started as "Moe" and I argued over who attended the better test pilot school. We were fast friends in no time.

Moe and I were assigned to the same test projects many times, especially since we were in the same unit at the Aerospace Engineering Test Establishment, or AETE, the only flight test organization in Canada, and also in the Fighter Evaluation group. Moe, as a test pilot, was triple qualified, which meant he had to fly a minimum number of hours in three aircraft types in order to maintain his proficiency. As a flight test engineer I had no such requirement other than to fly in any aircraft a minimum number of hours each month in order to maintain airmanship.

One day I would get the surprise of a lifetime. Moe and I were scheduled for a flight in the primary test aircraft, CF-18 tail number 907, which is the Canadian version of the US Navy's F/A-18 fighter aircraft. As we walked out to the aircraft, I reached up to the ladder and prepared to climb aboard when something caught my eye. I certainly never expected it, and I would never be so bold as to ask for such a thing, but there on the side of the cockpit near the rear seat, painted in white lettering, was, "Capt Jon Payne." Moe's name was painted similarly near the front seat.

I simply could not believe what I saw. Never in a million years did I ever think my name would be on a military aircraft, let alone a fighter. There was a time when I thought I'd never be able to fly for the military at all. But there it was—my name on a fighter jet. The Canadians will never know how much that meant to me.

One of Moe's favorite activities was to fly inverted, or upside down, which he did at every opportunity. One of the aircraft types we flew was the Tutor, a side-by-side two-seater used by the Canadians as a primary trainer for their up-and-coming pilots. Whenever we flew the Tutor together, Moe just had to flip us upside down. Then, when we rolled upright again, I almost always had to sneeze. In my feeble attempts at trying to be polite, I would fumble for the hot-mike switch to shut it off before sneezing into his ears over the microphone. It was the longest time before I realized the real reason he liked to fly inverted—he was intentionally making me sneeze!

But it wasn't all fun and games.

There was an incident at Moose Jaw involving a Tutor aircraft. Moose Jaw is the primary training location for new pilots in the Canadian Forces. Apparently, an instructor pilot was flying a training mission when he lost the engine and was unable to get it to restart. He followed his emergency procedures, but even with more altitude than supposedly necessary, he barely made it back. Clearly, something was amiss. Either the pilot had done something wrong, or the flight manual procedure for an engine-out landing was incorrect. They came to us to verify the proper procedures, and Moe and I got the project.

But I was in for another surprise.

One of the other test pilots assigned to our project decided I needed some "training." He didn't say anything about it during our pre-brief before a practice flight. He waited until we were strapped in the jet and taxiing to the runway. My training was to involve hands-on stick time, to include takeoffs and landings in the Tutor aircraft.

"Wait a minute," I said. "According to regulations, as an FTE I'm not supposed to have the controls at altitudes lower than three hundred feet above the ground."

His response surprised me, and I'll never forget what he said—or what we did.

"I'm fully aware of that," he said. "But I was once an instructor pilot, and the way I look at it, if I'm supposed to get in a jet with a brand new college kid with no flying experience whatsoever who doesn't know a wing from a tire, and I'm supposed to give him the controls of a jet for takeoff and landing, why can't I let you? At this point in your career, you're more experienced, and a graduate of the Test Pilot School to boot."

I began to see his point.

He continued, "Besides, the things we're going to be doing in this project are very much out of the ordinary. We'll be shutting down the engine and loosing cabin pressure, and if something should happen to my oxygen system and I pass out, I want somebody with me who can bring me home—all the way. Now, I'll talk you through everything. Take the jet."

Talk about a surprise! The trouble was, he was absolutely correct as far as I was concerned. It really was a safety issue, even if it was a stretch from the regulations.

I responded with the proper response, "I have control."

The Tutor was not much larger that the Cessna 172 I learned to fly as a private pilot, and was quite easy to handle, so the takeoff was uneventful. Landing, however, would require some practice.

But first, the pilot had a plan.

"Head over to those clouds," he said, and pointed in the direction of some clouds topping out at about seven thousand feet above the ground. They were puffy clouds, but one had a nice, flat top to it.

"That's your runway," he said.

For the next forty-five minutes or so, he talked me through one "landing" right after another using the top of that cloud as a runway. He never touched the stick, and I had the time of my life. I can honestly say I completely understand what people mean when they mention, "cloud nine." I've seen it. I've landed on it. Like the motto on my class patch from TPS, I guess I can say, "*Been There—Done That.*"

By the time that training session was over, the real landing was no problem. He was backing me up, of course, but he never had to take control. I did it all myself—and got a tremendous boost of self-confidence. That was a great day!

Our test plan involved many flights, all of which were considered "outside the envelope." Our approach was to develop the engine-out landing procedure from scratch, which meant we had to collect lift-to-drag data in actual engine-out conditions. We did it the old-fashioned way with pencil, paper, and a stopwatch. The difficulty was that the Tutor has only one engine. Since we had many, many test points to fly, which meant we had to fly the same descending maneuver at many different airspeeds, we needed to shut down the engine for each test point to mimic an engine-out emergency. There was an emergency battery on board, but it was good for two or maybe three engine restarts. That wasn't going to work, so we improvised.

Our solution involved an intentional dive toward the ground each time we needed to restart the engine to fly another test point. This action forced the engine to wind-mill fast enough to restart without the use of the battery. It involved a lot of ascending and descending, and while the engine was shut down we had no pressurization in the cockpit. We got cold, and our ears got a real workout from the constant pressure changes. But after dozens of flights, we finally had all the data we needed. Next was the final step to verify the emergency procedure—intentional engine-out, or dead-stick, landings.

As planned, each of our three dead-stick landings was entirely successful. We were able to verify that the emergency procedures in the flight manual were correct as written.

That flight test project was exciting and went exactly as planned. But it's when things don't go as planned that the real excitement occurs.

Another project involved a new G-suit. The G-suit is worn over the flight gear all aviators wear and contains bladders that inflate automatically during high G maneuvers. This action squeezes the legs and abdomen of the aviator. Its purpose is to help avoid G-LOC, or G-induced loss of consciousness, by helping to keep the blood from pooling in the lower extremities away from the brain. The traditional G-suit covered about forty percent of the lower half of the body. The new G-suit was designed to cover about eighty percent, a vast increase over the original.

However, there was a concern. If the new G-suit inflated too much, it might interfere with the pilot's ability to move the control stick to the extreme left, right, or back since the stick is located between the pilot's legs and the pilot's legs would be covered with many more, inflatable bladders. Our project would qualitatively evaluate the performance of the aircraft with and without using the new G-suit to see if there were any noticeable differences.

Seemed like a no-brainer.

On one test day, Moe and I headed out on a mission to take note of the performance of the aircraft during maximum stick deflections. We wore our normal G-suits.

We took off in a two-ship formation, and Moe and I were in the lead. Another CF-18 with two other members of our unit had their own qualitative analyses to make, and our plan was to separate after takeoff, fly our test points, then re-join and practice some basic fighting maneuvers before RTB (returning to the base).

After we reached an altitude between fifteen thousand and eighteen thousand feet or so, our two aircraft separated. Moe and I began to set up for some turns and rolls at maximum stick deflection.

After a few of these maneuvers, the next test point involved moving the stick all the way back and to the left. We set up at an altitude of about fifteen or sixteen thousand feet and entered a 4.5G turn to the right.

Once we were stable in the turn, Moe said, "All right. Max back and left. I'll hold for two seconds, then center the controls. Ready... ready... NOW!"

Moe jerked the stick back and to the left, and the aircraft protested—violently. It clearly did not like what we were doing.

Almost immediately, Moe said, "Oh, sh...!"

Before he could utter another word, we were slammed against the left side of the cockpit, and the aircraft gave us an audible signal telling us what we already knew—we had too much Beta. In other words, we were flying at too great an angle sideways instead of straight ahead.

It started out as a beep, but then became a steady tone. It sounded like, "*Beep. Beep. Be-be-be-be-be-be-be-BEEEEEEEEEEEEEEEEEEEEEP!*"

And just like that, we experienced a departure. We were no longer in control of the airplane, and we weren't flying. We were falling. Like a great, big, heavy, rock.

Looking outside, we saw ground, sky, lake, forest, sky, lake, ground, sky, ground, lake, forest, and so on. It was a sickening feeling.

Instinctively, I went straight to the altimeter. We were both aware that if we were still out of control by the time we descended to 10,000 feet above the ground, or by 11,500 feet according to our altimeter, it was time to get out.

"Fourteen thousand," I said.

As I verbalized our altitude, Moe did exactly what he should do in a situation like that—centralize and analyze. That meant he should move the flight controls to their central positions, then analyze the situation and try to determine what happened and what to do about it.

A couple of heartbeats later, I yelled, "thirteen thousand!"

We were descending rapidly, and it felt as though the aircraft was violently flopping around. It was very difficult to determine which way was up and which way was down.

Another second ticked by and I yelled, louder this time, "TWELVE THOUSAND!"

We had only five hundred feet to go when, just like that, Moe said, "Recovered."

We recovered in a slightly nose-down and inverted attitude. It's unusual to recover in an inverted attitude, and we were still descending, but at least we were flying again.

Moe slowly rolled us into an upright position and pulled the nose up to maintain our altitude at about 10,000 feet. The whole thing lasted only seconds, but it seemed like *much* longer.

Without a word, Moe jumped on the radio and said, "Two, lead."

"Two," came the immediate response.

Moe said, "Lead is RTB. We just departed the jet."

"What? Wow. Okay. See you on the ground."

We headed straight home. Clearly, we had to rethink the maneuvers we wanted to fly for our new G-suit evaluations. But other than our unexpected departure, there were no more problems—and the new G-suit worked beautifully.

∴ ∴ ∴

After many more flight test projects and the best three years of my military career, it was time to move on to another assignment. Joy wanted to finish her pharmacy degree, so I looked around for the possibility of being assigned to a base located near a pharmacy school. After narrowing the possibilities down, only one base filled our needs, and that was Offutt Air Force Base in Omaha, Nebraska. There are two pharmacy schools nearby, and the base had jobs I could fill, so I applied for a position and was accepted. We packed up Kitty, Buttercup, and our two boys and headed south—and there's a whole lot of nothing between Cold Lake, Alberta, and Omaha, Nebraska.

CHAPTER 6 –
NEBRASKA

In June 1996, we arrived in Omaha, and within a month we bought our very first house. It was brand new. We had a privacy fence put up for Buttercup, but since the house wasn't quite ready for occupancy, we decided to take some time and headed home to Alabama. It had been almost five years since we had visited anyone back home. Of course, Kitty and Buttercup joined us on the trip.

As soon as we arrived in town, we took Buttercup to my grandmother's house. Maw Maw had a large, fenced back yard, and even though she had two other dogs, Buttercup seemed to get along with them without any problems. Kitty went with us to my father's house because she needed more care and attention due to the stress of the move.

After we visited everyone else and just before we headed back to Nebraska, our last stop was back at Maw Maw's, where the 'Cuda had been stored for the last seven years or so, to pick up Buttercup.

Just minutes before we left Maw Maw's, something very sweet happened. As we packed the car with the last few items, we snapped Buttercup's leash on the hook of her collar and led her to the car. She jumped right in. Then suddenly, Maw Maw's two dogs, still behind the gate of the fence that ran across the driveway, started barking and barking and barking. Buttercup jumped out of the car with the leash still attached to her collar, trotted over to the gate, stuck her nose through the fence, and gave each dog a little goodbye kiss. Immediately, both dogs ceased barking. Buttercup turned, trotted right back to the car, and jumped in, all without a single word from any of us.

We stood there in awe. To this day, Maw Maw says, "If I hadn't seen it with my own eyes I wouldn't have believed it."

We had been living in Nebraska for less than a year when I received a very interesting letter in the mail. Bloomer had gone on to join NASA and was an astronaut. He was about to go up on his first trip to space and sent us an invitation to attend the launch. I was excited and heartbroken at the same time since I knew there was no way we could possibly attend. Joy was deep into schooling, and I was very busy at work, not to mention that the launch was about 1,600 miles away. I thanked Bloomer but declined and planned to watch the launch on television.

A short while later, launch day came. This one was a night launch, which was good because I was able to watch it live. About an hour before the launch, I ran to my computer and typed up a personal email for Bloomer. Then I just waited. I planned to send it precisely at lift-off. I knew he wouldn't see it until he returned to earth, but I wanted to send it anyway.

The launch countdown began, and with perfect timing, I hit *Send* precisely at lift-off and watched a brilliant launch of the space shuttle. I ached to be there, but Bloomer understood. I was sure there would be more launches anyway.

During the next couple of years, I was busy with work on the base while Joy attended school. She worked to complete her two-year pre-pharmacy program, while at the same time applying for admission to one of the pharmacy schools nearby. She was accepted to a school just before she completed the pre-pharmacy portion of her studies. But that led to another problem. Pharmacy school consisted of a four-year program, so in order for her to complete the pharmacy program, I had to figure out how to stay in Omaha for longer than the usual three-year assignment. Fortunately, I was able to find another assignment right there in the same building, but for a different military command. It seemed as though our problems were solved.

Since I knew we could stay in Omaha for at least another four years, which would take me through to retirement eligibility, I had the opportunity to do something I had wanted to do for decades—restore the 'Cuda. So at just about the same time Joy started pharmacy school, I drove the thousand miles back to Maw Maw's in Alabama to get the 'Cuda. After sitting in her yard for eleven years, it was a rust bucket, and I'm sure Maw Maw was happy to finally see it go after telling passers-by on a regular basis, "No, it's not for sale." It would have been cheaper and much easier to simply get another 'Cuda to restore, but this one was my first car. It was going to be this one or none at all.

During the summer of 1998, work on the 'Cuda began. I found a paint shop willing to take on the project, and I started the teardown. After about four months of steady work, primarily on weekends, I had the entire car disassembled and ready for the body shop. I even had a step-by-step list of everything I took off the car so I could easily put things back together.

I called my insurance company and asked about a tow to the body shop with the 'Cuda. Since I had been a member for decades, they graciously agreed to tow the 'Cuda one way for free. I thanked them, but insisted on a flatbed truck for the job. They sent one.

Just before the tow truck arrived, I had to get what was left of the car out of the garage and around the corner so the truck could load it. Two men were working on a new house right across the street, so I walked over to ask them if they would help me push the car into place.

As they walked toward the garage, one of the men saw the 'Cuda and asked, "Sending it to the junkyard?"

He was dead serious.

I answered, "Nope. Gonna restore it."

He gave me a look that clearly said, "*No way, man.*"

He didn't actually say "can't," but I took it that way. I was determined to prove him wrong.

Life went on, but Kitty had problems. She developed a liver problem and required medication twice daily. Otherwise, she was still her usual self, skittish and frail. As she got older, I noticed one very welcome change. She loved to jump in my lap. She still didn't like to be held or cuddled, but she was perfectly content to sit in my lap and be petted. She sat in my lap for hours, no matter what else went on around us. In fact, she was in my lap during one of my birthday celebrations, and instead of putting her on the floor, I simply held the cake in my hands as I blew out the candles. It didn't bother her a bit. She loved her Daddy!

As time passed, I wished for different medication that didn't require me to practically gag her with every dose. I decided to call the vet.

The vet explained that there were other medications available in liquid form, but in order to determine which one was best for her condition they would first have to do a biopsy on her liver. I didn't see a problem with that, so I scheduled an appointment.

After the surgery, I brought her home, but she was still mildly sedated and loopy. After sleeping one night on the couch to be near her I noticed no improvement, and I was worried. She barely moved all night, and only once tried to get up to eat. She just didn't have the strength. The sedative was still very much active in her little body, and she merely stumbled around and finally just urinated where she shakily stood. Bless her heart. I called the vet again.

They had me bring her back in right away. She was limp but awake when I handed her to the veterinarian who promised to keep me informed. That was a Friday morning.

When I had not heard from the vet by Saturday afternoon, I called to check on her. The vet's office was closed on the weekends, but I knew the veterinarian had taken Kitty home with her the night before. She had also given me her phone number.

"She passed away this morning," was the abrupt response.

I was shocked. I had no idea Kitty was in extreme danger, and we never even had a chance to say goodbye. I could barely speak, so I just said I'd be there shortly to pick up her body. When asked if I planned to bury her in the backyard, I told the vet I planned to do just that. She offered some tips to ensure no other animals dug her up. I hung up the phone and just stood there for a minute or two.

Brandon was the only other person home at the time. I slowly walked up the stairs to his room. He saw me coming with tears on my face and met me at the doorway to his room. We just hugged each other for a minute without saying much of anything, both of us still in disbelief.

We buried Kitty in the center of the backyard that very afternoon, right where she used to sit when she occasionally gathered the courage to go outside for a few minutes. The four of us huddled around her little grave and said a prayer on her behalf. A few days later we planted a tree right next to her as a reminder of her precious little life. May God bless her soul.

I carried this photo in my wallet for years. On the back I wrote:

Kitty
"Daddy's Little Girl"
Passed on to God
May 6, 2000.

About a week after we buried Kitty, we decided to go look for another kitten. We still had Buttercup, but I think even she felt Kitty's loss. We went to The Nebraska Humane Society, the largest pet store I had ever seen, right there in Omaha, to look for a new, furry addition to the family.

When we walked in, we headed straight to one side of the store where there was a relatively large, glass-walled room filled with kittens all over the place. According to the sign, all the kittens already had their first round of shots, were completely healthy, and were ready for adoption. There were chairs lining the wall, but I just walked to the center of the room and sat on the floor, Indian style. I didn't have to sit there long.

Less than five minutes later, a calico kitten, obviously female since male calicos are extremely rare, bounced over to me. She looked up at me for a moment, then without hesitation, crawled into my lap. She faced the wall, settled herself down, and then lifted her head to look at me upside down. She meowed, clearly saying, "*You belong to me. We can go home now.*"

I looked over at the rest of the family and simply said, "Well, I guess that settles that," and we took her home.

Buttercup seemed happy to see the new kitten, but the little fur ball obviously had had little contact with dogs at only six weeks old. At the first sight of Buttercup, she clawed her way right up on my shoulder, leaving marks all the way. I immediately knew what to name her. We named her Sunshine after the song by John Denver where he sings, "*Sunshine, on my shoulder, makes me happy...*"

In many ways, Sunshine was the opposite of Kitty in that she craved attention. At night, she slept on whomever she could get to first—right on their chest with her nose about a millimeter away from her victim's chin. And yes, just like the others, she was rotten in no time.

But I still missed Kitty. Several weeks went by before an interesting realization hit me, and on different fronts. First of all, Kitty would not have died so suddenly if I hadn't asked the vet about a different medication. She was fine the way things were. I just felt sorry for having to put her through the pilling twice a day, every day, for the rest of her life. But in addition to that, something else hit me. We knew Kitty had liver problems, even without a biopsy. Since the liver is used by the body to rid it of many medications, shouldn't the vet have known Kitty could have a serious issue with ridding herself of the sedative? And why didn't she say anything to me about such a possibility before the surgery?

Not only was I heartbroken over the loss of Kitty, I was extremely angry. To me, this seemed to reflect serious incompetency on the part of the veterinarian, or at the very least, an extreme lack of compassion. We dropped that veterinarian like a bad habit and never looked back. The search was on to find a new veterinarian.

Since I decided this time to choose a vet with office hours on weekends, the list was quite short. But we found just what we were looking for in Dr. Jennifer Wagner. She was one of several veterinarians at what was then known as VCA Rohrig Animal Hospital in Omaha. Sunshine's next visit to the vet was to see Dr. Wagner.

Not very long after we got Sunshine, a stray cat appeared out of nowhere. He was solid gray and probably the friendliest cat I've ever seen. His tail had a kink in the middle as though he had been injured, but it didn't seem to bother him. In fact, nothing bothered him at all. The boys occasionally wrapped him around their necks and walked around the house, but he just took it all in stride like there was nothing to it.

We had him for about a week and decided to keep him. We thought about names and discussed a few possibilities, but before we could decide, we got a call from a family friend. She saw an ad for a missing cat, and this one seemed to fit the description. One phone call later and the owner came and picked him up. Bummer. I decided I wanted to get another just like him one day ... a solid gray, male cat.

About two weeks went by and we realized we *really* wanted another "Kitty." We loved Sunshine, but she wasn't Kitty, and the next thing we knew we had another female cat with longer, gray fur. This one even *looked* like Kitty. We got her at the same pet store where we got Sunshine. We could tell she had recently given birth, but her kittens were nowhere to be found. Joy named her Sabrina, and the name fit. She was like Kitty in that she didn't like to be held, but she, too, jumped in our laps for a few minutes of petting on occasion.

MIGHTY LITTLE MAN

❧   ❧   ❧

As the weeks passed, Joy was busy with work and school, and I spent weekends in the garage working on the 'Cuda engine. The body was at the shop, and because of the difficulty in finding body parts, I was in for a long wait. In the meantime, I was able to concentrate on the engine rebuild, and while I was in there, I decided to make a few … improvements. Oh yeah!

It was during the engine teardown that I realized something about Brandon. Even at only eleven years old, he really had a knack for mechanical things. In fact, he helped me with the most difficult parts of the engine teardown and rebuild.

One afternoon, we had the engine almost completely torn down when we began removing the pistons from the exposed engine block. The engine was mounted on an engine stand, and we rotated it upside down to get at the connecting rods holding the pistons in place. Brandon tapped the bottom of each piston and I caught it as it plopped out of its hole, each of which faced toward the floor and the oil drip-pan.

We removed the first piston without difficulty. The second was a little more stubborn. Brandon was finally able to tap it out, and I caught it and placed it on a piece of cardboard on the floor.

As we turned back to the engine to begin work on piston number three, I noticed what looked like hydraulic fluid on the floor next to the drip pan.

"What's this?" I asked as I rubbed at a puddle of it with a finger on my left hand. "It looks like hydraulic fluid, but there's no hydraulic fluid in a car's engine."

Confused by the strange liquid, we stood there and looked around. Suddenly, Brandon yelled, "Dad!" and pointed at my right hand.

I looked down to find that the piston rings from the number two piston had sliced open all five of the fingers on my right hand. The cuts were deep, and I was bleeding all over, but I never felt a thing.

We were done for the night.

We kept at it for the next several days and had just about finished the engine rebuild when we got a phone call from Joy's family in Alaska. Her father was in a bad way, and we needed to get up there quick-fast-and-in-a-hurry. So we left and spent a few days in Anchorage. After visits to the doctor and lengthy discussions, it was determined that, even though he was in his nineties, Joy's father was in no immediate danger. We decided I would leave and return home and leave Joy and the boys there to visit for a little longer.

I returned home and finished the engine rebuild, which basically meant paint. The engine was still mounted on its engine stand, ready for installation back into the body, and I took several pictures for a photo album I used to document the restoration. I was still waiting for the body, so at that point there wasn't much left to do.

In the US military, there is an acronym, NUDET, which means, "Nuclear Detonation." Two days after I returned home from Alaska, on August 9, 2000, that's exactly what happened in my life. Although the damage was not physical, it was essentially just as devastating, and completely unexpected. It's amazing what can result from a simple phone call.

My marriage was in serious trouble.

After weeks and weeks of counseling, we decided to keep trying. Joy was still in school and working as her curriculum required, and I was busy at work. But I didn't touch the 'Cuda. In fact, even though the fully restored and painted body was back in the garage, it was a full year before I spent any time on it at all. As things slowly got back to normal, I decided to get back to work on it.

During the spring of 2001, I was notified that I was to participate in a military exercise in Australia. Well, actually, I was to fly to Australia and embark on a naval vessel for a ten-day "cruise" around the island.

"Um, say what?" I asked my commander when he gave me the news.

He laughed and said, "Yep, you and three others from our unit get to go."

"Are all four of us going to be on the ship?" I asked.

"No, only you and one other person."

"What about the other two?"

He paused, then with a mischievous grin, continued, "The other two will be in Hawaii."

"Lucky me," I replied.

It took three days to get there. We landed in Darwin, Australia, and embarked on the *USS Blue Ridge* a couple of days later. As the senior ranking officer of the two from our unit lucky enough to be the ones assigned to the ship, I got the day shift. My shipmate was stuck with the night shift. By the time our ten days were over, we both wanted nothing more than to get off the ship and go home.

Throughout the exercise, we communicated with the other two, Hawaii-based members of our unit via email from the ship. We were extremely happy to learn what *their* time was like: a couple of hours of participation each morning, then beach time for the rest of the day—for the entire three-week exercise. They apparently had a really hard time. But even after three weeks of "boredom" on the beach, they too were ready to get home.

As we suspected would happen before we left Australia, we disembarked in Cairns and were stuck for several more days waiting for transportation. But the delay gave me the chance to take advantage of a couple of once-in-a-lifetime opportunities. First, I went scuba diving at the Great Barrier Reef. Then my shipmate and I visited the Cairns Zoo.

The scuba trip started with a one-hour boat ride out to the reef. During the ride we were briefed on how to use the scuba gear and informed about safety and the fact that, since we were not certified divers, at no time would we be underwater without a licensed instructor nearby.

The first thing we did upon entering the water was check our equipment, then we headed to the bottom about thirty-five feet down. Our group of about eight students and two instructors formed a circle on our knees while the instructors signaled for "OK" signs from each diver. Suddenly, I felt a bump. It was Wally.

Wally was a Napoleon fish who lived at the reef. He was extremely friendly and a camera hog. He craved attention, and the more hands on him the better. He rubbed all over me, just like a puppy. If I turned to look away, he drove his snout straight into the palm of my hand and forced me to rub him from nose to tail, all the while flashing the cameraman who filmed the dive for purchase later on. We made two dives that day and I had a ball. Of course, I bought a copy of the video.

The day after the scuba trip was our scheduled departure date, but we wanted to at least briefly visit the Cairns Zoo before we left. We checked out of our hotel and left our bags at the front desk, then headed to the zoo where I fulfilled a life-long dream … I held a koala.

We got there shortly before opening time, about an hour or so before the first photo session with the koalas. In the meantime, I headed to the kangaroo pen after I bought some food to feed them.

Jonny feeding the kangaroos in Australia; 2001.

I must have been the first visitor in the pen that morning, because as soon as I entered I was surrounded by about a dozen kangaroos, and every one of them wanted to eat right out of my hand. In no time at all, my hands were covered with kangaroo slobber. I was pleasantly surprised at how friendly and non-aggressive they were. They ate like rabbits.

It seemed no time at all had passed when it was time to stand in line for my turn with the koala. What I didn't realize until I was almost to the front of the line was that there were actually two photo opportunities: one with a koala and one with a boa constrictor named Bo. I have to say that of all God's creatures, spiders and snakes are my least favorites. I had no intention of getting anywhere near Bo.

Directly in front of me in line was a young girl about ten years old. After her picture with the koala, she did not hesitate to allow the zookeeper to wrap Bo around her neck for another photo. I knew what was coming. Either I was going to have to man-up and take a picture with Bo, or I was going to be a wimp right there in front of strangers from all over the world. I clearly had a decision to make.

Inevitably, it was my turn. I stood next to the backdrop, and a zookeeper walked around the corner with a sleepy koala in her arms. She placed it in my arms and moved my arms and hands into the proper positions as she did so, and gently took the arms of the koala and placed them on my shoulder, both on one side of my neck. The claws of a koala are huge, and the zookeeper explained that the reason they do it that way is to prevent a koala from using someone's neck as a tree.

After the planned photo, I asked if my former shipmate could take one more with his personal camera. The zookeeper had no objection, so I turned around with my back to the camera in such a way that only the koala's head was visible over my shoulder, just like I was holding a baby, with the koala looking directly back at the camera. Immediately I heard several, "Oooo's," and "Ahhh's," and especially, "Oh, how cute!" sounds from other people in line behind us. We were a hit.

Jonny holding a Koala.

After the photo with the koala, the zookeeper took it from my arms. I took one indecisive step and got the palm of her hand right in the center of my chest.

"Not yet," the zookeeper said. Without warning, another zookeeper came from nowhere and wrapped Bo around my neck. Oh boy. The decision was made for me, and all I could do was play along.

Just before the photographer snapped the picture, I said, "Wait!"

I looked over at my shipmate and said, "Hey man, let me borrow your outback hat and sunglasses."

The zookeeper took them and put them on me while I fought Bo as he tried to wrap himself tighter around my neck. When she was satisfied with the way I looked, the zookeeper turned to the cameraman and said, "Now!"

Snap! The picture was done. She grabbed Bo from around my neck, and I walked over to the cashier to pay for the pictures. I shuddered involuntarily as I reached for my wallet, and the cameraman, the zookeepers, and the other people in line erupted in applause. Bo and I were a hit, too, but I had the heebie-jeebies. I was glad it was over.

Jonny and Bo.

At that point we had only minutes before we needed to head back to get our bags, but I wanted one more chance to be with the kangaroos. I walked quickly back to the kangaroo pen. I had no more food, but was surprised to see that they were obviously full from their morning feeding from me and some other early visitors, so they didn't surround me as before. In fact, some visitors were unable to get the kangaroos to eat at all, so I was happy to have been able to get there earlier and get all slobbery.

I walked around for a few minutes, then turned to leave. As I left the pen, I saw a mother kangaroo lying on the ground just inside the gate. She seemed very relaxed and was on her side but with both arms flat on the ground in a position similar to that of the Great Sphinx in Egypt. She seemed comfortable enough, so I knelt down and began to pet her. She didn't even open her eyes. She just let me rub her all over for a minute or two. Just before I stood up, I noticed an ear sticking out of her pouch. I scooted around to get a little closer, then reached over and gently rubbed the ear with my fingers. The little Joey started squirming. After rustling around a bit, the ear disappeared and two feet popped out. I guessed a foot rub was in order. I rubbed the little toes without so much as a twitch from the Joey, and all the while the mother never once opened her eyes. I guess she was tuckered.

Back at the hotel, the clerks politely asked about our trip to the zoo. I pulled out my picture of the koala and me and promptly got an obligatory, "That's nice," from one of the clerks. Then I pulled out the picture with Bo.

I got an immediate, "Wow, that's a great photo!" from both of them.

I thought for sure they would have preferred the koala picture. I guess in Australia a picture of a koala is cool, but a big-ol' snake, well, that's apparently something else entirely.

🐾 🐾 🐾

Back home, I was still trying to reset my sleep cycle, and Joy and I were discussing everyday things. The 'Cuda came up. She asked me about the progress of the restoration, but then she asked me something I hadn't really thought much about.

"So, which one of the boys will get the car if something happens to you?" Joy asked. Like I said, I hadn't really thought that much about it. Since my father gave me the car and I had kept it all these years, I just knew I would never part with it and that one day I would pass it on to the boys.

"Hmmm," I replied. "I don't really know. I guess I need to figure something out though, don't I?"

"Well, I'm not going to be the one to decide, so I suggest you come up with something," she said.

Almost as a joke, I suggested, "Well, I could always just get another one. That way, both of them would get one."

Surprisingly, she said, "You know, I think that's a good idea."

But I knew before I could get another car in the garage I had to get the newly rebuilt engine back in the 'Cuda in order to free up some space. Before I could do that, I started second-guessing myself.

It had been a year since I had finished the engine rebuild, and I couldn't remember if I had tightened the windage tray bolts properly. The windage tray is a metal plate which essentially straddles the crankshaft. It forms a barrier between the oil in the bottom of the oil pan and the whirling crank shaft and piston rods directly above. Its purpose is to prevent "tornadoing" of the oil during high engine RPM, as is common in some high performance engines. It's held on by four small bolts. For the life of me I couldn't remember tightening them to specifications. I knew I was going to have to crack open the oil pan again and double-check. It's not a tough job, especially with the engine still on the stand, but getting a proper seal when reinstalling it can be a challenge.

I rotated the engine upside down on the stand, loosened the multitude of oil pan bolts, and took the oil pan back off. Then I grabbed my torque wrench, made a quick check of the proper torque needed, and snapped the wrench on one of the bolts. It was as snug as a bug in a rug, as were the other three. I had just wasted my time, but at least I had peace of mind. After installing a new gasket set, the oil pan was back in place. A few days later, the boys helped me get the engine back in the car, and I was ready to find another 'Cuda.

It wasn't until about a year later that I actively looked for one. Luckily, I found one on EBay. I placed a bid lower than I thought the car was worth, but it was all I could afford. It wasn't in great shape, but it was restorable. My dream car had always been a 1970 Hemi 'Cuda. This one was a 1970 model, but had a 383 Magnum engine. So I planned to clone it into a Hemi 'Cuda—if I won the auction.

To my surprise, I won the bid. But there was a catch. The car was in San Francisco, 1,800 miles away. Oh boy.

I already had an enclosed, triple-axle car trailer, and even had it modified specifically for the 'Cuda body type with attachments strategically placed on the floor for strapping down the wheels, so I hooked it to the back of my diesel truck and headed out. I made the trip from Omaha to San Francisco in three days, averaging about six hundred miles a day.

CHAPTER 6 – NEBRASKA

When I arrived, one look at the car revealed I had made a good deal. The owner was a young woman in her twenties. She was teary-eyed when we signed the papers and explained her reasons for selling it. She had snagged a training spot as a NASCAR pit crew member and was leaving within a few days. Her new home had no garage space, so she had to give up her 'Cuda. She helped me load it in the trailer, and I drove a few miles down the road to a hotel with enough space to park my truck and trailer combination. I was ready for the return trip. Bright and early the next day, I was on the road toward home. I thought the hard part was over. I was mistaken.

After travelling only about one hundred and fifty miles, I was heading uphill into the Sierra-Nevada Mountains on Interstate I-80. Suddenly, I heard what sounded like a shotgun blast. I turned the radio down and immediately tried to determine the source of the sound, but I heard nothing out of the ordinary. Then I spotted something out of the corner of my eye. In the extended side mirror on the driver's side of my truck, I could see rubber flying in all directions. I had blown a trailer tire.

This really surprised me for a couple of reasons. First, the trailer had three axles and six tires. Second, it was capable of hauling much more weight than it currently carried. Nevertheless, I had indeed blown a tire. I was one mile from the summit of what is commonly known as Donner's Pass after the infamous, cannibalistic Donner Party from the 1840's. Eerie.

I pulled over to the side of the highway. The tire that blew was the middle tire on the driver's side toward the highway. Great. I whipped out my cell phone, not really knowing who I was going to try to call, only to find that I had no cell phone reception. Things were getting worse and worse. I grabbed the map I carried with me and discovered the next exit was just over the summit about two miles away, so I gingerly hauled the trailer to the next exit.

When I arrived at the exit, all that was there was a small, family restaurant. There was not even a gas station. But it had a big parking lot that was mostly empty. I walked in and spoke to the owner about my predicament, and he gave me permission to park the trailer there temporarily until I could get the tire replaced. He also told me there was a place that sold tires about fifteen miles up the road. I thanked him and headed back outside.

Since most of the tire was gone and what was left was not touching the ground, and because it was the one in the center on the left side, I had no need of a car jack to raise the trailer. I removed the wheel with the shredded tire, threw it in the bed of my truck, unhooked the trailer and made sure it was locked up tight, and headed down the road.

I found the place the restaurant owner told me about, and walked right up to the shop foreman dragging the blown tire with me. I briefly explained my problem.

After a quick look, the foreman said, "Well, I can tell you the problem right now. You've got passenger car tires on your trailer. If the rest of the tires are like this one, you're about to have a major problem."

And there I thought things were looking up. Yeah, right.

"Great," I said, and then asked, "Got any trailer tires?"

"Nope. All I have are some light truck tires, and I'm not sure if I have enough of those. Let me check."

He disappeared for about five minutes, then returned and said, "I only have four."

Then he paused for a moment, obviously thinking. He continued, "Look. I'm not trying to make a huge sale here. But you've got to have something or you'll never make it. I can put the four tires I have on there, and they should get you home. But you really need trailer tires."

"All right," I said. "Put one on the wheel I brought in and I'll take it back to the trailer and put it back on. Then I'll bring the trailer to you for the other three."

"That'll be fine. Since I know you won't make it far if you try to run off without paying...," at which point we both shared a much needed laugh, "...just settle up when it's all done."

A few minutes later I was back at the trailer with the new tire. It went back on with no problem, and I was soon on the road again for the short trip to the tire place.

Since the trailer was hauled in a slightly nose-up attitude, this put most of the weight on the tires to the rear, so we decided to replace the four tires on the center and aft axles. I called Joy and shared the wonderful news with her, then about an hour later I was on the road again toward home. With the delay, I was behind schedule, but I didn't want to push too hard since I still had a long way to go. I drove a total of about four hundred miles that day, then pulled over at a hotel and dove into bed.

The next day, everything seemed fine. In no time at all I found myself in the middle of the desert somewhere in Nevada with no exits in sight, just motoring along on my four new, but incorrect, tires.

BAM! It happened again.

"You've got to be kidding me!" I yelled aloud to no one.

This time, the front tire, again on the driver's side of the trailer, blew just like the other one had, and my fun meter was broken.

I again pulled over to inspect the damage. Sure enough, the guy at the tire place knew what he was talking about. Even with four new tires and two old ones, it was still too much for the two old tires on the trailer. I stood there on the side of the highway, without so much as a single car going by, and began to regret buying this car and braving so long of a drive. This trip was terrible. Again, I whipped out my cell phone. At least I had reception. I called Joy.

"Hey," I said when she answered. "You're not going to believe this."

"You didn't break down again, did you?" she said in disbelief.

"Yep. Blew another tire. One of the old ones. But this time, I'm literally in the middle of nowhere."

I grabbed my map. A quick look revealed more good news: I was miles and miles away from the nearest exit with nothing but desert in both directions.

I said, "I need you to get on the phone and find any place that sells tires. I'm somewhere in the middle of Nevada on I-80."

"Okay. Give me a few minutes and I'll call you back," she said.

Then she said, "While I've got you on the phone and before I forget to ask, do you remember a while back when you said you wanted to get a gray, male cat someday?"

The very, very, very last thing on my mind at that moment was getting another cat. But I answered with a sigh, "I remember."

"Well, a classmate of mine has a cat with a litter of kittens. One of them is gray and a male. He sounds like he's just like what you've been wanting. What do you want me to tell her?"

I really was not in the mood to discuss a new addition to the family and was more concerned with getting the conversation back to tires. I had no idea at the time, but my answer was about to change my life forever.

I said, "Yeah, tell her we'll take him. Now find me some tires!"

I was bummed to say the least, and what made matters worse, it was a Sunday. I was sure Joy was going to have a very hard time finding someone open, especially a place with tires for sale. But I had no other choice but to get in the truck and head on down the highway. I drove at a snail's pace at the minimum forty-miles-per-hour. I was getting nowhere fast.

A few minutes later, my cell phone rang. It was Joy.

"Great news!" she said. "I found a place. They're open and they have tires!"

The place she found was about thirty miles down the road. A little under an hour later, I arrived. This time, trailer tires were available. But my luck was still in full swing. They weren't the right size.

"They'll fit your wheels, but you really ought to have the next larger size," the guy said. "What do you want to do?"

"I don't have much choice, do I?" I responded. "Go ahead and put them on, please."

"No problem. Give me about an hour and we'll have you back on the road," he said.

An hour later I was once again on the road in an attempt to get home. By that time, I had spent over seven hundred dollars on new tires, none of which were the correct ones. The cost of the trip seemed to get higher and higher, and on top of the cost of the "good deal" I made on the purchase price of the car I was hauling made me wonder if any of it was a good idea after all.

I arrived home six days after I left. I drove a total of about 3,600 miles and averaged about 600 miles a day. It was almost dark when I walked in the door. I headed straight to the kitchen table, just to sit for a minute, when my cell phone rang. It was one of the guys from the office. He and several others wanted to see the new 'Cuda and check out the progress on the restoration of the other one.

"Tomorrow after work," I said, "and tell the boss I won't be in tomorrow either. I'm beat."

The next day after work, several of the guys from the base dropped over to drool over the cars. Jonathon and Brandon had already helped me unload the car from the trailer and it was in the garage next to the other 'Cuda. We were just standing around chatting about the cars when Joy pulled in the driveway. She got out, walked around to the passenger side, opened the door, and pulled out a small kennel with a kitten inside. I got only a glimpse, but I could tell this was the kitten she told me about during my second blown tire fiasco. She took him into the house while I remained outside with the guys.

About a half-hour later, the guys left for home and I headed into the house. Inside, the new kitten romped around and investigated his new home. Sunshine was unimpressed, but Sabrina seemed curious enough. Buttercup walked right up to the kitten and seemed to wonder if it was some sort of plaything. I walked over to the kitten and picked him up. He wasn't exactly what I had in mind in that he wasn't solid gray; he was more like a gray tabby. But the connection was immediate, and his name was obvious. Even though he was smaller than the others, he was the only male in a house full of female pets.

I named him Little Man.

CHAPTER 7 –
LITTLE MAN!

As the story goes, Little Man was born in a barn somewhere in rural Nebraska and was promptly stepped on by a horse. He was uninjured, surprisingly enough, which should have been a clue as to his nature. We got him two years and one day after Kitty's death, which meant he was likely born sometime in early April 2002. Born as a barn cat, he needed his first round of shots and a checkup, so I took him to Dr. Wagner. He needed to grow a little more before we could get him neutered, but otherwise he was given a clean bill of health.

Little Man as a kitten drinking from Buttercup's water bowl.

Part of Joy's pharmacy curriculum required her to attend a three-day seminar in Denver, Colorado. She scheduled her attendance for the seminar that began just a week or so later, and I decided to go along for the break. The boys were old enough to stay home on their own, so it would just be the two of us—almost.

I decided to take Little Man along, too. As small as he was, I was afraid he would become breakfast for the other pets if we didn't lock him up in a separate room the whole time. The boys would be there when they weren't at work or school, but teenagers being the way they are, I didn't want to take the chance they might forget to lock him up and leave him to fend for himself. So Little Man got to go to Denver.

It was full day's drive, but the little fur ball did fine on the trip. We got to the hotel and dragged our luggage, Little Man, his kennel, food, and litter pan up to the fourth floor, and then began to settle in when we decided to go get something to eat. After we unpacked, we put the DO NOT DISTURB sign on the outside doorknob and started to close the door behind us.

That's when it started.

Little Man was not happy about being left behind. Just as we closed the door, he tried to scamper out. I blocked him with my hand and promptly got a verbal thrashing.

"*Wait! You can't leave me here! Come back!*" Little Man meowed at the top of his little lungs.

We continued down the hall toward the elevator. We heard, "*Come back! Come back! Come back!*" all the way down the hall. We stepped into the elevator and the door closed behind us.

"*Come back!*" We could hear him all the way down.

When the elevator door opened, we stepped out into the lobby.

"*Come back!*" We could still hear him.

As we walked across the lobby to the hotel entrance, we intentionally avoided looking at the clerk. Just as we stepped outside, we heard still another "*Come back!*" all the way from the fourth floor.

"I guess we better make this quick," I said to Joy. She agreed.

CHAPTER 7 – LITTLE MAN!

We drove around for only a short time and found a little, family restaurant. We had a quick supper, paid the bill, and turned to leave. When we arrived back in the hotel parking lot, we parked the car, got out, and headed for the hotel entrance.

As soon as we walked through the door, we heard more, "*Come back! Come back!*"

"He's still screaming?" I said. It was more of a statement than a question.

"I think we may have a little problem," Joy said. "They're going to kick us out if this keeps up."

"Looks like I'm going to get to spend some time in the room while you're at the seminar, huh?"

"Looks that way," she said.

We got to the elevator and heard still more, "*Come back! Come back!*"

The doors opened and we stepped inside. The doors closed and I punched the button to the fourth floor. The elevator started moving up.

"*Come back! Come back!*"

We reached our floor, the elevator stopped, and the doors opened.

Sitting right in front of his room directly across from the elevator door was a man, probably a truck driver. He didn't look happy. He had pulled one of the chairs from his room out into the hallway and just sat there. I'm sure he didn't know who was at fault, and I don't know if he was upset because of the noise or because someone was, in his opinion, mistreating a kitten. But we stepped into the hallway and turned toward more "*Come Back! Come back!*" from Little Man. I did not look back, but I could feel the man's eyes on me all the way down the hall. I fumbled for my key and unlocked the door without looking toward the man who sat just down the hall and stared us down.

As we entered our room, the crying ceased. I sat down on the bed and said, "Little Man! What's the matter?"

He did not respond. He just jumped up on the bed, sat next to me, curled up, and started purring.

Looks like I've got a buddy, I thought.

A few minutes later, I bravely poked my head out the door. Sure enough, the man was gone.

For the next two days, I didn't leave the room. I spent my time surfing the internet, relaxing, watching television, and playing with Little Man. It's amazing how something so small can have so much energy. Little Man certainly seemed to enjoy the attention, and he wore me out. Each night, Little Man slept right next to me, all cuddled up and purring. I loved every minute of it.

🐾 🐾 🐾

Once we were back home, Little Man, Sabrina, Sunshine, and Buttercup attempted to get along. Sabrina decided right away that Little Man was the replacement for her missing babies; therefore, he required mothering—especially at bath time. It was hilarious watching her chase him down. He resisted of course, but he was still small enough for her to handle easily. She held him down with one paw, then licked him all over until she was satisfied he was clean enough. At times, if this process took too long for Little Man's comfort, he squirmed and tried to get away. But the look on Sabrina's face clearly revealed she was thinking, *"Come here you little …,"* as she forcibly mothered him to death. Eventually, Little Man learned to just deal with it and let her do her thing.

Buttercup, being Buttercup, wanted to play with everything and everybody. I'm sure she missed Kitty, especially since she and Kitty actually played together on occasion. But without Kitty, she needed to find someone else to entertain her. Little Man was still too small. Sabrina was simply uninterested. Sunshine, however, made it very clear that Buttercup was not to even suggest such a thing. So Buttercup found something else. What she found was a complete surprise.

Buttercup could be very skittish at times, especially if there were any loud noises, but she was a sweetheart. She was also very protective, as long as there was a pane of glass separating her from any perceived threat. Otherwise, she was little more than a scaredy-cat. But for one and only one thing did she ever show any real watch-dog type of behavior. It wasn't when the mailman came. It wasn't for the trash collectors. It wasn't for the occasional service man that came to work on a problem at the house. Nope. It was the most horrific of all things: a mother pushing a stroller down the sidewalk.

CHAPTER 7 - LITTLE MAN!

If Buttercup caught the sight of a young mother pushing her baby in a stroller, she went absolutely nuts. She growled and barked with her nose pressed firmly against the window glass and followed the "perpetrator'' all the way around the corner with her eyes, and since we lived on a corner lot, that meant she could see her all the way around as the young mother approached, turned the corner, and kept on going. It became a joke. As soon as I spotted the "threat" heading toward the house, I grabbed Buttercup and held her next to the window. She remained quiet until she caught sight of her perceived monster, then the racket started. I growled right along with her as we moved from window to window. Soon the whole family laughed so hard I could barely participate, and all the while the young mothers pushing their strollers had no clue they were the target of such hilarity.

Sunshine, on the other hand, was still very unimpressed with the latest addition to the family. She tolerated Little Man, but that was all. If he came too close, she hissed and slapped at him, but all Little Man did was look at her as if to say, "*Whaaaat?*" However, Sunshine's time was coming.

I'm sure jealousy was part of the problem between Sunshine and Little Man, so I made sure to pay attention to all of the cats as much as I could. Soon Sunshine was happier, and in her own way claimed me as her human and developed a morning ritual.

It became routine for Sunshine to join me in the bathroom every morning as I got ready for work. First, there was the shower, and it was the same every time. As I showered, Sunshine ran to the glass shower door, pawed it ferociously, and screamed as if saying, "*He's drowning! He's drowning!*"

And every response from me was the same. "It's okay Sunshine. Daddy'll be out in just a minute."

This usually happened the entire time I was in the shower.

When I finished and Sunshine heard me turn off the water, she jumped on the toilet lid, which was right in front of the shower door, and waited until I dried off. Then she simply watched as I stepped out, dressed, shaved, and prepared for the day.

One day was very different from all the rest, however. Normally, I dried myself *before* I stepped out of the shower. But for some unknown reason, on that particular day I did things a little out of order. After I turned the water off and Sunshine jumped on the toilet, I grabbed a towel, opened the shower door, and began to dry myself *after* I stepped out of the shower.

I should have realized that there is a certain part of male, human anatomy that is right about eye level for a cat sitting on a toilet lid.

BAP-BA-BA-BAP-BA-BA-BAP-BA-BA-BAP-BA-BA-BAP! My nether regions got knocked around like a punching bag.

"Oomff...," I yelped, threw my hands between my legs, and hit the floor on my knees with the towel still over my head. After I composed myself for a minute, I gently reached up and pulled the towel off my head only to find myself eyeball to eyeball with Sunshine. I had her right where she wanted me.

"Sun...," I squeaked, and then cleared my throat before continuing, "Sunshine! What did you do that for?"

Sunshine looked straight at me, reached out with her nose and kissed me right in the mouth, then rubbed me under my chin with her head, back, and all the way to the end of her tail. She then turned around, settled herself back down on the lid, and purred.

I thanked God she didn't have any front claws.

CHAPTER 8 –
LITTLE MAN, THE MASCOT

When Little Man was still less than a year old, he had already grown to a size larger than all the other cats in the house. In fact, anyone visiting us would laugh when they heard his name. He certainly seemed more like a Big Man. He also had a strange habit, something I had never seen a cat do before. He loved to lie on the floor with his hind legs straight out behind him and his front legs straight out in front of him. Naturally, I took a picture.

The picture that started it all. Note the prominent "M" on his forehead.

A few days after I took the picture of Little Man in his prone position, I was at my desk at work thumbing through the pictures I had just picked up from the Base Exchange. Just as I came across the picture of Little Man, one of the young officers happened to walk by my desk. His name was Kevin, and since he was the second Kevin in the office, his nickname became "K2." The first Kevin, another young officer, was nicknamed "K-Naught," as in the "original" Kevin.

As soon as he spotted Little Man's picture, K2 asked, "Sir, may I borrow that picture?"

"Sure," I replied. "Just make sure I get it back."

I handed him the photo and he walked away.

The next day, K2 walked right up to my desk shortly after we all arrived at work and handed me the original photo plus another one. Being the computer guru that he was, I shouldn't have been surprised at what I saw. It was awesome.

Our unit was responsible for planning the routes for Conventional Air Launched Cruise Missiles, or CALCMs, as we called them. K2 had taken the picture of Little Man and scanned it into his computer, and then with some editing magic he had placed Little Man on the top of a cruise missile in flight, put a superhero cape on him, saved the new photo as a new file, and printed it out for me. Way cool.

Little Man, the superhero.

Soon, everyone in the office was talking about Little Man's photo. In no time at all it got the attention of our unit commander, another lieutenant colonel.

He walked up to my desk and said, "What's this I hear about a cat flying one of our missiles?"

I laughed and said, "K2 had a field day with a photo I took of my cat, Little Man. Here, check this out," and I handed him the photo.

He was very impressed. He immediately had a thought.

"You know what? This is our new mascot!" Everyone's eyes lit up and we all had a good laugh.

Then he asked, "Aren't some of you heading out to Korea for an exercise soon?"

"Yes, Sir," a couple of people answered.

"All right then. Here's what I want you to do."

He explained that he wanted someone to go to one of those shops in Korea where they made stuffed toys. He wanted to get about a dozen, stuffed, toy cats, with Little Man's coloring, and have them add a little cape with his name embroidered at the bottom. Then one of those would belong to the unit while the rest would be available for purchase by unit members. But he had something special in store for the "virtual" Little Man.

After the exercise in Korea, a couple of unit members came back with several Little Man stuffed toys. At my request, they also bought a cat-sized cape for Little Man himself. I paid for a couple of the toys and his cape, and the rest of the toys sold out in a hurry. The one belonging to the unit was designated as the travel companion for anyone going on an official trip. Whoever took "Little Man" along was to take a picture of him near something identifying the location, then the photo was pinned on the bulletin board at the office. It wasn't long before Little Man had virtually been around the world, with the photos to prove it! He was barely a year old, and he was already famous.

🐾   🐾   🐾

After I saw what could be done by a smart computer user, I had a thought. I decided I wanted to make a video of the 'Cuda restoration, complete with background music and driving scenes. K-Naught was my editor while I was the director. In our spare time we took videos of me doing one thing or another on the car. I had already taken photos of the teardown, primarily as an aid to help me get the thing back together, but the videos were going to add a whole new dimension. I couldn't wait to video the very first time I cranked the engine after the rebuild. It had not been cranked for almost fifteen years, and I was dying to hear her run!

When the day finally came to crank the engine, I was so excited I could barely think. We had everything set up. K-Naught was in the car with me with the camera trained on the oil pressure gauge. Another friend stood in front of the car, and Brandon was next to the driver's side door. Since I wanted to make sure the engine got oil before I cranked it for the first time, I had Brandon pull the coil wire off the distributor. This way the engine would turn over with the starter and I could see pressure on the gauge, but it would not be able to start until I made sure there was adequate oil pressure. Even Little Man wanted to get in on the action. He screamed at the door to the garage from inside the house, but with everything going on I felt it was not the best place for him. Besides, the garage was a wreck with oil, grease, parts, and tools everywhere. No, he would have to stay in the house.

I turned the key and heard the engine turn over, and K-Naught recorded the whole thing. After several seconds, I saw oil pressure registering on the gauge. So I turned the key to OFF and had Brandon reconnect the coil wire. We were ready for the big moment.

"Everybody ready?" I asked, with a slightly excited voice.

"Let's fire her up!" was the response in unison from everybody else.

I turned the key and … nothing. The engine turned over fine. The oil pressure was there. All the wires seemed to be connected properly. It just wouldn't start. I grabbed my phone and called my father.

"Check the rotor under the distributor cap. It's very easy to install backwards. See if that helps," he said.

"How can I tell if it's backwards?" I asked.

The rotor had a long neck with a large flat end, like that of a screwdriver, which sat in a grove on top of the oil pump. It can be placed in only two ways: the wrong way and the right way.

Daddy said, "Disconnect the coil wire and take out the number one spark plug. Stick your thumb over the spark plug hole and turn the engine until you feel pressure on your thumb. As soon as you feel pressure, turn the key immediately to OFF. Then pop the rotor cap off and see which way the rotor head is pointing. If it's pointing at the number one cylinder, it's good. If not, it'll be pointing backward toward the windshield."

Simply amazing. I'd heard stories about Daddy before, but I'd never seen it for myself. I'd heard he could do things like time an engine without a timing light, just by feel, by literally placing his hand on the engine and adjusting the timing until it felt right. But to be able to pinpoint a problem over the phone from one thousand miles away … I was in awe.

Sure enough, we did just as Daddy said, and the rotor head was pointing at the windshield. I lifted it up, turned it one hundred and eighty degrees, and stuck it back in its grove. Then we put everything back together. We were ready for another try.

"Here we go again! Everybody ready?"

This time, the response was more of a muffled, "Yeah."

I turned the key. The engine started turning. The oil pressure was coming up. I pumped the accelerator a little and …*VAROOOOOOOOOM!!*

My baby was running for the first time in fifteen years, and it was all caught on tape!

I left the engine running and K-Naught and I got out and walked to the front of the car. We wanted to *see* the engine running. It was a beautiful sight. I had chill bumps. But then I made a discovery which brought me right back down to earth.

I couldn't believe what I saw …there was a huge puddle of oil under the car. I had an oil leak. A bad one. After the way I painstakingly rebuilt the engine and meticulously followed all the rebuild instructions, I simply couldn't believe I had blown it so badly. To say I was bummed is an understatement.

I walked around to the driver's side, stuck my hand through the open window, and shut off the engine.

"Guess I have more work to do before we can continue with the video," was all I said.

We were done for the day. But the worst part was not that I had a leak. The worst part would be the guys in the office. They were going to have a field day with this, and I was certain I would never hear the end of it.

The following weekend I decided to try and determine the cause of the oil leak. I crawled under the car and sure enough, there was oil all over the back side of the oil pan.

That's it! I thought. *It's just a bad oil pan seal.*

Then I remembered taking the oil pan off to check the windage tray bolts several weeks earlier. I was convinced I messed up the seal when I put it back on.

I bought a new oil pan gasket set, pulled the oil pan off, cleaned it up, and replaced the seal, but this time I was especially careful not to over-tighten the twenty or so bolts. I knew that over-tightening can cause the seal to be squished out of place and result in an oil leak. *Yep. That must be what I did.*

When everything was put back in place, I crawled out from under the car and jumped inside to crank her up.

Just before turning the key, I heard Little Man, screaming at the top of his lungs, *"Let me in!"*

"Sorry, Little Man, this is not the place for you," I called to him.

Little Man was not convinced. He kept on, and on, and on, and on. But it couldn't be helped.

Trying to ignore the screaming, I turned the key and cranked the engine. She fired right up, and sounded *great*, by the way. I let her run for a few minutes, then shut her down and crawled back under the car.

Another puddle of oil, just like before. And it seemed to be coming from exactly the same place—the back of the oil pan.

How hard can this be?

I jumped up and checked the manual to make sure I was using the proper amount of torque on the bolts. As far as I could tell, I did everything correctly, so the only thing I could do next was replace the gasket and seals all over again. Back to the auto parts store I went.

When I returned with yet another gasket set, I went immediately back under the car and heard Little Man screaming at me just as before. But this time, he was even louder. Finally, Joy had had enough.

Without warning, she opened the door to the garage and said, "Can't you hear this baby screaming?"

Little Man ran into the garage and Joy closed the door behind him.

"Little Man, what are you doing in here? You can't be in here! There's junk and mess everywhere!" I said.

He ignored me and gingerly walked around every grease spot, every drop of oil, all my tools and parts, and found a nice clean spot under the car right next to me. Then he plopped himself down, yawned, and watched my every move without uttering a sound. I was completely but pleasantly surprised.

"All right then. We'll give it a try," I said. "But please stay out of the mess."

I did a quick look-around to make sure there was no antifreeze anywhere. That stuff kills. I didn't see anything I thought would hurt Little Man, so I let him stay for a while.

Back to the oil pan, I repeated the process all over again ... and the leak was still there.

Little Man and I replaced the oil pan gasket and seals four more times to no avail, and I was utterly frustrated. Little Man, however, loved every minute of it. He was finally in the garage with Daddy, and from that day forward, if I was in the garage, Little Man was in the garage with me.

I didn't know what else to do, so I called the service department of the nearest Dodge dealership. When the service manager came to the phone, I explained what was going on.

"You can certainly bring it to us and we'll have a look," he said, then continued, "but in all honesty, I think you'd be better off taking it to T&M Automotive. Tim's the owner, and he specializes in muscle cars. I'm sure he can fix it."

I was about to make one of the best friends I've ever had.

T&M was on the other side of town. I called and spoke to Tim, and we made arrangements for me to get the car to him the next weekend. Since the car still wasn't finished and had no lights installed yet, I loaded it on my trailer and hauled it over bright and early the next Saturday morning.

When I arrived, we introduced ourselves and got right to it. I explained in more detail what I had done and why.

"Little Man and I have done six oil pan changes over the last few days, and we still can't seem to get a good seal," I explained.

"You and who?" Tim asked.

"Never mind," I said. "But I'm at a loss as to why I can't seem to fix the problem."

"All right then. Let's have a look," Tim said with a puzzled look on his face.

He had a lift in his garage, so up the 'Cuda went. We could clearly see the oil on the back of the oil pan, and it certainly seemed to both of us that the pan was the source of the leak.

"Let's replace the gasket and seals," he said to one his employees. I stepped back to watch. If I was doing something wrong, I wanted to know what it was so I wouldn't do it again—ever.

In short order, Tim had the new set installed and was ready for a test. We cranked the engine and … there it was, still leaking.

Tim was deep in thought. "Hmmm. Maybe we just don't have a good oil pan. This one is clearly new. Do you still have the original one?"

"Yes, but it's at the house and still dirty and a little rusty on the outside."

"Go get it, and bring some paint to match the engine color," he said.

Off I went.

When I got back, Tim cleaned up the original oil pan, and then hit it with some paint. We waited a while to let the paint dry to the touch and started all over again with a new gasket and seals.

Strangely enough, we felt more confident that this was going to work.

We were wrong.

We cranked the engine and let it run for a few minutes, but the leak was still there.

"See what I've been going through?" I said.

Tim did not respond.

We both stood under the car and looked up at the oil pan. After eight attempts, six by Little Man and me, and two more by Tim, we were no closer to solving the problem. Several minutes later, Tim seemed to brighten up a bit.

He leaned toward me and said, still looking up at the oil pan, "Hand me a screwdriver and a paper towel."

I reached over to his tool chest and grabbed a screwdriver, then walked to his work bench and snatched a paper towel. I handed him both.

He wrapped the paper towel around the tip of the screwdriver, then stuck the screwdriver up into the space between the flywheel and the engine block, well above the top lip of the oil pan. When he brought it down, there it was— covered with oil.

Tim said, "I think we found the problem. It's one of the oil gallery plugs on the back of the engine block."

I knew what that meant. It meant the entire drive train had to come out so we could get to the back of the engine. I could see dollar signs and hear the sound of, *Cha-ching, cha-ching.*

"Well," I said, "I guess we better get at it." I just shook my head and turned away.

About forty-five minutes later, everything was removed—the drive shaft, transmission, bell housing, clutch, and flywheel—and we had a clear view of the back of the engine. It was plain as day. One of the oil gallery plugs was the source of the leak. A few taps with the screwdriver and out it came, completely dry of any sealant.

"There's the problem right there," Tim said. "There's supposed to be sealant on this plug to prevent this very problem. Why didn't you put sealant on it?"

I just smiled.

"You seem awfully happy. Is there something I don't know?" Tim asked.

"Yep," I responded. "This means it wasn't my foul-up. The oil gallery plugs were installed by the machine shop when I had the engine block cleaned and bored before I rebuilt the engine."

I was happy I wasn't a screw-up after all.

We applied about two cents worth of sealant to the plug and everything went back together. A quick run of the engine confirmed we had solved the problem, and to the tune of only a few hundred dollars of labor charges. It's something I'll never let happen again.

Soon Tim and I were fast friends. I made regular trips to his shop with the 'Cuda for help with one thing or another, mainly for things that were just too difficult for me to do in my cramped, two-car garage. But on one of my trips out there, I was presented with a little memento in memory of the oil pan fiasco.

One of Tim's employees was also a sign-maker. He made a sign for me. It reads, *Think Outside the Pan*. At the bottom of the sign, Tim glued yet one more oil pan gasket set—just for an emergency. Wise words, indeed.

It hangs in my garage to this day.

Call it a guy thing, but as soon as I got back at work, I made certain to inform the whole gang that I did not screw up my engine rebuild. I also passed on that Little Man was the supervisor throughout most of the ordeal. Soon, the status of the 'Cuda and the adventures of our mascot became daily reports. Most of the guys seemed genuinely interested, but the lone female in our group, a lieutenant named Becky, had little to say although she too seemed interested and laughed at some of my reports.

But one day she said, "When you can show me a video of Little Man driving the 'Cuda, then I'll *really* be impressed."

Hmmm. Guess I'll have to work on that one of these days.

Before long, K-Naught and I were back to work on the video, which I named *The Cuda Kid* after my citizens' band radio handle from my high school days, which was simply, "Cuda Kid." Even K2 got in on the action. We shot several scenes in the garage, and I had the background music all picked out. I had the driving scenes I wanted to shoot all planned out in my mind. I even planned to hire a pilot at the Aero Club on base to assist in getting some aerial shots. But alas, it was not to be. K-Naught and K2 were both notified they were due to move on to their new assignments. As a result, *The Cuda Kid* took a backseat to just about everything else. Also, I had another issue which took my attention away from anything to do with the 'Cuda. Buttercup was seriously ill.

Her illness really snuck up on us. Since she was a Sheltie, she had beautiful fur, and lots of it. One day, I picked her up to give her some Daddy loving and noticed she had lost weight. In fact, she was like a bag of bones. She didn't look ill, and she ate normally, but off to Dr. Wagner we went.

To our dismay, she was diagnosed with something similar to what happened to Kitty—more liver problems—and soon even her appetite dwindled to practically nothing. This time, treatment involved much more than just a pill twice a day. Her condition affected other systems in her body, and it was serious enough that Dr. Wagner recommended we seek some specialized care. The nearest facility capable of handling the job was the College of Veterinary Medicine at Kansas State University about three hours away.

After several trips and various treatments, which included a feeding tube that allowed us to feed her through her side via a tube in her stomach, Buttercup's condition seemed to be under control. She was still on medication, but she gained back some weight and ate on her own.

With Buttercup's condition under control, I was able to get back to the 'Cuda. But with the other 'Cuda in the garage and all the parts from the one in restoration all over the place, it became increasingly difficult to get much done. I needed more space.

In short order, Joy found a beautiful home for sale on five acres in north Omaha. It was classified as an earth home with two sides underground. The house itself was actually smaller than where we lived at the time but was built on the extreme north end of the property with a beautiful view of a wide open field that faced south—right over an in-ground pool. But the best part was the garage, or rather, the *two* garages. One was essentially a storage garage with enough room for one car. The other was a three-car garage with a doorway to the interior of the house. We took a drive to take a look, and decided on the spot we wanted it. We contacted the realtor and made an offer. It was accepted. The closing date was a short two weeks away.

But then we got more bad news: Buttercup's condition deteriorated again. Her appetite dwindled and she began to lose control of her bodily functions. We made one more trip to Kansas State, but there was nothing more that could be done. We knew we were going to lose her.

After a long discussion with Dr. Wagner, we set a date to take her in for the last time. But before that time came, we decided to give her a treat. She always loved to run around in wide open spaces, so a couple of hours before we were due at Dr. Wagner's, we cooked a small steak for Buttercup, piled in the car, and drove over to our new property. It was the day before we were scheduled to sign the papers for the house.

When we arrived, we opened the car door and turned Buttercup loose. She had a ball. She ran around and jumped and chased birds to her little heart's content. For a time, she showed no indication she was so seriously ill. But she soon tired and wandered back over to where we stood near the house. After she rested for a few minutes, we gave her a bowl of water and placed a dish with her steak on the ground. It was her last meal.

Every one of us dreaded what was about to happen, but we couldn't delay any longer. We scooped up Buttercup, loaded her and all of us in the car, and drove to see Dr. Wagner. Dr. Wagner took Buttercup to the laboratory to insert an IV through which to administer the necessary drugs, and brought her back to the examination room where we waited.

"Take all the time you need," she said. "Just let me know when you're ready."

There was not a dry eye in the room.

We all took turns with Buttercup and told her we loved her. It was one of the most difficult things I've ever faced, and no matter how hard I tried, I could not stop the tears. It occurred to me at that moment that I had never done that before. Every other family pet I had ever known either passed away suddenly and unexpectedly or disappeared never to be seen again. This was something altogether different. And I hated every second of it.

About fifteen minutes passed in the blink of an eye, and we all knew it was time. I opened the examination room door, nodded to Dr. Wagner, and closed the door. She came in a few seconds later with two syringes. She hesitated, and I nodded again. With every one of our hands on Buttercup, Dr. Wagner injected the first into Buttercup's IV and quietly explained that the first drug simply calmed her down and made her very sleepy. Before all of the drug was injected, we could see it taking affect, and Buttercup simply rested her head on the table between her paws. Then, the second drug was administered. This one stopped her heart. Dr. Wagner placed her stethoscope against Buttercup's chest and then nodded.

Our Princess Buttercup Boo was gone.

Buttercup.
Photo courtesy of James F. Pyrzynski.

We buried Buttercup in the backyard right next to Kitty. They were together their entire lives and travelled with us from Montana to California to Canada and finally to Nebraska with a trip to Alabama in between. Even though we were about to move out of one house and into our new one, we felt it was only fitting that Kitty and Buttercup rest in peace together where they spent their last days. As with Kitty, we all gathered around Buttercup's grave and said a little prayer. Then we all cried.

The next day, we closed on our new home.

🐾 🐾 🐾

It took many trips over several days with my car trailer to move all our things, but before long, Joy, Jonathon, Brandon, Sunshine, Sabrina, Little Man, and I were all settled in.

After a mere two nights in the new house, reality struck. We had five acres—with nothing more than an old push mower. We needed something bigger. I called Tim for advice.

Tim lived only about two miles from our new home, and he was also on a five-acre plot. He knew just what to tell me.

He said, "Don't do this the way I did it. Don't go buy a riding lawn mower, because pretty soon you'll want something bigger. You'll avoid getting what you really need because they're so expensive, but you'll wind up spending a ton of money only to bite the bullet and get a tractor later when all the money is gone. Meet me at the John Deere place."

Seems he's thought this through before, I thought.

As promised, Tim met me at the John Deere place. I walked out with copies of the signed paperwork for a 4210 model, complete with material collection system, mowing deck, loader (bucket), and rear blade for snow. It was delivered the next day. I had never been on a tractor before, but soon I drove like a pro. That thing was great. Even the boys got so they could handle it with ease, and we all *loved* it.

As was our habit, I would cut the yard around the house and then let Brandon jump on the tractor to cut the field. One day, before our first winter in the new house, I cut the yard and asked Brandon to do his thing out in the field. I had been back in the house for about five minutes when Brandon ran up to the kitchen window and pounded on it from the outside. He held a bloody, white, little ball of fur.

"Oh my God! Brandon hit a cat with the tractor!" I yelled to Joy and ran outside. She was right on my heels.

"What did you do?" I asked Brandon.

"Nothing, Dad. Before I even cranked the tractor I saw this kitten in the middle of the driveway. I think a dog got it or something."

I took a closer look. The kitten wasn't more than a week or two old. It was white with a few grayish areas, and there was blood all over its back.

"Give him to me," I said. We jumped in the car with the kitten and headed to Dr. Wagner's office.

"Well, what do we have here?" she asked when she came in the examination room.

"Brandon found this kitten in the driveway when he was about to get on the tractor. He said he didn't do anything to it. He just found it this way. I have no idea where it came from or who it belongs to. I just knew it needed your help," I explained.

Dr. Wagner just laughed. "I know exactly who this little guy belongs to."

"You do?" I asked. "Who?"

"He belongs to you!"

Translated, that meant I was going to be responsible for the bill. Just what I needed – another vet bill – on top of the new house payment and a brand new tractor payment. Yippee.

"Oh, all right. Go ahead and look him over, then give me the bad news."

Dr. Wagner said, "I'll be right back," and she headed off to the laboratory with the kitten in her hands.

A few minutes later, she strolled back in with a fluffy, little, pearl-white kitten. He was all cleaned up. Dr. Wagner had a mischievous grin on her face.

I looked at her quizzically and asked, "What's up?"

She looked at me and said, "You have no idea what you're in for, do you?"

"What do you mean?" I asked.

She said, "This kitten, a male, is only about two weeks old. As best I can tell, he was attacked, or rather, stolen from a litter by an adult male cat. He'll be fine. He has some punctures on his back, but they aren't bad at all. I'm not even going to prescribe any medication for them. Brandon must have come along just in time."

"Why would another cat do that?" I asked.

"They do that sometimes. They try to get rid of the kittens in the litter of a strange female so she'll go back into heat faster. It's a survival-of-the-fittest kind of thing."

"Single-minded little turd," I smirked.

Dr. Wagner laughed, "You're probably right. But you haven't heard the best part."

"Uh-oh."

"Uh-oh is right. You still have no idea, do you?

"Ummm, no. I guess I don't. What am I in for?"

"You're going to have to bottle feed this little guy …"

"Well, that's not so bad," I said and smiled.

"…every three to four hours. Not just during the day and when you go to bed and get up the next morning. I mean every three to four hours."

"You've got to be kidding."

"Nope. And there's more."

"There's more?"

"Oh yeah," she said. "You're going to have to help him go to the bathroom."

"Excuse me? I have to do what?"

"Come here and I'll show you," Dr. Wagner said as she took the kitten over by the sink in the examination room.

She said, "Hold him on his back like this."

She held him in the palm of her hand with his head toward her wrist.

"Turn the tap water on so that it's lukewarm with a slow, steady stream, stick his bum under the water, and gently massage like this with the thumb and fingers of your other hand."

As she rubbed him, he urinated right there in the sink. She made it look easy. I suddenly gained a whole new appreciation for mama cats.

"Good grief," I said. "How often do I have to do that?"

"Every time you feed him."

"Great." I had no idea how much work a practically newborn kitten could be.

"And it's a good idea to put him on a heating pad for a little while, but only on the lowest setting, and even then only if you can check on him every few minutes. You don't want him to overheat."

Things just kept getting better and better.

"I'll write down the formula you'll need and the amount he should have."

I'm sure she could tell I was feeling a bit overwhelmed.

"Anything else?" I asked.

"Good luck!" was all she said.

After we bought bottles, nipples, and formula at a pet shop, we took the little thing home. We decided to take turns feeding him in the middle of the night. During the day, especially on weekdays, Joy suffered the brunt of the effort since she could take him to work with her. On weekends, I took over most of the feedings.

He got his name at his very first feeding just minutes after we got home from the pet store. To keep his front legs under control, we wrapped him in a hand towel so that only his little head stuck out. Then we gave him his bottle. As he sucked, his ears wiggled. He was the cutest thing. But that's not why he got his name. He got his name because he looked just like the polar bear cub on the Coca Cola commercials.

We named him CoCo. After a couple of very long weeks of feeding and helping him go to the bathroom, CoCo was old enough to fend for himself and grew cuter by the day. And, just like all the others, he was rotten in no time.

Surprisingly, Little Man had no problem with the newest addition to the family even though CoCo was a male. In fact, by the time CoCo had grown to about half Little Man's size, they were best buddies. I never would have guessed it, but they were the first to cuddle together for a nap. But when Little Man wasn't cuddling with CoCo, he was cuddling with me. He was the only one of the four who would let me cradle him in my arms. He would lie on the couch right next to me with his head on my arm and snooze away. In that position, he would stretch his hind legs straight out with his feet around the center of my thigh. He was a big boy, and still the king, a point Sunshine was about to learn the hard way.

By the time Little Man was about two years old, he was noticeably larger than the other cats. He wasn't fat, just large. He was longer, taller, and heavier than any of the others. In fact, I considered the possibility that he was part Maine Coon, a very large breed of domestic cats. He has what looks like an "**M**" on his forehead, and for the longest time I thought that was a characteristic of Maine Coons. However, since then I've learned it's common to tabbies, and there are all kinds of folklore tales about how that came to be.

Since Sabrina took over as his adoptive mother when he was very young, there was no tension between them. Sunshine, however, had an attitude.

One afternoon, Little Man was on the floor just sleepily looking around. Then along came Sunshine, apparently jealous to the end. Defiantly, she walked up to Little Man, sat right in front of him, tapped him on the head with her paw, and hissed at him. At first, Little Man just closed his eyes and attempted to lean back away from her as if to say, "*Please leave me alone.*"

But Sunshine just wouldn't give it up. She kept popping him on the head.

Finally, Little Man opened his eyes, took a deep breath, and let out an audible sigh. Then, very slowly, he lifted his right front paw as though he was about to throw a baseball, and pulled the trigger. He hit Sunshine square on the side of her face and knocked her about two feet away. She landed flat on her side—and never bothered Little Man again. Oh yeah. Little Man is king.

Even though Sunshine and Little Man didn't get along very well, Sunshine loved her Daddy and all the attention I gave her. She came to me in the middle of the night, crawled up on my chest, and settled herself down about an inch from my face. That was the signal. I was supposed to pet her, and for as long as she wanted me to. If I dared to fall asleep, she let me know the error of my ways in a very peculiar way—she clamped her teeth on my chin.

"Yes, Sunshine, Daddy loves you," I said as I pet her with both hands.

She responded by purring as only she could with quick, short, shallow breaths.

Then I fell back to sleep.

Clamp.

"Okay, Okay, Sunshine, Daddy still loves you," I said again as I resumed my petting while she continued with her purring.

Back to sleep I went, and—*clamp.*

"Yeah, yeah, Sunshine, Daddy loves you," I said again and again.

After a while, I rolled to my side, which forced Sunshine to get off my chest. That was fine as long as I understood that it was her decision, not mine, to stop the show of affection. At least I got a little more sleep.

🐾　🐾　🐾

I came home from work one day and received a troubling report from Joy about Little Man. His right eye always seemed to ooze a little bit, but now it was worse. Joy was convinced he had some type of an infection, so back to Dr. Wagner we went.

Joy was correct, unfortunately. In fact, the infection was fairly serious and Little Man stayed overnight in the hospital and received heavy doses of antibiotics. He recovered, but to this day he gets "eye-boogers," those little globs of dried stuff in the corner of his eye. Dr. Wagner said she believes he's fine and that it's nothing to worry about. She explained that he may have a duct partially blocked by some scar tissue left over from his infection. I occasionally have to get a damp napkin and wipe his face, but Little Man doesn't seem to mind much. Besides, it makes him look tough.

🐾　🐾　🐾

Two of my usual chores around the house were to deal with the litter pans and feed the cats. With four cats, we went through a ton of litter and a ton of food. In all honesty, I really didn't mind. But since they all had good appetites, the litter pans got a lot of use. Feeding time was frenzied with all four cats eating at the same time out of four different bowls. Unfortunately, we didn't notice until too late that Little Man ate not only his own portion but any remainder the others left behind—and he got bigger and bigger.

About three months after Little Man's eye trouble, what I saw in the litter box gave me cause for yet another concern. I wasn't absolutely certain I knew who was responsible, but I had a hunch it was Little Man. I was correct.

By that time, Little Man was about two-and-a-half years old. One day after supper as I scooped the litter pans I noticed a couple of huge clumps of urine in the litter. They were softball size. I had no idea what that meant, but I knew it wasn't normal. So, the very next Saturday morning Little Man and I took another trip to see Dr. Wagner.

I think Dr. Wagner had a pretty good idea what the problem was right off the bat, but she probably wanted to confirm her suspicion before she said anything to me. She had me leave him with her. A couple hours later, she called with the bad news.

"I just wanted to call and give you a quick update. I'm amazed you caught it so quickly, but Little Man has diabetes."

I knew only enough about diabetes to know it's a bad disease, and I thought it was a death sentence.

She continued, "I'll understand if you want to do this. Many people put down their pets after getting this kind of news, especially if their pet is older. Treatment can be expensive. But Little Man is still young. You don't have to decide right now, but I wanted to let you know."

"Um, okay," I said. I think she could tell I wasn't happy with the news.

She said, "Give me a little time to clear some things up at my end and I'll call this afternoon. We can talk some more then."

"Okay. Thanks, Dr. Wagner," I said and hung up.

I didn't know what to think. I called Mama to give her the news.

"Oh, Mama, not Little Man," I said. My voice quivered a little.

"I know, honey," Mama said. "But she did say Little Man doesn't have to be put down, just that treatment is expensive."

"You're right, Mama, and as far as I'm concerned, as long as Little Man can still lead a normal life, he's not going anywhere."

Later that afternoon, Dr. Wagner called again.

"Like I said earlier, diabetes is treatable, but it's expensive and takes quite a bit of dedication. He'll likely need an insulin injection twice a day for the rest of his life," she said.

"Just how expensive is it? Will he be able to live normally?" I asked.

"Many cats live a completely normal lifespan, even with diabetes, so that's not a concern. The insulin bottles run about ninety dollars each and can last a couple months or so depending on how much we need to give him."

I could live with that and immediately felt better.

"I suppose you'll have to show me how to do all that," I said.

"Of course. Come on down here and we'll go over everything."

I was about to get one heck of an education on this disease. When I got to Dr. Wagner's office, she showed me which syringes I needed, how to draw up the correct dose, and even trained me how to give Little Man his injection. She had me practice on him using a syringe with sterile water.

"Always feed him first," she said. "Never give him insulin unless he eats. Too much can cause hypoglycemia, or low blood sugar. That can result in seizures and even death if it's severe enough, so it's better to give not enough than too much. After you've made sure he's eaten enough, give him his injection while he's still at his food bowl. He probably won't even notice."

She made it sound so easy.

She demonstrated with a syringe of sterile water. "To give an insulin injection, pull up right here between his shoulders so his skin forms a little tent, then just poke in a direction parallel to his back, squeeze, and withdraw the needle."

Seemed simple enough, but then it was my turn. I was able to do it without difficulty, and Little Man didn't seem to mind being used as a pincushion.

"Now we need to talk about diet," Dr. Wagner said. "Little Man needs special food for diabetics. We have just what he needs, but we'll need to determine a specific amount, and he *cannot* eat the regular food you give to the other cats. You're going to have to figure out how to feed them separately."

Per Dr. Wagner's guidance, we changed our daily routine so that Sunshine, Sabrina, and CoCo were fed in a separate room behind a closed door, and we continued feeding Little Man in the kitchen near the refrigerator where his insulin had to be kept. A month or so later, Little Man went back to Dr. Wagner for a checkup and a glucose curve. This involved testing his blood sugar levels every couple of hours during the day in an effort to determine if he was getting the correct dose of insulin. He was. Before long, our routine was established. All was well.

🐾 🐾 🐾

In the fall of 2003, I got some professional help finishing the 'Cuda. All that remained was some work on the interior, but I knew getting the headliner in place properly was going to be a bear. My hired help had a lot of experience and came highly recommended by Tim, so I turned him lose. About a week and several "tweaks" later, he was finished.

The very next Sunday morning, I awoke everyone at six-thirty. I was sure that was a good time—when there would be little to no traffic—for the first drive in the fully restored 'Cuda. I had not driven it in sixteen years.

The restored 'Cuda.

We hit the freeway and headed east on I-680 to the north of Omaha, then merged onto I-29 headed south. We planned to loop around Omaha, freeway all the way, and come back home from the west. As we headed south down I-29 on the Iowa side, a young girl in the only other car for miles came flying up behind us in her beat-up clunker. We were doing seventy miles per hour, the speed limit, but she easily passed us at about eighty-five. Suddenly, she hit the brakes, slowed to allow us to come along beside her, and then gave us a great big smile, flashed a thumbs-up, and then hit the gas and took off again.

That made every penny, every ounce of blood and sweat, and every excruciating effort completely worthwhile.

The 'Cuda restoration was complete—except for one minor thing.

I began to grow concerned about Maw Maw. She was getting on up in years, but her mind was as sharp as ever. Still, I wanted her to see the car before anything happened to her. After all, she put up with it in her yard for eleven years before I took it away for the restoration. Besides, Daddy hadn't seen it either. I decided to make the whole visit a surprise.

My cousin, Sonny, lived very close to both Maw Maw and Daddy. I called and explained what I wanted to do and we agreed to meet at Maw Maw's the following Saturday—one thousand miles away. I loaded the 'Cuda in my car trailer on Wednesday night after we dropped Little Man at Dr. Wagner's for boarding, and on Thursday we all hit the road for the two day drive from Nebraska to Alabama. A neighbor cared for the other cats since they didn't require any special attention.

Even my former stepfather was in on the action. On Saturday, we pulled up to his house and unloaded the 'Cuda. We stored the trailer under the deck on the side of his house, then jumped in the 'Cuda and headed to Maw Maw's.

When we arrived, she couldn't believe her eyes. "Is that the same car?" she asked.

"One and the same," I replied.

"Your Daddy's gonna love it," she said.

We decided to hide the 'Cuda in Maw Maw's garage and have Sonny call Daddy to come over. He gave Daddy some made-up excuse for needing him to drop by—and it worked.

About twenty minutes after Sonny's call, Daddy pulled in the driveway. We watched through the window in the closed, garage door. Sonny met him outside and drew his attention toward the street away from the garage. At the signal from Sonny, we hit the button to open the garage door. It was practically fully open before Daddy noticed a thing.

"Oh my God," he said as he turned and saw the 'Cuda.

We all ran out to give him a hug since we hadn't seen him for some time, but soon everyone stood around the 'Cuda.

"All right, Daddy, you and Maw Maw are coming with me. We're going for a little drive," I said.

With Maw Maw in the front and Daddy in the back, I cranked up the 'Cuda and headed out. We drove over to a private airport about five minutes from Maw Maw's house, and along the way, I played a very special song on the CD player I had installed instead of the old AM radio. It's one of their favorite songs of all time, *My Way*, by Elvis Presley. I'm not sure, but I think I saw a tear in Maw Maw's eye as we drove along and listened to the song.

At the airport, I got out and asked Daddy to do the same, then I handed him the keys.

"Here. You can take us back," I said. He smiled as I crawled into the back seat.

Just as he pulled us back into the driveway, Daddy said, "Wow. This thing drives as good as it looks."

When we got out of the car, someone suggested we take some pictures.

"Not yet," I said.

"Why not?" Daddy asked.

"Because the restoration is not actually complete yet."

He just looked at me with a confused look on his face.

The 'Cuda is the sports version of the Barracuda. There are a few differences which make the 'Cuda stand out from the Barracuda, the most noticeable of which are the Rallye hood with the two air scoops sticking up and the two holes in the rear valance under the bumper through which the exhaust tips exit. By contrast, the Barracuda has a flat hood and the exhaust comes out underneath the valance rather than through it. But another difference is an emblem on the tail lamp panel right next to the license plate. It simply says, "Cuda." Daddy never noticed it was missing.

I reached in my pocket, pulled out the emblem, handed it to him and said, "I want you to finish the job."

With tears in his eyes, he pealed the backing off the emblem, stood at the back of the 'Cuda, and meticulously placed the emblem in its rightful place on the tail lamp panel.

After over five years of blood and sweat and more parts and money than I ever dreamed possible, the 'Cuda restoration was finally complete.

Left to right: Brandon, Jonathon, Sonny, Jonny, Daddy, and Maw Maw in front of the restored 'Cuda.

I retired from active duty during the winter of 2004. I didn't know it at the time, but two of my former TPS classmates, CJ and Rex, both astronauts, jumped in a NASA T-38 and tried to surprise me with a visit to my retirement ceremony. They made it about halfway from Houston to Omaha before they had to stop because of the weather. But a couple of weeks later I got a neat retirement gift in the mail. Rex sent me a signed photograph of himself on a spacewalk, and inside the envelope with the photo was a mission patch from every space shuttle mission flown by one of our TPS classmates. It was a remarkable gift. I called Rex to thank him, and promised to one day frame the photo and all the patches, once all of our classmates finished their NASA careers, and display it in a prominent place in my home.

Another gift I received from my unit was a framed cover of *Time* magazine. At the start of the second Gulf War, our unit planned the cruise missile strikes during the "shock and awe" period, and one of the hits was photographed and placed on the cover of *Time*. A couple of lieutenants in the office contacted the magazine staff and received permission to modify the cover so it included the name of our unit, but only for the purpose of producing copies for the members of our unit to hand out as going-away gifts. All the members of the unit signed it for me. Becky had something very interesting to say.

On the back, she wrote, "What am I going to do without my daily dose of 'Cuda and Little Man stories?"

It hangs in my room to this day.

Shortly after retirement, I started a new job as a contractor for a small company there in Omaha, and I found myself looking for a new hobby. The 'Cuda was finished, but even though I had another one to restore, I didn't have the time, the money, or the energy to tackle such a project again anytime soon. I'm not sure what made me think of them, but I wound up starting a collection of action figures, specifically Johnny West and GI Joe, my favorite toys as a boy. Before long, I had a nice little collection that continued to grow over the next few years.

One of the items I found is a Jeep for GI Joe. I bought it from another collector. When it arrived, I couldn't wait to get it out of the box. I was like a kid at Christmas.

"Hey, Brandon! Check this out," I called to him as I opened the box.

Everything was there, even the cannon with four projectiles, and this particular set was an early one with the battery-operated engine sounds. It was over forty years old, and the spring for the cannon was a little rusty. Still, it seemed to function just fine.

I decided to test it.

I cocked the firing mechanism, dropped a projectile into the barrel, but then paused.

The plastic may be brittle, I thought.

"Brandon, stick your finger right here. You'll heal. The plastic won't."

He understood and agreed completely.

"Okay," he said and placed his finger so that when I released the firing mechanism his finger would take the impact, not the barrel.

I let her rip.

The projectile flew all the way across the room and put a ding in the wall on the far side.

"Whoa! That was cool!" Brandon said. "No wonder you guys only had three television stations when you were growing up. You didn't need any more. You had such cool toys to play with!"

Ain't it the truth.

In November 2005, I received some very bad news. Pop died. I was a thousand miles away at the time. I knew he was in the hospital, but he had been there other times for one thing or another without difficulty. This time was clearly different. Had I known he was in such bad shape I would have been right by his side.

Pop meant the world to me. No matter where I was, no matter how far away, Pop and I spoke on the phone or in person at least once a week since as far back as I can remember. He was the single, most influential person behind my decision to become an engineer. He was always there for me—first when I was a child and then later as an adult. I could always count on Pop.

But now he was gone.

Jonathon was away in the Army, and Joy was on a girls' trip to Savannah, Georgia, so Brandon and I dropped Little Man, Sunshine, Sabrina, and CoCo at Dr. Wagner's office that evening, then jumped in the car at 4:00 the next morning and hit the road to Alabama. We got to Pop's house a little over eighteen hours later, exhausted.

Joy could not get a flight so quickly out of Savannah, so she rented a car and drove to Augusta, Georgia, to pick up Jonathon after he was released from duty for a family emergency with the help of the Red Cross. They arrived shortly before Brandon and I did. Caroline, Pop's stepdaughter, was already there also with her two children, Lauren and Matthew. Her husband had died young a couple years earlier. I had not seen her in twenty-five years, so I walked over to give her a hug. It was like hugging an ice sculpture. I didn't understand at the time, but later I would understand perfectly. It was very late in the evening and the memorial service was scheduled for the next morning, so we all went straight to bed.

It seemed as though nearly everyone who was or had been a part of my life at one time or another came to the memorial service. My former stepfather, my cousin Sonny, and people I hadn't seen in years all came to bid Pop a fond farewell. Pop was going to be cremated so there was no viewing. At the appropriate time during the service, anyone with something to say about Pop was given the opportunity to do so.

I went first. I could barely speak and cried through most of my little speech.

Caroline went next.

A day or two after the service, Caroline and I met to identify Pop's body. After the cremation, we buried Pop's ashes next to my grandmother, Wanna, as Caroline's mother suggested. All seemed well, so a couple of days later I returned home to Nebraska. But while everything else seemed to be fine, I was anything but.

With all the stress of Pop's death, I finally became aware of my true feelings regarding my marriage. I realized I was in denial about the issues that began five years earlier. I'm not sure, but I think Joy felt the same thing. Although we gave it our all, we knew it simply wasn't going to work out. We talked and decided to divorce. But we also decided to wait until after Christmas to take any action. Still, I was a mess.

That Christmas will always stand out for me, but not because it was our last as a family. By that time we were both well aware our family was fractured, so that wasn't it. What made it so memorable was what happened on Christmas Eve.

Pop's death and burial interrupted much of our normal Christmas decoration activities. In fact, it was Christmas Eve before we had a chance to complete decorating the tree. So that night, we all began to do just that.

That's when I decided to build a fire in the fireplace.

The previous summer, I had helped a neighbor cut down and chop up some trees on her property. In return, she said I could keep all the wood I wanted. I bought an outdoor stand and filled it to the brim with all the wood it would hold. It was from that pile I retrieved some wood for the fire. But there was a problem. The wood wasn't exactly seasoned yet enough to burn, as I was about to find out.

After several attempts, I finally got a small fire going. But before anyone knew what was happening, the house filled with smoke. Normally, the heat of the fire would start the flow of smoke up the flue and out the top of the chimney. But because the wood wasn't quite dry enough to burn, the heat just wasn't there, and the smoke filled the house.

Every smoke alarm in the house went off at the same time.

Not really knowing what to do, I tried to fan the fireplace hoping the fire would catch better and grow the flames. All that did was make it worse. Everyone was coughing and yelling, our eyes were watering, and the noise was unbearable.

I yelled at no one in particular, "Open the doors and windows!"

Everyone scattered like cockroaches and did as I said, only to allow even more smoke to travel through the house instead of up the chimney.

But that created another problem. During the cold winter months, mice were notorious for sneaking into the house, and especially the garage, to get warm. With all three doors leading to the outside wide open, we were inviting trouble. On top of that, the cats all wanted to go outside. So we had to stand guard at the doors to keep the mice out and the cats in.

But the smoke was still there.

I knew I had to get the fire out, and quickly, so I did the only thing left to do—I grabbed the tongs. I reached into the fireplace, picked up one of the pieces of smoking wood between the fingers of the tongs, and headed for the nearest door.

"Everybody get out of the way!" I screamed as I ran through the house with the smoldering smoke generator and prayed I wouldn't drop it on the carpet. I ran out the door and dropped the wood in the snow, then headed back to the fireplace for another log.

Two more trips for two more pieces of wood and the fire was gone.

By then, the smoke was clearing, but the house was getting cold. We waited just a few more minutes before closing the doors and windows. When everything was almost back to normal, we gathered in front of the fireplace and just stared at the mess on the hearth, and every one of us burst into laughter. We felt just like the Griswold's in *National Lampoon's Christmas Vacation.*

So we watched the movie—and never did finish the tree.

After the holidays, I filed for divorce and got the process started. As if the stress of divorce wasn't enough, I had other problems. As a defense contractor, my job was dependent upon contract renewal, and in my case, the renewal was supposed to happen again just a few months later. But my company leadership was concerned it may not happen due to cutbacks in government funding. Things were stressful indeed, but we tried to remain upbeat for another reason— Brandon was due to graduate from high school in just weeks. It was tough to do.

Through it all, there was Little Man.

    🐾   🐾   🐾

For some reason, Little Man became somewhat of an anchor of reality for me. He was a constant reminder of better times and a brighter future. In a way, he was what kept me grounded and hopeful. Jonathon was away in the Army. Brandon was heading off to college soon after graduation. Joy and I were divorcing. There was a good chance I was about to lose my job. But Little Man was always there to perk me up, and sometimes his presence and the feeling of him leaning against me while napping were just enough to give me a reason to smile. In his own way, he was invaluable to me. No matter how I felt, no matter what was going on around me, Little Man had a way of making things seem better. He was a rare flicker of light that shone brightly during my darkest hours, and I loved him for it.

🐾   🐾   🐾

By June 2006, the divorce was final, Brandon graduated and made plans for college in Colorado, but my job was still in question. Realizing that my future in Nebraska as a defense contractor was bleak, I researched the possibility of a position closer to home. I found several possibilities at Oak Ridge National Laboratory, about thirty minutes from Knoxville, Tennessee, and only about three and one-half hours from "home" in Alabama.

Even though Oak Ridge is a Department of Energy facility and my experience involving nuclear systems was by virtue of my work in the Department of Defense, I was already very familiar with the processes and procedures in operations and security and felt I was indeed well qualified. Believing a job offer was imminent, I quit my job as a contractor and decided to move out there. Besides, under the circumstances, I really needed to leave Nebraska.

But there was a catch.

In the divorce decree, Joy specified that she would maintain custody of the cats—even Little Man.

I was heartbroken. However, I didn't fight her decision. By that time Joy was a pharmacist and perfectly capable of caring for the cats. It really was the best solution, especially since I had no job waiting for me. Of course I was extremely sad to be leaving Little Man behind, and I felt guilty since he was right by my side during the most difficult period of my life. But I was confident he was in safe hands.

So my departure from Nebraska was bittersweet. I was embarking on a new life, but I had to say goodbye to my Little Man.

Sometimes, life just sucks.

CHAPTER 9 –
A NEW LIFE ...

The first thing I did when I arrived in Tennessee was look for a place to store the 'Cuda. After all, first things first. Fortunately, Caroline lived in Knoxville, so she suggested a couple of places.

Then seemingly out of nowhere, our relationship began to grow.

The 'Cuda itself even played a part.

Shortly after my arrival in Tennessee, there still was no job offer and I grew concerned. Well, in truth, I was more confused than concerned since I knew I was qualified for many available positions. I still had my military pension which was enough to exist, but not necessarily enough to live on. I was fine, but understandably bummed out after everything that had happened recently. In an effort to cheer me up, Caroline mentioned the Rod Run.

The "Shades of the Past Rod Run" is one of the largest car shows in the country and is held annually around Labor Day in Pigeon Forge about an hour and a half from Knoxville. However, my version of the story seems to be a little different from hers.

One day she said, "Jonny, I think we should take the 'Cuda to the Rod Run in Pigeon Forge."

"What's that?" I asked.

"Only the biggest car show you've ever seen."

I looked outside. The one thing I never do with the 'Cuda is drive it in the rain, and there were many clouds overhead.

"No, I don't think so. It looks like it might rain."

She responded with an eye-roll. Then she said, "You'll love it. There will be literally thousands of cars there. Everyone just pulls in whatever parking lot they can find, they pop the hoods of their cars, and then they walk around drooling. It's awesome. Everybody will love your car. Besides, it's not going to rain."

With that, she says I puffed out my chest, changed my entire expression, and couldn't wait to hit the road, but I seem to remember that I merely reluctantly agreed.

After breaking the car out of storage, Caroline, her children Lauren and Matt, and I arrived in Pigeon Forge about two hours later. I found a nice spot facing the road in a grocery store parking lot, parked the car, and popped the hood. But there was no way I was going to walk off and leave the 'Cuda unattended. I insisted we each take turns staying with the car while the others walked around.

It was just like she said it would be. There were six lanes running through town, and by mid-afternoon there was not one more parking spot available anywhere along the two- or three-mile stretch of town. I saw some unbelievable cars, and while I was out walking around, Caroline said at least three different people stopped and tried to buy the 'Cuda from her.

She knew that would happen only over her dead body.

When we were ready to leave, she begged me to let her drive.

"Can you drive a stick?" I asked.

Another eye-roll. "Yes, of course I can," was the response.

I hesitated for a moment. I looked her over and tried to assess whether I thought she was up to the task. After all, the 'Cuda is not an ordinary car. And it's my baby.

Again, I reluctantly agreed.

I drove to the nearest gas station to fill up, then let her get behind the wheel when it was time to leave. Lauren and Matt were in the back seat.

When everyone was strapped in she cranked the car and pulled away from the pump. We had to wait a while for a break in traffic, but soon a spot appeared. She pulled into traffic with no difficulty—then stalled the car right there in the middle of six lanes of muscle cars zipping by. All we needed was for someone to ram us from behind and my car would have been a mess.

Caroline went into a full-blown, four-alarm, all-out *panic*. She was crying, screaming, and blubbering to the point I couldn't understand a single word.

From the back seat, Lauren and Matt screamed in unison, "Mommy, please let Jonny drive!"

I held my hand up to gesture to them it would be okay, then very calmly said to Caroline, "Everything's fine. Take a deep breath. Now, push in the clutch. The car can't start unless you push in the clutch."

She was still crying a little bit but followed my instructions and pushed in the clutch.

"Okay," I said, "now make sure you're in first gear before you crank it back up."

She checked and satisfied herself she was in first gear, then cranked the car and seemed to collect herself a little.

"All right. Now give it a little bit of gas and let the clutch out a little bit at a time. A little gas, a little clutch, okay? Just a little gas and a little clutch."

The car slowly started to move—in third gear.

"A little gas, a little clutch," I said again.

She practically burned up the clutch, but she did it. She drove us all the way home without any more trouble.

She told me later that was the event which drew her to me more than anything else. It was because I was so calm when my 'Cuda was stalled in the middle of all those cars, and because I didn't scream at her for messing up in the first place. In her words, it was my "confidence under stress" that made the difference.

Yeah, the 'Cuda was the catalyst that sparked our relationship. Caroline's been driving it quite well ever since.

As time went on, we became closer and closer. But she noticed something else about me: I simply would not shut up about Little Man.

I told her everything. I told her he was the mascot for my old military unit, commonly called, "Det 1." I told her how he helped me finish the 'Cuda restoration. I told her about waking up in the middle of the night to find myself nose-to-nose with Little Man. Not only did I tell her everything … I told her over and over and over again.

And she rolled her eyes at every story.

But she took it to heart.

A few weeks went by, and still there was no job offer. I kept busy with routine maintenance on my truck. I also made a couple more trips out to Nebraska to pick up a few personal items and some furniture I had left behind. The 'Cuda took up all the space in my car trailer during my first trip out to Tennessee, so some things had to wait.

While I was away on one of my trips to Nebraska, Caroline called to tell me she had a little surprise for me when I got back to Tennessee. I didn't have a clue what it could be, and I certainly never expected what it was.

Caroline got me a kitten. She and Lauren and Matt had gone to the pet store to pick up some food for their beagle, Ginger, when a man walked in with a litter of kittens he wanted to give away. One of them, a male, was white with some gray spots, and since Little Man was gray and was all I talked about, they decided he would be the one. They named him Tiger. What made this so sweet was that Caroline is allergic to cats—and Tiger had to stay in her townhouse.

I tried to spoil him right from the start.

About a week later, Caroline had to go on a business trip for a full week.

"Surprise!" she said when she told me. "You get to watch the kids. And by the way, they're both grounded."

At the time, Lauren was seventeen and Matt was ten. School started just days earlier and already they were in trouble at home for one thing or another. They had never been grounded before. I was in for a rough time. To this day, I call it, "Hell Week."

Right off the bat on Monday morning, just minutes after Caroline left on her trip, things started happening.

CHAPTER 9 – A NEW LIFE …

First, Ginger started acting very strangely. She squealed at even the gentlest efforts to pick her up and soon threw up everywhere. We locked her in the spare bathroom downstairs next to the kitchen and felt confident she had just eaten something to upset her stomach and that she would be fine after a few hours. But in all the excitement, Matt missed the bus to school. So I loaded him in my truck and dropped him off.

When I got back to Caroline's townhouse, Lauren told me that she too missed her bus. So, another trip to drop off Lauren and I was back.

I figured I had better get to work on some things, so I started a load of clothes in the washer, then headed to the upstairs bathroom—Ginger was in the other one—only to find the toilet stopped up.

I looked all over the place for something to use on the toilet, but all Caroline had was one of those snake things. So I went to work.

I fought with that stupid toilet for about two hours to no avail. I decided to take a break and go downstairs to put the clothes in the dryer and start another load in the washer.

Just when I rounded the corner in the kitchen and could see into the laundry room I noticed the washer. It had "walked" about two feet from its original position. Since I still had the toilet on my mind, I didn't think much of it. I just pushed it back into place, unloaded the clothes into the dryer, and started another load.

Back at the toilet, I tried again for a few minutes, but finally decided to head to the hardware store for a plunger. It was only about ten minutes away so I was there and back in no time.

As soon as I walked back into Caroline's townhouse, I again noticed the washer, still running, and trying its best to jump out of the laundry room.

I ran over and shut it off. I soon discovered the only thing that kept the washer in the room at all were the water hoses attached to the faucets on the wall and to the back of the washer. I had no idea how long this had been going on, but I knew that unless I could figure out the problem it was about to become one big giant mess.

I stepped back from the washer and gave it a good hard look.

Is this thing alive? I wondered.

Then I noticed a large piece of gray plastic on the bottom of the washer. I stooped down, tilted the washer backward toward the wall, and peeked underneath to find a shipping tray still screwed to the bottom of the washer. In big, bold, block letters I found the word, R E M O V E. Even though Caroline was nowhere around, I gave her my own eye-roll.

Two can play at that game, I thought.

I went out to my truck for some tools, and in short order, I had the washer back in place and ready for use.

On my way back to the truck with my tools, I noticed the plunger.

Oh yeah, I thought, *the toilet.*

I stopped dead in my tracks, grabbed the plunger, and headed upstairs.

A few plunges later and the toilet was running again. But it was running, and running, and running. It wasn't overflowing. It just wouldn't stop running.

Back downstairs for my tools, then back upstairs to the toilet.

Fortunately, no new parts were necessary. A minor adjustment to the chain attached to the handle and the problem was solved.

I headed back downstairs and heard Ginger whining. I peeked in on her and saw she wasn't getting any better.

Oh, brother, I thought. *Now I have to go to the vet.*

I grabbed Ginger's leash and walked her to my truck. The vet was just down the road.

This shouldn't take long, I thought.

I was wrong.

I waited for what seemed an eternity, then got the news: Ginger had eaten some cat litter, poop and all, compliments of Tiger. She was going to be fine. She might still throw up for a while, but she would be okay—except for the fact that she was never potty trained. Oh boy.

Back at the townhouse, I put Ginger back in the spare bathroom and headed to the laundry room. Then I noticed the time. I realized school would be out shortly and I had no idea what to do for supper. But at least I wouldn't have to go pick up Lauren or Matt. They would come home on the school bus.

As I was going through the kitchen looking for something to make for supper, Lauren walked through the front door.

"Where's Matt?" she asked.

"You mean he doesn't come home on the bus?" I said.

"No. He has to be picked up in the afternoon."

Good grief, I thought.

Back to the elementary school I went.

At least Caroline had remembered to inform the school that I would pick Matt up instead of her. I just wish she had remembered to tell me.

A few minutes later, everyone was back at the townhouse. But I was exhausted. Too tired to even think about cooking, I decided to go get some burgers.

I said to both of them, "All right. I'm going to go get us something to eat. In the meantime, your Mom said to make sure you get all your homework done before any playtime. Okay?"

"Okay," Lauren said.

"I don't have any," Matt said.

"All right then. I'll be back in a few minutes. Don't open the door for anyone but me."

About twenty minutes later, I got back with some burgers. We all ate, then Lauren and I cleaned the kitchen. By the time that was done, it was well past eight. Matt's bedtime was at nine.

"Matt, it's time for a shower. Run on upstairs. Don't take too long, it's almost bedtime," I said.

"Okay," he said and disappeared.

Just a few minutes before nine, the phone rang. It was Caroline.

"How was the first day?" she asked.

I took a deep breath and relived the whole day. I explained everything that happened. Caroline laughed so hard it sounded like she was crying on the other end of the phone.

"At least it's finally over, except for the clothes," I said.

Then right at 9:00 PM, Matt walked into the room.

"You know, Jonny, I did have some homework," he said.

Caroline heard him. All I heard from the other end of the phone was a screech of laughter. Since Matt was still standing right there, I bit my tongue.

"I guess the day ain't over yet," I said to more laughter and hung up.

Oh, Caroline, you're gonna owe me big-time, I thought as I helped Matt finish his homework before finally getting to bed about 10:00 PM. The first day was finally over.

I've been through military survival training twice, once during the summer in the mountains of Colorado, and again during the winter in the frigid, far north of Canada. Both times were picnics compared to Hell Week.

•ꞏꞏ•   •ꞏꞏ•   •ꞏꞏ•

Toward the end of August, I received some terrible news. Daddy had cancer. It started in his lungs, but by the time it was discovered it had spread to his brain. He immediately started treatment.

If ever there was a perfect time to be unemployed, that was it. I was able to get to Birmingham and stay with Daddy in the hospital whenever other family members couldn't. Treatment started with radiation. Next, a port was placed in his chest to be used for chemotherapy treatments. He responded well to the radiation, but then his body started to fall apart. By mid-September he was back in the hospital—and it didn't look good.

I headed down as soon as I could. My stepmother, a few of my siblings, Caroline, and I met with the oncologist who explained some good news and more bad news. The good news was that the cancer in Daddy's brain was gone thanks to the radiation treatments, and the cancer in his lungs had stopped growing. From that standpoint, it looked like he was going to win the battle. But then there was another problem. The placement of the port for the chemotherapy resulted in a staph infection, and his whole system was in sepsis. Essentially, the infection was poisoning him.

After our meeting with the doctor, we went to Daddy's room to see him. He was "out of it" for the most part, but still able to communicate. We visited for a while, and then got into a discussion amongst ourselves about who would stay overnight with him. Everyone else had been there off and on for days at a time already, and they really needed to get back to work. So the choice was obvious. I would stay until he either went home, or ...

He had been in the hospital for several days already. For a time, it was just the two of us. We talked a little, as best he could, and then I said I wanted

120

to head down to the cafeteria to get a bite to eat. Just before I walked out of the room I reached in my pocket and pulled out the keys to the 'Cuda.

Several years earlier, I bought a keychain in the shape of the emblem on the tail lamp panel on the back of the car, just like the one Daddy put in place to officially complete the restoration. It simply read, *Cuda.* There were only two keys on it: the ignition key and the trunk key.

I took Daddy's hand, placed the keys in his palm, wrapped his fingers around them, and then said, "Here Daddy. I need you to hang on to these for me."

"What's this?" he mumbled.

"The keys to the 'Cuda," I said.

"I can do that," he said, and gave me a little smile.

Then he said, barely audibly, "I'm proud of you."

I smiled at him and said with a little laugh, "Yeah, the 'Cuda turned out pretty good, didn't it?"

"No," he said, nodding his head, "the 'Cuda is just a car. But what you did to it is a reflection of you. That's what I'm proud of."

That brought a tear to my eye.

Throughout the night, Daddy tossed and turned and said very little. The nurse came in several times to check one thing or another, but specifically checked the oxygenation of his blood. I had no idea what a normal level should be, but I could see on the meter that the values were in the seventies. The nurse didn't seem to make much of it, so I didn't either.

Early the next morning, the oncologist walked in. She spoke with the nurse about several things, most of which I barely understood, but then she asked about Daddy's oxygenation levels.

I don't know what made me speak up, but I interjected, "The levels I saw just about every time they were checked were in the seventies."

The doctor just stood there with a concerned look on her face, then turned to the nurse and said, "Intensive care, STAT."

I would later learn that anything lower than the nineties was too low for oxygen in the blood.

If that's the case, I wondered, *why wasn't it a concern last night?*

Nevertheless, in short order Daddy was wheeled down the hall to the intensive care unit.

I called my stepmother. She arrived shortly thereafter.

Daddy made a rebound after about two days in intensive care. By that time, practically the whole family had arrived from various parts of the country, and there was cause for hope. His kidneys kicked in and he was urinating like crazy. He was on a respirator which made communication impossible, and was heavily medicated as a result, but he was awake just enough to nod his head. I waited for an opportunity when we were alone to let him know what was going on.

"Daddy, can you hear me?"

He just nodded.

"All right then. Has anyone told you what's going on?"

This time, he shook his head, *no.*

"Okay. Right now, things are looking better. The last I heard from the oncologist, the cancer in your brain is gone, and the cancer in your lungs has stopped growing. It looks like the radiation worked. Do you understand?"

A nod, *yes.*

"Another good thing is that even though you weren't urinating much before, now you're pissing like a race horse. But now is not the time to ease up. It looks like you're going to beat this, but you've got to keep fighting. Understand?"

He nodded again.

Then I continued, "Now, the reason you're here in intensive care is because you developed a staph infection from the port in your chest …" I tapped his chest to help him understand what I was talking about, then said, "… and you're all doped up from the medication they're using to fight the infection. Hang in there, Daddy. I love you."

Another nod. He understood.

The next day, just when we thought things were going to be fine, Daddy took a turn for the worse. His kidneys stopped working and it was apparent to everyone we were going to lose him. The doctors assured us there was nothing more they could do, but that at least he could breathe on his own. He was taken off the respirator and an oxygen mask was placed over his nose and mouth. He was in his last hours.

Everyone was there. I am the oldest of Daddy's eight kids from multiple marriages and was standing right next to my youngest half-brother, Darrell. All my other brothers and sisters stood around the hospital bed. Caroline had come down from Knoxville, and she was by my side. My two boys, Jonathon and Brandon, and Caroline's kids, Lauren and Matthew, were also there, as was our cousin Sonny and my stepmother, Jean.

About two hours after the respirator was removed, Daddy took his last breath. He was surrounded by all of his children, and every one of us had our hands on him the moment he died.

The room was full of tears.

I was standing to Daddy's left, right next to his left hand. Darrell was standing there too. Without a word, Darrell reached down and took Daddy's left hand in his—and the keys to the 'Cuda were still there. He gently pulled the keys from Daddy's grasp, turned, and slowly handed them to me. We hugged. And we cried.

Daddy was gone.

Daddy's six sons and our cousin, Sonny, were pallbearers at his funeral a couple of days later. At six-feet, three-inches tall, Daddy was a big man. His grave was about one hundred yards from where the hearse parked, and by the time we carried him about halfway to his gravesite, we were all grunting.

Suddenly, somebody said in between grunts, "I guaran-damn-tee y'all one thang ..."

Even under the circumstances, that got chuckles from the rest of us since that's exactly how Daddy used to talk.

"... Daddy's up there right now lookin' down at us and sayin', '*Y'all better NOT drop my ass.*'"

We almost dropped him right then and there.

CHAPTER 10 –
... AND A NEW BEGINNING

Three months after Daddy's death, Christmas came and went. Understandably, it was quite different without him. It seemed to be harder on Maw Maw than on anyone else. There is something terribly unnatural about losing a child, especially one with grandchildren of his own. Children expect parents to pass away before they do. Parents, on the other hand, never expect their child to pass away first. It's still very hard for her, especially around Christmas.

As for me, Pop died just before I came home after spending over twenty years away in the military, then Daddy died just after I returned. I had hoped to make up for lost time, but that opportunity was gone now. I missed them both terribly.

On the flipside, my relationship with Caroline had grown even stronger; we decided to marry and planned the wedding for the following summer. In a way, I was surprised at how far our relationship had come, especially considering that "ice sculpture" hug I got when I first saw her again after twenty-five years. One day, I decided to ask her about that.

We were discussing wedding plans, and I asked, "By the way, do you remember that hug you gave me when I got to Pop's the day before his memorial service? What was that all about?"

She looked at me and smiled. Then she said, "You really don't know, do you?"

"Not a clue."

She proceeded to tell me about life with Pop after I started school again and was unable to visit. All Caroline heard about over the years was me. Pop kept her abreast of all my activities and accomplishments. When I graduated with my bachelor's degree, Pop told her about it. When I became an officer, Pop told her about it. Even after she married and came to visit with her husband and children, all she heard from Pop was, "Jonny got promoted again," or "Jonny got his master's degree," and even, "Jonny went to Canada and flew fighters."

As she was telling me that, she ended by saying, "All I ever heard was, 'Jonny, Jonny, Jonny!' Even though we had not so much as spoken on the phone for all that time, I was sick of you!"

We both burst into laughter. Who knew we would "click" after all these years?

🐾   🐾   🐾

In November I finally landed a job working for the US Army at Redstone Arsenal in Huntsville, Alabama, less than one hundred miles from where I grew up. My first day on the job was scheduled for early January 2007, so right after Christmas I found an apartment nearby. Brandon was out of college and living with me, so he and I, along with Tiger, all moved to Huntsville just before the start of the New Year.

Brandon and I tried our best to spoil Tiger. I bought him some of that wet food cats love, and Brandon even let him eat at the table while I was away on a couple of business trips, but he never really took to either of us. Still, we kept trying.

Caroline is a planner. She loves to plan. Planning for the wedding was right up her alley. Between January and June, she kept herself busy after work planning for the wedding and honeymoon.

We also did some house hunting and found a model home with the only thing I wanted: a room for a man-cave. There was one lot remaining in the subdivision under development, so we took it. We met with the builder and discussed a few minor changes to the model, one of which was an electrical outlet to be placed one foot from the ceiling in what would become my man-cave. The builder thought I was nuts, but he put it where I asked. So in addition to all of her other planning activities, Caroline was also busy picking out colors for the house and loving every minute of it.

We married a month before we closed on the house. The ceremony included just the two of us and our four kids and it was beautiful. We married in Tennessee at Whitestone Country Inn, the perfect place for a wedding. We had dinner that night in the gazebo overlooking Watts Bar Lake, and to this day, the staff at Whitestone refer to our big day as "the purple wedding" since Caroline had so many things decorated in purple—my favorite color—and the color of the restored 'Cuda.

The day after the ceremony, we kissed and said our goodbyes. Caroline went back to Knoxville and Brandon and I went back to Huntsville. The closing on the house was scheduled for the middle of June, and our honeymoon was scheduled for just after that.

We decided that when the time came, we would move Brandon and me out of our apartment first. To keep Tiger out of the way, we took him back to Caroline's townhouse the weekend before we closed on the new house. He had not been there for about six months, but Ginger remembered him. As soon as I walked in and dropped Tiger on the floor, Ginger ran up to him and gave him a friendly sniff, then turned and ran off. She returned seconds later with a stuffed toy in her mouth and dropped it at Tiger's feet. It was the sweetest thing. Everyone immediately erupted with, "Awwwwwww!"

Before we knew it, moving day arrived. We moved everything with my car trailer. As planned, we moved my stuff first.

That's when we got another addition to the family.

Brandon, the cat magnet, found a kitten. It was a solid black female. Without a word he walked up to me with the kitten in his arms.

"No," was all I said.

"Aw, c'mon Dad," Brandon replied.

"Brandon, we have to move all our stuff, then Caroline's stuff, and it's going to take several trips for each place. We don't have time to deal with another cat right now."

"Please, Dad?" he said.

"No. Go put her somewhere where her mama can find her." I looked around for a spot out of the way where I thought she wouldn't get hurt.

"Go put her over behind that dumpster. It's out of the way, and I've seen other cats over there before. Maybe one of them is her mama."

Brandon walked toward the dumpster at the end of the parking lot, and I went back to loading boxes.

When he returned, he brought reinforcements. Caroline, Lauren, and Matt were with him. They had been conspiring.

"Dad," Brandon said, "There's no way I can put her back there. Her name is Zoe."

He just stood there, along with all the others, giving me the soulful eye routine.

I relented. "Okay, okay, okay, but we've got to get to work!"

After my apartment was emptied and multiple trips to Knoxville and back, we finally had everything moved in. Then it was time to start on my man-cave and make use of that outlet near the ceiling.

It was for a model train.

🐾   🐾   🐾

My boss owns a shop, complete with wood-working equipment, metal-working equipment, and every hand tool imaginable. He decided to help, and in short order the two of us cut out the shelving for the track. I took the pieces home for staining. Before I could do anything with my room, I had to get the track built, so everything else was piled in the center of the room or in the closet.

It would all have to wait.

🐾   🐾   🐾

We took our honeymoon in Hawaii. It was the best trip either of us had ever taken anywhere. Our room was on the fourteenth floor with a view of the ocean, the beach, and even Diamond Head crater. The bellhop told us that every afternoon at about 3:00 PM the sea turtles can be seen in the water not far from the beach. I couldn't wait to get out there and swim with the sea turtles!

Caroline had planned all kinds of activities. We visited the USS *Arizona* memorial, attended a Polynesian dinner, took bus tours all over the island of Oahu, hiked to the summit of Diamond Head, and of course went swimming at every opportunity. The most fun was the luau.

The price of the luau included several drinks. Caroline soon learned she loved the drink called Lava Flow. I stuck with the Mai-Tai. Dinner was absolutely incredible, but Caroline loved her Lava Flows.

After the first drink, she walked up to the bar and said, "I'd like another Lava Low, please."

The bartender replied, "Don't you mean Lava Flow?"

"Um, yes, that's the one."

But it got even better.

For her third, and subsequent, drinks, she simply walked to the bar and said, "I need 'nother Lava Lamp, right here, thank you."

The bartender just rolled his eyes. I was sure he'd heard that one before.

But of all the things we did in Hawaii, the most memorable involved— what else? Animals.

One of the activities included in the package we purchased was a day trip to Hanauma Bay. The bay is horseshoe shaped and is actually the crater of an ancient volcano. It is absolutely beautiful. The water near the beach is only about waist deep, but gets a little deeper toward the center of the bay. There's a reef throughout most of the swimming area, and the fish are so used to people that they just swim around and through the reef paying no attention to the human invaders. We rented some snorkel gear and hit the beach. We took along some disposable, underwater cameras we bought at the hotel.

After snorkeling for an hour or so, I got out of the water to sit on the beach for a few minutes. Suddenly, Caroline ran up to me.

"Come here! Come here! Baby (my nickname for her) found an octopus!"

"You found *what?*"

"An octopus! Come here! I want to show it to you!"

"There's no way you'll ever find it again," I said, firmly believing we would never find it, if in fact it had ever been there at all. As far as I knew, there were no octopi in Hanauma Bay.

She dragged me out to where she had seen it earlier, and sure enough, there it was. I couldn't believe my eyes. It had found a crack and was nestled in-between a couple of boulders of the reef. I whipped out my camera and snapped a few pictures, and all the while Caroline and I just floated about five feet over the top of it.

That was definitely a first for both of us.

For our last afternoon in Hawaii, we decided to snorkel right off the beach in front of the hotel. I still had not yet seen a sea turtle and was hopeful at the possibility of spotting one. The water was much deeper of course, but it was clearer than and nowhere near as crowded as Hanauma Bay. It was absolutely beautiful. We took our cameras along just in case.

We were not disappointed.

We had been in the water for only a few minutes when I heard someone swimming nearby say something about a sea turtle.

"Where?" I shouted.

"Over that way," he said, and off I went.

Within minutes I spotted a sea turtle about the size of a couch cushion. It didn't seem to care that I was within arm's length and snapping pictures like crazy. Caroline and I followed it around for the better part of an hour.

Then it headed for a large boulder on the sea floor. We followed it, but still kept a safe distance. We had been told we were not to frighten the turtles.

Suddenly, the boulder moved. It was not a boulder at all, but another sea turtle. This one was the size of a living room recliner. It was huge!

Frighten the turtles? I thought. *Yeah, right.*

This one let me get very close. It wasn't as friendly as Wally at the Great Barrier Reef, but clearly it had no fear of me. I took some fantastic pictures, including close-ups of its head. At one point, I got close enough to slide the tips of my fingers across its shell. It felt like a giant sand dollar. What a blast!

It wasn't until the eight hour flight to the mainland, while looking over our pictures, that we realized what we had done. As we talked about the fun we had, we realized how stupid we were to get so close to that octopus.

"If that thing had lifted just one tentacle toward me, they would have had to close Hanauma Bay," I said to Caroline.

"Why would they do that?"

"Because I would have polluted the entire Pacific Ocean."

Caroline was building a photo album of our trip right there on the plane. As we laughed about everything we had seen and done, we came across a picture of the crack in the rocks where the octopus was hidden.

As we looked closely at the picture for the first time, we discovered it revealed a remarkable scene. Grainy because of the cloudy water from the sand having been churned up by so many people swimming nearby, the picture showed a barely visible, curled tentacle coming straight out from the crack between the rocks.

It's a good thing I hadn't noticed that at the time.

To this day, if I say to Caroline, "Baby found an octopus," the response from her is always the same: "Baby did."

CHAPTER 11 –
REUNITED!

Soon after our honeymoon, the routine of everyday life began. Brandon went back to Nebraska. He missed his friends and a very special young woman in particular. Lauren stayed in Knoxville to attend the Tennessee School of Beauty, but also to remain near friends. So it was just the two of us and Matt, Ginger, Tiger, and Zoe. Ginger stayed outside, so that left Tiger and Zoe to rule the house. However, Tiger wanted nothing to do with Caroline or me. But he loved Matt.

Tiger was … different. He had a habit of lying on the floor propped up on one front leg. He looked terribly uncomfortable, but he would lie like that for an hour or more at a time. He also had a favorite place to hide: on top of the kitchen cabinets.

Tiger.

We didn't think much of it at first, but it soon became apparent that Tiger was upset about something. He developed a habit of charging out of nowhere and nipping us on the backs of our legs. If we tried to pick him up, he didn't bite, but he let it be known he wanted nothing of the sort. With Matt, on the other hand, he would rub and purr and let Matt hold him without any resistance. We were at a loss to explain it.

Zoe was the baby. She loved to cuddle and be held. She was rotten.

Still, I missed Little Man.

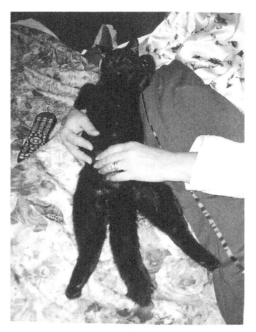

Zoe cuddling with Mommy.

Then on a Wednesday in October, I got a call from Brandon.

"Dad, Mom wants to know if you can take Little Man back."

I couldn't believe my ears. "What? Why?" I asked.

"She still has Sabrina, CoCo, Sunshine, and Little Man, but her hours at the hospital make it really hard to take care of Little Man's diabetes. She said she knows you'll be able to take good care of him now."

CHAPTER 11 – REUNITED!

As it turned out, Joy had moved back to Alabama herself and was only about forty-five minutes away.

"I'll call you right back," I said and hung up.

I ran to Caroline and explained the situation. She was hesitant at first, especially with her allergies and the fact that we had two cats already. But one look at me and she knew she could only agree.

"All right. Make arrangements to go get him," she said.

"Thank you!" I said and gave her big kiss, then grabbed the phone.

"Brandon, tell your Mom I'll come and get him."

Two days later, Caroline went on a planned trip to Birmingham to help her mother with some things. She took Matt along while I stayed home with our four-legged children. I had made arrangements with Joy to meet at her apartment that Friday afternoon to pick up Little Man. I could hardly wait.

When I arrived at Joy's apartment, the first thing I said after she let me in was, "Little Man?"

"Oh, he's probably on the floor behind the couch. It's his hiding place," she said.

I walked toward the couch, but was met about halfway by Sabrina. I picked her up and loved on her a bit, then put her back down and continued toward the couch. I walked over to the side, peered around the back, and saw Little Man.

"Little Man!" I said.

"Little Man, look who's here," Joy said.

Little Man stretched and yawned, then looked up at me.

"*Daddy!*" he meowed as he squirmed to get out from behind the couch.

I had not seen him in about sixteen months, and I was in for a surprise.

As he came out from behind the couch, I was shocked to see that he had ballooned to over twenty-three pounds. I picked him up and gave him some long overdue Daddy-lovin'.

It was feeding time, so Joy fed him and the other cats. She explained his insulin dosage, which was eleven units twice a day, the food he needed, and gave me the latest copy of his veterinary records. I gathered his food and things next to his kennel while I waited for him to eat.

In the meantime, I tracked down CoCo and gave him a long overdue squeeze, then looked for Sunshine. She was under another piece of furniture, so I fished her out and gave her a rubdown too.

By then, Little Man had finished eating, so it was time to take him home. I picked him up and put him in his kennel, said goodbye to Joy, and reached to pick up the rest of Little Man's things when Sabrina walked over to Little Man and gave him a kiss right through the kennel door. I petted her one last time, then picked up the kennel by its handle, loaded Little Man and his things in my truck, and headed for home.

In an effort to ease Little Man's transition to his new home with other animals, I set him up in a spare, upstairs bedroom. But first, I wanted him to get a feel for the rest of the house without Tiger and Zoe, so I locked the two of them in the laundry room while I let Little Man roam around for a few minutes.

It wasn't long before Little Man caught a whiff of Tiger through the laundry room door.

He immediately made his feelings known. He sniffed and growled and almost talked. I had never seen him do that before, and it certainly sounded to me like he was saying, "*Daddy, something evil lurks therein, and it needs an ass-whoopin'. Just open the door Daddy. Open the door. Just open the door.*"

I picked him up and said, "C'mon, Little Man. Let's go upstairs."

He grunted and looked toward the laundry room all the way up the stairs.

We walked into the spare bedroom and I closed the door behind us, then put Little Man in his litter pan so he would know it was there. I sat down and leaned back on the bed with my legs dangling off the side. Little Man jumped up on the bed. He walked over to me and, without a sound, put both front paws on my chest and began to knead. After a few seconds he stopped, then stepped off my chest and settled himself in a ball under my arm. He placed his head on my shoulder and closed his eyes, then purred in utter contentment.

I found this selfie on an old flip-phone. The picture quality is awful, but the content is priceless!

He had never done anything quite like that before. It seemed to me he really had missed his Daddy.

Little Man was home.

The next day, Caroline returned home. As soon as she walked in, I ran upstairs to get Little Man. As I carried him to the top of the stairs and headed down, Caroline stood at the bottom. She was finally going to meet Little Man.

Little Man is home!

"Oh my God!" she exclaimed at her first glance of the cat I had been talking about for months. "He's huge!"

Little Man was quite large anyway, but now he was severely overweight. He was so fat I could barely pull up enough skin to give him his insulin injections. He needed to go on a diet, but I didn't want to change too many things all at once. I felt it best to wait until his transition into his new family was complete.

Fat Little Man.

For the next few days, we kept the cats separated. Then with supervision, we let them mingle. There were surprisingly few tiffs between Tiger and Little Man, and soon all the animals got along just fine. Apparently, Little Man and Tiger had a "conversation" when we weren't looking, and I'm sure that meant Little Man did all the talking and Tiger did all the listening. I'm convinced this happened because it wasn't long before we noticed something quite interesting. Not once after Little Man's arrival did Tiger ever again attack us and nip at our legs. Not once. Clearly, Little Man was recognized by the others as the alpha male.

Little Man is king.

CHAPTER 12 –
LIFE WITH LITTLE MAN

Once the wedding, the move, and the honeymoon were over, it was time to get to work on my room. It was also time to get Little Man's weight and insulin under control.

The elevated track for the train still required much work. I tried to keep Little Man out of the garage while I stained the shelves, and for the most part I was successful. But Little Man soon figured out he could bulldoze his way past me whenever I opened the door to the garage—his most favorite place in the whole world. To this day, there are paw prints on the garage floor where Little Man ran across a freshly stained shelf only to leave his prints behind as he headed for his spot on top of the 'Cuda—after I wiped his feet of course.

In the meantime, I cut back Little Man's food portion a little. He wasn't happy with that, but went along with it.

One day I made my usual trip to the grocery store. Naturally, cat food for Tiger and Zoe were necessary items while Little Man ate a diet prescribed by the veterinarian for diabetes. As I put the groceries away, I decided to hold off filling up the food container for the other cats until it was empty, so I simply put the new bag under the kitchen counter in a cabinet.

Apparently, Little Man saw me do it.

The next thing I knew, the cabinet door was open, the bag was on the floor with a hole in the bottom, and Little Man was chowing down. Little stinker. I knew it would happen all over again unless I did something to prevent it, so

I patched the hole in the bag and put it back under the cabinet. But this time I wrapped a rubber band around the knobs.

That'll keep him out, I thought.

Yeah, right.

The next day, I got a call at work from Caroline.

"This has got to be the smartest cat I've ever seen," she said.

I knew she was talking about Little Man.

"What did he do?" I asked.

"Well, first thing this morning I walked into the kitchen to find the cabinet door open again and cat food all over the floor."

"I guess the rubber band I put on there didn't last long," I said.

She said, "After I cleaned everything up, I put a twist-tie wire on the cabinet door knobs."

"That should do the trick," I said.

"Well, that's what you'd think," she said.

"Uh-oh. What did he do?" I asked.

"Well, about an hour later, I walked into the kitchen again and the wire was gone. I turned around and Little Man was standing in the doorway from the kitchen to the living room just looking at me, and the little rascal had the wire dangling from his mouth."

I laughed. "I guess you got there before he got the doors open again."

"Yeah, but it was the way he looked at me, like he was thinking about something."

I laughed again because I knew exactly what he was thinking.

I said, "I can tell you what he was thinking. He was thinking, '*Look, Lady, I don't know who you think I am, but my Daddy didn't raise no dummy.*'"

🐾 🐾 🐾

For the next several weeks, Little Man and I spent a lot of time in the garage working on the shelving for the track. Once the track was up, we arranged things in what was now *our* room—the man cave. I hung photos and military decorations, built shadowboxes for an old World War II Grand rifle and a matching set of Winchester rifles Daddy left me, and displayed my GI Joe and Johnny West collections in display cases. I even displayed the GI Joe Jeep I bought years earlier on a cabinet near the wall. All we needed was a big-screen television and a few pieces of furniture and the room would be ready. Those would come later.

In the meantime, I looked for but still was not settled on a steady veterinarian in Alabama, so I called Dr. Wagner's office in Nebraska. She called back a couple of days later and gave me some advice for Little Man's diet. The decrease in Little Man's food intake not only meant weight loss. It also meant changes in insulin dosage were necessary. He needed more glucose curves to see how his levels were reacting to the new diet and reduction in insulin.

I finally found a veterinarian with weekend hours and took Little Man there for his curve. Unfortunately, this meant he would have to be poked several times throughout the day for blood tests, so I had to leave him there all day. He hated it, but soon both his weight and his insulin dosage were coming down.

The following fall, I got a letter in the mail. It was from NASA. Rex, my classmate from TPS, was scheduled to fly on his second space shuttle mission. The launch date was scheduled for December 2007, and we were invited. Not only that, but Rex had given us multiple slots. Since Jonathon, Brandon, and Lauren were busy with work or school, they wouldn't be able to attend. So in my response to NASA, I included Caroline, Matt, Mama, and my stepfather Ronnie. Since I was not able to attend Bloomer's launch years earlier, I was determined not to miss this one. We made our plans to head to Florida.

Two days before the scheduled launch, we hit the road. Of course, Little Man had to be boarded again. Rather than have him make even more trips later, I had them run another curve while he was there. As I should have expected, he began to associate every trip to the vet with being poked over and over again. Unfortunately, this would become a bigger problem later.

We arrived in Florida only to be notified of a delay in the launch, but Caroline was unfazed. She had already planned for such a contingency. Since we had a couple of days until the new launch time, we decided to take advantage of the many recreational activities in the Orlando area.

My favorite was Discovery Cove. There's a waist-deep pool there with stingrays that swim around and rub all over everybody. The staff hand out raw shrimp and show each person how to feed the stingrays. As we held shrimp in our hands, the stingrays would swim over their treats and suck them up like vacuum cleaners. They were like puppies. They loved to be petted, but especially loved to be fed.

Discovery Cove also gave us the opportunity to do something I have wanted to do for as long as I can remember: swim with dolphins. Of course we bought the package of photographs that showed each one of us as we swam with a dolphin by holding on to its fin as it swam across the pool. Awesome.

Back at our hotel, we received notification of yet another delay in the launch. So, it was another day, another delay, another theme park. One of the places we visited has a stable for none other than the Budweiser Clydesdale horses. Talk about monsters. Those horses are huge, and they are some of the most beautiful of all of God's creatures.

We spent a week in the Orlando area and wound up visiting every park imaginable until word came that the launch was on an indefinite hold due to a mechanical problem. We went home tired, broke, and never got to see the launch, but at least I got a patch with Rex's name on it for my mission patch collection. Rex finally launched on his mission the following February. Sadly, we were unable to attend.

One day that February, Caroline had plans to attend a school function at Matt's school. She called me just before she left the house. About ten minutes later, I got a call on my cell phone. It was our security company. They had received an alarm notification. Thinking Caroline had tripped the alarm accidentally, I asked them not to call the police, then immediately tried to reach Caroline. When she didn't answer, I called a neighbor and asked her to check the house just in case.

It was not a false alarm. Someone had broken into our home. Fortunately, no one was there except the cats and the dog.

I called the police as I ran out to my truck, and a few minutes later I finally got Caroline on the phone. By the time I arrived, Caroline and the police were already there.

The door to the garage had been kicked in, as was the door from the garage into the house. The damage was such that neither door would close and the house was wide open. No one ever heard a sound from Ginger who was still in the backyard. Tiger and Zoe were nowhere to be found. Little Man met me at the door.

Normally, Little Man would have been the first to run outside. He loves to lie in the driveway, roll on the concrete, and sit with his eyes closed as he sniffs his kingdom, but never without one of us nearby since he's an indoor cat.

Little Man outside sniffing his kingdom.

This time was different.

As I walked in, I heard Caroline upstairs calling for Zoe and Tiger. She even had one of the police officers—after he cleared the house of course—scour the woods next to our yard looking for "her babies." He was still out there looking.

I looked at Little Man as he stood guard at the door. He had a strange look on his face.

I asked, "What happened, Little Man?"

He didn't make a sound, but took a deep breath and sighed. It was as if to say, "*Fine, it's fine, everything's fine. It was just some punk. He didn't take nothin'.*"

"Did you scare off an intruder?" I asked.

Little Man just sat there.

"Where's Zoe and Tiger?" I asked.

Little Man slowly turned to look back into the house, then looked at me and yawned.

We continued to look around and finally found both of them. Zoe had crammed herself under the dining room cabinet near the front door. Tiger had hidden himself at the top of the kitchen cabinets, out of sight.

After the cats were found, Little Man jumped on the couch, looked at me as if to say, "*Told ya,*" and settled down for a nap. It was the weirdest thing.

Umm, oooo-kay, I thought.

Sure enough, nothing was taken. Thanks to the alarm, and maybe even Little Man, the burglar apparently ran off after he broke in. The police completed their report and gave us some advice regarding the doors. They suggested we replace all the short screws on every doorknob that led to the outside with three-inch screws. They also suggested we get some of those bars that brace under the doorknobs from inside, making it virtually impossible to break through those doors again.

After the police left, and since we couldn't close the door all the way, let alone lock it, we had to barricade the door to the outside with boxes and things inside the garage to get through the night.

Up to that point, Caroline had never been a fan of guns. But the next day, after new doors were installed and all repairs were completed, we went to an indoor shooting range—at her request. I took a revolver I bought many years earlier and used it to teach Caroline how to shoot. We left the range only after we had bought Caroline her own gun and stopped at the sheriff's office on the way home to get our concealed carry permits. We would not be caught off guard like that again.

A couple of days later, a realization hit me. When the alarm went off at about ten minutes after ten that morning, Caroline had just left the house. That meant one of two things; either the burglar saw Caroline leave, or he broke in anyway with no thought to whether anyone was home since there were other vehicles in the driveway. Either case was unacceptable. But I chose to look on the bright side. Now I was "cleared hot" to buy more guns with no objection from Caroline. Hooray for me!

After the dust settled, I actually felt proud of Little Man, and told him so. He has always been very stoic anyway, but especially on that day he, more than all the rest of us, seemed to be the one most capable of keeping it together. He showed almost human characteristics. I'll never forget that look he gave me at the door.

If he had been in the Air Force, he would have said, "*Don't worry buddy. I've got your six.*"

Over the next several weeks, Little Man became very accustomed to our daily routine. Each morning after I kissed Caroline goodbye, I told Little Man, "Daddy gotta go work. I'll be back after 'while."

Every afternoon when he heard me arrive back home he met me in the kitchen. He always did the same things. First he plopped down on his right side. Then he stretched. Then he yawned. Finally, he looked at me. That was the signal—it was time for some Daddy-lovin'.

"Did you miss your Daddum's today?" I asked him every time as I bent down to pet him. Caroline just rolled her eyes.

Then one day I had to go on a week-long business trip. I left the house at o-dark-thirty Monday morning, after I told Little Man goodbye of course, to catch a plane to California for a conference. It took me all day to get there. By the time I was settled in my hotel room and called Caroline, it was well after suppertime and long after I would normally arrive home.

When Caroline answered the phone, there were none of the usual questions like, *how was your trip*? Or, *are you staying in a nice place*? There was nothing of the sort.

She went straight to, "Talk to this cat! He's driving me CRAZY!!"

"What's he doing?" I asked.

"He's running all over the house, crying and looking for you! First he'll …"

"Put me on speaker."

"… go up to y'all's room and cry …"

"Put me on speaker."

"… then he'll go to the garage door and paw at it …"

"Okay, okay. Put me on speaker."

"… then he'll look at me and cry some more …"

"OKAY! Put me on speaker!!"

I heard her push the button on the phone, and then she said with a disgusted tone, "All right. You're on speaker. I'm holding the phone down to him."

"Little Man?" I said into the phone.

"*Daddy?*" he meowed.

"Hey Little Man. Daddy's on a trip. I'll be back in a few days, okay? You be good boy for Mommy. See you on Friday, okay?"

"*'kay*," he meowed.

And that was all there was to it.

When I got back home that Friday, Little Man met me first. He heard me come in and came running. When he saw me in the kitchen, he stopped dead in his tracks.

Plop. Stretch. Yawn.

I bent down and loved all over him.

"Somebody missed him's Daddum's," I cooed to Little Man just as Caroline walked in.

She said, "Oh, gooby-gooby-gooby-doo. Dooby-dooby-gooby-goo. That cat gets more loving than I do."

"Hey! That rhymes!" I said.

"Hmfff!" she said and stormed to the bedroom.

146

I decided to lay it on thick. "Say, I'n dus a baby boy, Mommy. I dus need sum Daddy lovin'."

"I hear you!" Caroline yelled from the other side of the house.

"Of course she heard us, didn't she, Little Man. That's why we said it, so she could hear us, yes sir. Him's dus Daddy's baby boy, dat's all. Him's such a good boy, jes him are. Doodness dacious, sakes a-wive."

By that time, Little Man was purring up a storm. But I was in trouble. I waited a few minutes before heading off to the bedroom.

Caroline had worked in the yard all day, so she had jumped in the shower. While she was still in the bathroom, I unpacked, then sat down and took off my shoes and socks.

I heard the water to the shower turn off.

A few minutes later, Little Man walked into the bedroom. He rubbed all over my legs, cried, and finally plopped down and rolled over on my bare feet with his belly up.

I bent down, rubbed him some more, and said, "I guess somebody wasn't done, no sir."

Right in the middle of purring, Little Man suddenly stopped, looked toward the bathroom door, got up, and walked out.

I swallowed hard.

I looked over at Caroline. She was standing at the door to the bathroom, all fresh and clean and dressed after her shower, with her hands on her hips. She was staring me down. If looks could kill ...

Suddenly, she ran over to me, plopped down on the floor, rolled over on my feet, stuck her hands and feet up in the air, and made purring sounds.

We both burst into laughter.

She got her attention.

Since "our" room was essentially complete in that I had nothing else to build, there was little reason to spend much time in the garage. Still, Little Man tried to get out there every time the door was opened for anyone who came or went. His favorite place was on top of the 'Cuda. I was afraid his collar, which was actually a dog collar Caroline bought for him as a joke, could scratch the paint, so I put a fender blanket up there for him. He spent hours and hours up there.

Little Man on top of the 'Cuda. Note the sign on the garage wall.

One day the next summer, after a lazy drive in the 'Cuda, I noticed the turn signal switch was broken. I was not surprised. After all, the car was about thirty-five years old and it was still the original switch. It needed to be replaced. I ordered the part and it was delivered within a few days.

The very next weekend I grabbed the switch and said to Little Man, "C'mon Little Man. Let's go work on the 'Cuda."

He seemed genuinely happy to help.

In the garage, I grabbed my tools, opened the driver's side door, and sat down. Little Man jumped in the car, ran across my lap, and settled himself in the passenger's seat to watch while I worked. I removed the steering wheel and some other parts to gain access to the turn signal switch and placed them on the floor in front of Little Man.

As I pondered how to get the wiring bundle out without disassembling the steering column, Little Man got up and walked over to me, curled up in my lap, looked up at me, and purred. Clearly, he was happy to be working on the 'Cuda again, happy to be in the garage, and happy to be with his Daddy. He's definitely a man's cat.

"Talk to the paw. I'm nappin'."

I wound up taking a lot longer than really necessary to get the job done.

Later that same summer, Brandon came back to live with us for a while. He got a job at an oil change place and loved every minute of it. I think he was especially proud of the fact that my father, his grandfather, was a mechanic when he was Brandon's age. Like Daddy, Brandon excelled. He really had a knack for cars.

A couple of months later, Brandon was at work when he heard a faint little cry. He investigated and determined it was coming from a storm drain nearby. He walked over, dropped to the ground, looked inside, and found a tiny kitten, solid black, screaming her little lungs out. Brandon reached down to grab her and got a finger full of the sharpest teeth in the entire world. But he got the little thing out of its predicament. Since we already had three cats, one of Brandon's co-workers took the kitten home.

Then one evening in October, Caroline asked me to run to the store for a few things for supper, so off I went. When I returned, Brandon was gone.

"Where's Brandon?" I asked.

"Oh, he just went to a friend's house for a few minutes. He'll be back soon."

I didn't give it any more thought—until he got back.

He walked into our bedroom with a box. Inside the box was another cat. It was the one he found at work that the co-worker had taken home. By then, the little thing was about two months old.

I realized Caroline, Brandon, and Matt had conspired again. Once they explained everything to me, I understood. The children of that co-worker were simply too young to care for a cat, so Brandon asked Caroline if he could go get her. Of course, Caroline agreed and told him to go get her before I knew anything.

Brandon named her Boo October since we got her in October, it was almost Halloween, and she was solid black. It was a weird but appropriate name. We just called her Boo.

Left to right: Little Man, Boo, and Zoe. Zoe has a much bigger tail than Boo. That's how we tell the two of them apart.

CHAPTER 12 – LIFE WITH LITTLE MAN

With four humans and four cats, the house filled up fast. Caroline had more allergy trouble with all the cat dander. She decided our bedroom would become her safe haven—no cats.

At bedtime one night, she closed the bedroom door to keep them out.

That lasted for only a few hours. Before it was time to get up the next morning, the cats made their displeasure known. They pawed at the door and cried. We yelled at them, and they stopped for a minute or two, but then they started all over again.

After a couple weeks of this, Caroline had had enough.

One Saturday morning we tried to sleep in a little. The cats were at it again. After yelling at them several times to no avail, Caroline jumped out of bed, ran to the door, jerked it open, and yelled, "Get away from this door!"

I heard nothing but thumps and thuds and nails scratching on the floor as all the cats desperately ran away.

Caroline slammed the door and came back to bed.

For the next little while, the cats seemed to get the message. Every morning I heard them at the door, but they didn't paw at it, cry, or make any noise other than an occasional, quiet shuffle.

I lay in bed and imagined what they said to each other.

"*Knock on the door.*"

"*You knock on the door.*"

"*You're the oldest.*"

"*You're the youngest.*"

"*Go on, knock on the door. We're tired of being locked out.*"

"*Are you kidding? I'm not knocking on that door. That crazy woman lives behind that door.*"

But soon everything started all over again. Only this time was a little different.

Early one morning, just as before, I heard a cry. It was Little Man.

"*Daddy?*" he meowed, softly.

Caroline woke up and said, "Go on, Little Man."

Another cry.

Frustrated, Caroline said to me, "You tell him this time."

"Little Man, go on now. We'll be up in a few minutes," I said.

A few minutes later, Little Man had enough.

BAM!

"Good grief! What was that?" Caroline asked.

A few seconds ticked by.

BAM!

"What the ..." I said, then, "... Little Man?" I called toward the door.

BAM!

"Holy crap!" I said, "I think he's head-butting the door!"

"You gotta be kidding!" Caroline said.

Needless to say, the cats eventually won. The bedroom door is now open all night long, and Caroline takes allergy pills.

🐾 🐾 🐾

Around Thanksgiving, Brandon left to go back to Nebraska. He wasn't going to school, but he had other plans. He called one day to announce he was getting married some time during the next year. He also wanted to enlist in the military. I thought it was a good idea.

Just after Thanksgiving, Caroline made her own little announcement. I was to hand over the key to my man-cave and not go in again until Christmas Eve. I was excited, but concerned at the same time, especially when she asked about my tools.

"What are you up to?" I asked.

"It's a surprise. You'll just have to wait."

I gave her a look, but handed over my key.

About a week before Christmas, she and Matt headed up to the room.

"All right," she said to me, "I need a drill, a hammer, and a saw."

"You want *what?*" I exclaimed.

"You heard me."

"Why don't you just let me help? I don't want you guys tearing up my room."

"Nope, we got it. Just get the tools."

I sighed and stormed off to the garage. Little Man went with me.

"Little Man, what are they up to?"

"*I don't know*," he answered with a meow.

"Good grief," I said aloud as I gathered the tools Caroline requested.

When I handed them over, I said, "At least let me make sure you know how to use them. Here's how you figure out which drill bit you need," I said as I explained how to do it.

"Thank you," she said with a mischievous grin and disappeared.

The next weekend, right before Christmas, Caroline and Matt headed back to my room. I stayed downstairs. Soon I heard the drill. I heard the hammer. I heard the saw. And I couldn't stand it anymore.

"Little Man, they're destroying our room!" I said to him as I bounded up the stairs. He was hot on my heels.

We got to the door and I started pounding.

"Me and Little Man want to know just what in the world y'all are doing in there!"

Silence.

"Answer me!"

Still nothing.

"Fine," I said as I headed back down the stairs. Little Man stayed behind. He just pawed at the door.

Just as I reached the bottom of the stairs, I heard Caroline open the door and say, "C,mon, Little Man! Hurry!"

I turned and ran up the stairs just as she slammed and locked the door in my face with Little Man inside.

"All right now. This ain't funny. What are y'all doing?"

I heard the hammer again. Then I heard a very loud crash.

"WHAT was that?" I screamed, terrified I already knew what it was. I had visions of my GI Joe Jeep smashed into a million, irreplaceable pieces.

"Was that my GI Joe Jeep?"

"Um," Caroline said through the door, "well, um, at least we had good intentions."

"GOOD INTENTIONS!?! Is that what you just said? Good INTENTIONS?"
Silence. I was about to blow.

"I'm going to the store!" I yelled and ran out of the house.

I decided to go to the shooting range and blow the ever-loving stuffin's out of some paper targets. I stopped at Wal-Mart to pick up some ammunition, then headed to the range. But by that time it was almost time for supper and I was hungry, so instead of going to the range I turned and headed for home.

When I walked in, Caroline and Matt were in the kitchen. Matt was setting the table. A few minutes later we all sat down. I asked the blessing, and without another word we all started to eat.

Breaking the silence, I said, "You know, it's not like I can just run down to the nearest toy store and pick up another forty-five-year-old Jeep for GI Joe."

Caroline and Matt both laughed. Laughing is what Caroline does when she's confronted about anything, and it gets on my very last nerve. I simply could not believe they took everything so lightly. I became livid. I found out later that Caroline saw the muscles in my jaw tighten and veins pop out all over my head. I also turned blood red from anger.

Finally, Caroline turned to Matt and said, "All right. Go on and get the bag."

"IT'S IN A BAG??" I yelled with steam coming out of my ears.

Matt left the table and returned with a grocery bag. He handed it toward me. I jerked it from his hands and looked inside. There was a piece of wood at the bottom of the bag. It was covered with indentations from being hit with a hammer. On top of the wood were the remains of an old, glass, and now broken, Christmas tree ornament.

I looked up at the two of them and knew I had been had. They both burst into laughter. I almost cried.

On Christmas Eve morning, I was delighted to find no damage to anything in my room. Caroline had bought me two leather recliners, some matching furniture with drawers for my collections, and a big-screen television, and since she had overruled me and put a Christmas tree with all white lights in the living room downstairs, she also bought me my own Christmas tree, complete with multicolored lights. She and Lauren even put matching garland all around the room for a nice, cozy feel. The room was perfect, bless her little wretched heart.

She and Matt then proceeded to tell me about the day they broke the ornament. As I was outside the door demanding answers, they were doing everything they could to keep from laughing and giving away the prank. Caroline fell on the floor while Matt collapsed in my recliner, and both of them had placed their hands over their mouths in attempts to keep quiet. Apparently, even Little Man was in on everything.

Oh yeah, they got me. They got me good.

CHAPTER 13 –
MORE AMAZING LITTLE MAN

On New Year's Eve, 2008, the weather was unusually warm, but still cool. It was a bright, sunshiny day, so we decided to take the 'Cuda out for a spin. We hit the freeway and drove about a half hour out of town. Caroline drove first. Then we swapped seats and headed back.

Just a few minutes from home, we zipped past a Harley-Davidson dealership.

Caroline said, "You know, I've always liked Harleys. Can we stop and just look around?"

I should have known.

That was more than one brand new motorcycle, a ton of clothes and accessories, and thousands of miles ago. We wound up joining the national Harley Owners Group, or HOG, as well as the local HOG chapter. Neither of us had much experience on motorcycles, so we took a rider's safety course before we hit the road on motorcycles for the first time. We became friends with many of the bikers in the group and went on many beautiful rides through the countryside with other chapter members.

The funny thing is, I never knew I wanted a motorcycle until I bought my Softail. I named it Sir Cedric. But it was Caroline who bought a bike first. It was a Sportster she named Racey Red. I didn't get Cedric until three months after she bought Racey, not until the day before we took our safety course.

Just a couple of months after we got our bikes, we rode up into Tennessee to check out the Tennessee HOG Rally. It was only about ninety minutes away, and by that time we felt comfortable enough on our new bikes to make the trip. We didn't attend the entire multi-day event, just the afternoon on the last day.

As we returned home, we stopped at the third or fourth traffic light into town. I was "leading," and by leading I mean only that I was in front of Caroline, not that I was making the decisions as to where to go as anyone who's ever ridden with Caroline can attest. We were in the right lane of a four-lane road. We stopped side by side.

While the light was still red, two guys on crotch rockets, aka speed bikes, pulled up next to us in the left lane so that there were four bikes across all waiting for the light to turn. The other two guys laughed and jawed and had a good time, and then waved at us as we all waited for the light to change. We waved back.

At that point, I had no idea what was about to happen.

Suddenly, the light changed. As lead, I was supposed to launch first. But Caroline took off on Racey like a rocket and left the other three of us to wonder what she was up to. In seconds, she was through the intersection and going strong.

What is she DOING? I almost asked aloud.

Then I heard one of the other bikers next to me say, "Aww, hay-ell no!"

He took off in hot pursuit. Apparently, he wasn't about to let a Harley, let alone one with a woman riding it, get the best of him. I heard the whine of his engine as he flew through the intersection after her.

The other guy and I just shook our heads as we rode through the intersection at normal speed.

As Caroline approached a residential area, she slowed down to keep from breaking the speed limit. The guy in pursuit saw her decelerate, then popped a perfect wheelie and passed her. Then he dropped his front wheel, drew up right next to her, and they laughed and pointed at each other and had a rip-roaring good time. Caroline gave us all a sucker punch, and the other guys knew it, but it was beautiful.

I laughed all the way home.

That summer we made our first overnight trip on our bikes. We rode up to Whitestone where we were married to celebrate our anniversary. It was a beautiful trip.

We were gone only two nights. Lauren came down from Knoxville to stay with Matt. But with Little Man's diabetes, I decided it would be best to board him while we were away. It was also the perfect time for another curve to see how the insulin was controlling his diabetes.

While we were away, Little Man's appetite problem resurfaced. He simply didn't want to eat while we were gone. He eventually ate a little on the last day shortly before we picked him up, but the veterinarian let us know about it so we would be aware.

The results of his curve showed his diabetes was very well under control. In fact, another reduction in his insulin dosage was warranted. Once we got him home, his appetite returned. Guess he just missed his Daddy.

In the fall of 2009, the invitations went out—Brandon was getting married—in Nebraska. This, of course, meant Little Man had to be boarded again. We had a neighbor come over to the house to feed the other cats every day just as we did for them occasionally. That time, we were gone for three nights. The time and expense of the trip were well spent. The wedding and reception were wonderful.

While we were in Nebraska, I got the chance to pay someone a little visit. One night while there was still light out, I left the hotel in our rental car to run a quick errand and drove right by the house where I lived years before with Kitty and Buttercup, and then with Sunshine, Sabrina, and Little Man. As I passed the house, I slowed down to get a closer look at the backyard where Kitty and Buttercup were buried.

I was elated to see the tree we planted next to their graves had grown with no apparent problems. I stopped in the middle of the street and just sat there for a moment looking at the tree and remembering my sweet little girls.

Then just before I drove away, I mouthed to both of them silently, "Hey baby girls. Daddy loves you."

God bless their souls.

When we returned home we were told once again by the veterinarian's office that Little Man, as before, would not eat while we were away. He seemed to suffer no ill effect, but I grew concerned. I didn't like leaving him behind, and I especially didn't want his blood glucose to get too low as can happen if he doesn't eat. But for the most part, he seemed fine once he was back with his Daddy. He's just a little rotten.

After his wedding and a honeymoon, Brandon started his basic military training. He had enlisted in the US Air Force just before the wedding, and then the really fun part began. I'll never understand why he chose to do so when he did, but he chose a training class that occurred so that he missed Thanksgiving, Christmas, and New Year that year. We were invited to attend his graduation—in Texas. Oh boy ... another plane trip.

Once again, Lauren came down from Knoxville to stay with Matt and the other cats while Little Man was boarded. We were gone for four days. That time, things got a little scary for Little Man.

During our return trip home, we had a layover in Atlanta. We got something to eat and sat down to wait for our connecting flight. I called the vet to check on Little Man. I had already called several times during the trip, so I was aware he wasn't eating again. A technician answered the phone.

"Glad you called. He seems to be doing better now, but we had some trouble a few hours ago," she said.

"Uh-oh, what happened?" I asked.

"You know he doesn't eat well at all when he's here."

"Yes, and I've been worried about that."

"Well, this morning one of the technicians just happened to walk by his kennel and noticed he was in a little trouble," she said.

"What do you mean by a little trouble?"

"He was noticeably lethargic and shaking. His blood glucose dropped dangerously low. As soon as we became aware of it we placed him on a glucose drip to get his levels back up. Don't worry. He's fine now."

I was scared and relieved at the same time and couldn't wait to get home. I made the decision right then and there. Little Man would not be boarded again.

Once we got home and back to our routine, Little Man was just fine. He seemed particularly happy to snuggle with me in our room upstairs in our double-wide, leather recliner. I put a thick, velvety pillowcase on his side of the seat. He loved it. At times, I had to turn up the television to hear over his purring.

Little Man cuddling up to his Daddy.

❀   ❀   ❀

Late one night the following winter, Little Man acted very strangely. He cried constantly. He didn't seem ill at all. He was just unusually vocal, like he was trying to tell us something.

"What is it, Little Man?" I asked.

He walked into the bedroom, looked at us and cried, then walked back into the living room and cried again.

"Little Man, what is it?" I called out.

This happened again a couple of times until I finally got out of bed to investigate. I walked all over the house. Little Man quietly followed me everywhere. I could find absolutely nothing wrong. I even looked outside. Nothing was amiss.

Finally, I went back to bed. But again, Little Man walked in, cried, and left just like he had before.

"Little Man, what IS it?"

He continued acting this way until he finally gave up at about ten-thirty, and we all went to sleep.

At two-fifteen the next morning, the alarm system went off. The sound reverberated all throughout the house and was absolutely deafening. Every living thing in the house was awakened immediately.

I bolted upright in the bed and said to Caroline, "Someone's trying to break in again!"

We had guns readily available. We both jumped out of bed and, without bothering to get dressed, we each grabbed our guns. I also snatched my cell phone. One of the panels for the security system is in the bedroom, so we ran over to it. It read, ALARM – ZONE 8.

I had no idea where Zone 8 was. Each area of the house was identified by its own zone number, such as the living room window or overhead garage door. But Zone 8 was unidentified.

I shut off the audible alarm, turned to Caroline and said, "Stay here."

Just then my cell phone rang. It was the security company.

"We have received an alarm notification at your address. Do you require assistance?" a female voice asked.

"I don't know yet," I said. "I don't see or hear anything wrong right now, but give me a minute to walk around and check things out."

"All right, Sir. I'll stay on the phone with you until you decide if you need me to send the police."

"Thanks. Just hold on a second."

I did a quick walk-around. Little Man walked right behind me, oddly indifferent about the whole thing. All the doors were closed and locked. No windows were broken. I even looked outside. Nothing was wrong.

I said into the phone, "Okay, I've checked the house and nothing's wrong. I don't think we need the police. But where is Zone 8? That's what our alarm panel says."

"Not sure, Sir. Every system is specific to the home where it's located. It depends primarily on the number of sensors you have installed. It might be a problem with your system. Would you like me to have a technician come out tomorrow to check it out?"

"Yes, thank you."

We agreed on a time for the technician to drop by. Then we reset the alarm and went back to bed.

The next day, the technician came by and discovered the problem without much difficulty. The system was designed to send alarm signals via landline simultaneously with a cellular backup. In our case, the cellular backup malfunctioned. The system detected the malfunction and set off the alarm to let us know. The technician replaced the unit, ran through all the necessary checks, and left.

About an hour later, I walked through the house and spotted Little Man. The look on his face gave me the answer. I had seen that look before. It was the same look he gave me after someone had actually broken in a couple of years earlier.

Once again, it was as though he was trying to say, "*I was TRYING to tell you!*"

It became apparent to me that Little Man must have been able to tell the security system was about to fail. That was the reason behind his behavior the night before. He indeed tried to warn us, but not one of the other three cats acted any differently. In fact, when the alarm sounded, every one of them scattered like cockroaches. Not Little Man. He's always right there.

Yes, there is something very special about this not-so-little guy.

··· ··· ···

One afternoon when I arrived home from work, I walked in the door and immediately knew something was wrong.

"What is it?" I asked.

Caroline said, quietly, "It's Patches."

Patches was our neighbor's cat. He was old and frail, but a sweet guy. Matt cared for him and the neighbor's other cat a few times while they were away. I went with him a couple of times just to make sure everything was all right.

"Is he okay? What happened?" I asked.

Caroline told me about the attack. I ran next door.

My neighbor told me that some people rented the house on the other side of their lot. The new tenants had two pit bull terriers. Patches was relaxing on his own front porch when the two pit bulls ran over into the front yard. Frightened, Patches took off across the yard in an attempt to escape.

He didn't get very far. One of the dogs caught him, shook him like a ragdoll, and had a death grip on him. Some kids ran to the door to let our neighbors know.

With tears in his eyes, my neighbor said, "I kicked that dog at least ten times before he let go of Patches. By that time, it was too late. Patches is gone."

After we talked, I walked slowly back home.

When I walked in the door, Caroline was cooking dinner.

"I hate that," she said.

"I do, too." I said. "And I'll tell you one thing. If those dogs had gone after Little Man I would have killed them with my bare hands."

She knew I was as serious as a heart attack. "I don't doubt that for a minute," she said.

I meant every word. Of course, that would have necessitated "a few words" with the dogs' owners as I viewed them as the real culprits, not the dogs. Things would have gotten ugly.

Rest in peace, Patches.

Not long after the alarm incident, Caroline grew tired of her job working from home. In no time at all she landed the job of her dreams. It was at none other than the Harley-Davidson dealership where we bought our motorcycles. She became the Retail Manager and loved it. She was in charge of motorclothes, parts, and accessories.

Caroline can be very demanding, to say the least. One of the guys working for her even gave her a new nickname: "Whip-Cracker."

It didn't take long for me to become the de-facto handyman for the dealership. Caroline called me about twice a month to come fix something or other. I repaired the legs of a display table. I hung displays. I replaced broken mirrors. I just called her, "The General."

One of the benefits of working at the dealership was being able to see the new motorcycles when they were delivered.

That's when Caroline met Saucy Celeste.

Saucy is the name Caroline gave her new motorcycle. Her boss called it, "the big mac-daddy of all Harleys." It has the big 110 engine and all the bells and whistles. It's painted with fantastic graphics in blue with black accents and is absolutely beautiful. But the fact that it has a bigger engine than my Cedric thrills Caroline to no end.

Just days after Caroline rode Saucy home for the first time, I got the necessary stickers to allow her to ride it on base. Rather than put the stickers directly on any of the chrome parts, I bought a metal plate about the size of a 3 x 5 card at the Harley place just for that purpose. I decided Little Man was going to help me mount it on her bike.

"C'mon, Little Man, let's go fix up Mommy's bike."

He followed me into the garage.

I paused at the bottom of the steps to read the installation instructions.

"Okay, Little Man. Says here the plate is to be mounted on the bottom bolt of the front brake caliper."

We walked around all the other stuff in the garage to get to her bike, which was parked among two cars, my Cedric, a riding lawn mower, my roll-around tool chest, an air compressor, and tons of other stuff. We could barely get around. I located the proper bolt on the bike, then stepped around all the junk to my workbench for a socket. Little Man just sat down near Saucy.

I picked a couple of sockets, certain that one of them would be the correct size. Rather than walk all the way around to the other side again, I just stepped to the near side of the bike to reach over the front wheel. I couldn't see the bolt from where I stood, but I could feel it.

I took one of the sockets in my right hand, reached over the wheel, and felt for the bolt. The first socket I tried was the correct size, so I just left it on the bolt as I stood up and turned to get a socket wrench.

Little Man started fussing.

"I'm right here, Little Man. I just need to get a socket wrench."

He kept on.

"Little Man, give me a minute. I'll be right there," I said as I fumbled around looking for the wrench.

He was still at it, crying and crying over and over again.

"Aw for heaven's sake, Little Man, I'm coming."

He wouldn't stop crying.

I found the wrench and turned to walk around all the stuff to get to the other side of Saucy with Little Man still jabbering away.

I got to the other side and said, "Good grief, Little Man, what is it?"

I stooped down to place the wrench on the socket only to see that I had put the socket on the wrong bolt. I had put it on the top bolt, not the bottom one. They were both the same size, and I'm sure either one would have worked fine, but the instructions said to mount the plate on the bottom bolt. So I moved the socket from the top bolt to the bottom one.

Little Man immediately stopped crying.

It took a few seconds for me to realize what happened. I froze right in the middle of removing the bolt. I looked at Little Man. I looked back at the bolt. I looked back at Little Man.

I snapped to my feet in disbelief and said, "Little Man, there's no friggin' way."

He plopped down on his side, took a deep breath, and sighed, giving me that same *I told you so* look I had seen more than once before.

"Holy crap!" I said and ran in the house to tell Caroline.

All I got from her was another eye-roll. I don't think she believes me to this day.

🐾   🐾   🐾

Spring arrived. Lauren hadn't been home for a visit since Christmas, so she came down for the weekend. Besides, it was her birthday. We went out for dinner, bought her a cake, and had a nice time.

That was about the time we noticed Tiger. He began to act up more than usual. We discovered months earlier that he enjoyed going outside. He never left the yard or jumped over the privacy fence, so we just let him roam around out there occasionally. It seemed to make him a little happier. But now he definitely seemed upset about something. Since he had been around all the other cats for some time, we didn't think they were the cause. Whatever it was, it came to a head that weekend.

On that Saturday morning, with all of us nearby, Tiger walked over to a potted plant, jumped up on it, looked directly at us, and before we could stop him, urinated on the floor. He had done this once before without anyone seeing him, and we had him tested for a urinary tract infection. He was fine. There was no medical explanation for what he did, and it could not be tolerated.

Several of us yelled in unison, "Tiger!"

Reluctantly, Caroline said, "I'll put him outside for now until we can figure out what's up."

She walked over to Tiger, picked him up just as she had many times before, and walked with him to the back door.

Tiger exploded in anger. He hissed and clawed and growled and attempted to bite Caroline's hands. It happened so fast I could see fear and confusion in Caroline's eyes.

Little Man appeared out of nowhere. From a distance of about seven feet, he launched himself, flew through the air, landed right on top of Tiger, and proceeded to beat the crap out of him; Tiger was attacking Mommy and clearly had to be stopped.

Suddenly, Caroline had a full-fledged catfight happening right there in her arms. I had never heard such kitty-cussing in my life, and fur flew everywhere.

I yelled, "Little Man!" and ran over to Caroline.

I grabbed Little Man and pulled him off Tiger. He didn't resist. Caroline opened the back door and dropped Tiger on the ground. I put Little Man on the floor and went straight to Caroline to see if she was all right. She was fine, but soon we were all upset. We knew what was coming, and there didn't seem to be any alternative. Tiger had to go.

A few minutes later after the dust settled, we noticed Little Man. He just stood at one of the kitchen windows, swished his tail back and forth violently, and looked outside at Tiger. He snorted and grunted. He was *pissed*.

Caroline walked over to him, reached down and patted him on the head, and said, "Thank you, Little Man."

Little Man looked briefly at her, then turned back to the window and resumed his watchful duties without making another sound. He eventually walked away from the window, at which point I said, "C'mon Little Man, let's go upstairs to our room and just watch some TV."

We slowly walked upstairs together. When we entered the room, I sat down in the recliner and Little Man jumped onto to his pillowcase right next to me, turned around in circles a couple of times, and finally settled down. He took a deep breath and audibly sighed.

"I know what you mean, Little Man, I know what you mean."

He blinked in response, plopped over on his side right next to my leg, and went to sleep.

We gave Tiger up for adoption, but felt terrible about it. It certainly seemed to me that Tiger must have been mistreated somewhere along the way. I held him completely blameless, but all that did was make me feel worse about letting him go. All we could do was hope he found happiness with another family.

In April 2010, it was time again for Little Man to get another glucose curve. Every curve over the last couple of years showed his glucose was a little too low for the veterinarian's comfort. In fact, just about every time she told me, "This is the most tightly controlled diabetic I've ever seen. Let's drop his dose another unit."

Rather than go through all that just to hear the same thing all over again, I decided to just reduce his dose by one unit without doing another curve. I paid special attention to his urine output to see the effect. If his urine output increased drastically and remained at that level, I would know he wasn't getting enough insulin.

Interestingly enough, after I reduced Little Man's insulin, his urine output increased for the next couple of days, but then tapered off to normal levels. I decided to just leave it alone for a while. If the past was any indication, I figured I would probably reduce his dose again later.

Summer rolled around. Matt was out of school, and Caroline was getting *the fever*—beach fever. We made plans to head to Florida for a few days. That time, however, I did not intend to board Little Man. Caroline wasn't exactly happy about it, but I was not about to put him through that again and take the chance that he wouldn't eat and drive his glucose levels too low. Cats can tolerate high glucose levels much easier than low levels. Too low can kill.

Little Man went to the beach.

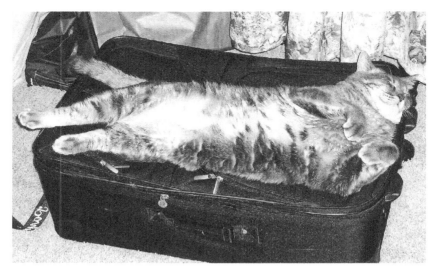

"I'm all packed an' ready to go, Daddy. Y'all wake me up when it's time to go."

He did just fine on the trip as long as he was in my lap while we were in the car. At the hotel, we put the DO NOT DISTURB sign on the door whenever we weren't in the room to keep Little Man from escaping. Fortunately, there was no repeat of the last time I left him alone in a hotel room.

We had a great time in Florida, but Little Man had an even better time. He had two queen size beds to roll around on, no other cats to bother him, and all the attention he could stand from the four of us. He was rotten to the core.

Back home, there were no other pressing projects, so I decided to do something I had wanted to do for a long, long time—I watched the entire series of *Star Trek*. That's exactly what Little Man and I did at every opportunity over the next few months. Sometimes, all I had to do was head toward the stairs and Little Man was right on my heels without a word from me.

We watched every single episode while curled up together in our recliner—just the two of us. Sometimes I had to turn up the volume to hear over Little Man's purring. In fact, one day I decided to make a recording of his purring. I grabbed the old camcorder I used to record some of the video I made of the 'Cuda restoration years before, muted the television, and recorded several minutes of Little Man's sounds of utter contentment.

Apparently, he enjoyed our time together so much he developed an interesting habit; he brought me his toys. I began to find his toys everywhere—at the top of the stairs near the door to our room, in the hallway outside our bedroom door, and even on the floor next to my side of the bed—just about anywhere Little Man thought I would find them. Well, that's how it seemed to me anyway.

He did have a favorite toy: a little, one-eared, baby blue, stuffed mouse. Sometimes, he cradled it between his paws as he napped. Priceless.

One day when Caroline saw how much Little Man and I loved to spend time in our room, seemingly away from her and everyone else, she decided she had something to say about it.

"It amazes me that you would be perfectly happy to spend the rest of your life in your room with that cat watching *Star Track*."

"That's not true," I said, reassuringly.

"Yes, it is."

"No, it's not."

"Yes. It IS."

"No. It's NOT."

"Okay, give me one good reason why it's not true that you'd rather spend time with the cat watching *Star Track* than spend time with me."

"You mean other than the fact that being with you means watching reality shows? Which I can't stand, by the way," I said.

"Yes, other than that," she said with a smile.

I paused for a moment or two as I tried to think of a good answer, preferably one that would get under her skin. I should have known by doing so I was just getting myself deeper into trouble.

Finally, I thought of an answer and said, "It's not true because it's Star *Trek*, not Star *Track*."

Caroline didn't talk to me much during the next couple of days.

A short while later, Caroline decided she wanted her own room, too. She took over the spare bedroom across the hall from the man-cave and declared it the Barbie Room. I had my Johnny West and GI Joe collections, and she had Barbie. She started decorating it.

Every afternoon, the sun shone through the window in the Barbie Room, which caused it to be uncomfortably warm. I decided to mount a shade over the window to help block the sun and keep the temperature down.

I went to the garage, grabbed some tools, and walked back inside. I walked by Little Man who was apparently headed to his litter pan, and said, "Daddy's gotta go fix Mommy's room."

He kept going and I headed upstairs.

While I was in there mounting the shade, my cell phone rang. It was Caroline. She was downstairs in our bedroom.

"Can't you hear your cat screaming?" she asked.

"What are you talking about? Who's screaming?"

"It's Little Man. He can't find you and he's running all over the house calling for you. Where are you?"

"I'm in the Barbie Room hanging the shade. I'll stick my head out the door and call him," I laughed and hung up.

I walked to the door of the Barbie Room, which was the first door at the top of the stairs, stuck my head out, and looked down the stairs. Little Man stood nervously at the bottom looking in the opposite direction.

I called out, "Little Man!"

He whirled around, saw me at the top of the stairs, and meowed excitedly, "*Daddy!*"

He sprinted up the stairs, into the Barbie Room, and began to rub all over my legs. Then he proceeded to "help" me mount the shade.

Little Man sure loves his Daddy.

🐾 🐾 🐾

One day toward the end of our *Star Trek* episodes, Little Man and I were snuggled up in our recliner when I realized we hadn't spent much time in the garage lately. I glanced around the room. I looked at various things and fixed my eyes on my GI Joe collection. Then an idea struck me for a new project. It was a small one, but it would give me something to do in the garage—with Little Man, of course.

I decided to build a weapons locker for the GI Joe accessories I had stuffed in plastic baggies in boxes in the closet. My collection had grown over the years and I put most of it on display, but many things like rifles, pistols, spare uniforms, etc., were not easy to display other than on or in the arms of a GI Joe. The extras wound up in baggies out of sight.

I drew up some plans, bought some wood, hinges, paint, and other things at the hobby store, and set to work. I built my own miniature gun rack for the center of the box, made miniature pegboards complete with miniature hooks and brackets, and even made some one-sixth scale coat hangers for spare uniforms. About two weeks after I started, the box was finished.

I took several pictures of the box and decided to send them to a friend of mine, Dan, in California. Dan is very knowledgeable about GI Joe. I had purchased a few items from him in the past and we struck up a friendship. I sent the pictures to him and a couple of other people via email to see what they thought.

Dan called me almost immediately.

"Do you have drawings of this thing?" he asked.

"Yes I do. That's the only way I could figure out some of the dimensions."

"Did you send pictures to anyone but me?

"Yeah, I sent it to a couple other folks. I've bought a few things from them in the past and thought they might like to see it."

"Could be a problem," Dan said.

"Why? What's the matter?"

"I want you to do exactly as I say, understand?"

"What's going on, Dan?"

"I'll explain everything when you get back from the post office."

"Why do I need to go to the post office?"

"No questions. Just take the drawings and stick them in a manila envelope. Take the envelope to the post office and mail it back to yourself via certified mail. Call me when you get back."

"What?" I asked again.

"Just do it, and do it right now. Call me after it's done." He hung up.

I did as Dan said. I put the drawings in an envelope, took it to the post office, and paid for it to be mailed back to me via certified mail. I called him from the parking lot.

"It's done. Now, what's going on?" I asked when he answered the phone.

"I forgot to tell you one thing. But first, do you have a safe?" he asked.

"Yes."

"Good. Now when the package is delivered back to you, put it in the safe. What I forgot to mention before is that it must be left unopened, do you understand? Unopened."

"Will do. Now, what is going on?"

"I think you have a marketable idea," Dan said.

"What?"

"Yes. I think there are a ton of people out there who will love this thing. Once you get the package back and stick it in your safe, you have proof that you came up with the idea first. Good job, man. I think it's great. You should sell them."

I talked things over with Caroline, and we decided to take Dan's advice. We started our own little side business selling action figure display lockers. We even came up with our own trademark: *STOW-N-SHOW*. Our motto is, "Why just 'stow' it when you can 'STOW-N-SHOW' it?"

I spent countless hours in the garage, with Little Man of course, designing jigs and cutting pieces for the boxes. But soon the job became too big for the garage. Some things I still do in the garage, but others require more space.

My boss' shop came back into play. When he learned what I was doing, he offered to let me use his shop for the bigger jobs. I jumped at the opportunity. I bought my own saws and drill presses, and the two of us gutted a room next to his machine shop and made it into a woodshop. We built shop tables and mounted my saws on them, and soon Caroline and I were in business.

I make the smaller things at home in the garage, like the little coat hangers and gun racks. Little Man is usually either right there on the workbench, at my feet on the floor lying on the mat that reads, "MY WORLD MY UNIVERSE MY GARAGE," or on top of the 'Cuda. He loves being in there with me, but sometimes stays for hours all by himself just sprawled out on the 'Cuda. The garage is his favorite place in the entire world.

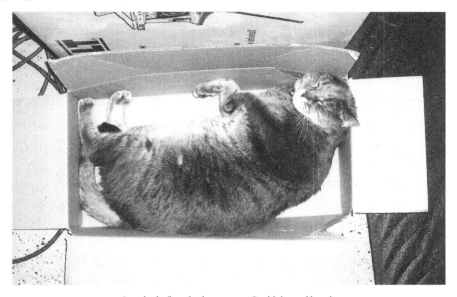

Somebody found a box next to Daddy's workbench.

For the bigger jobs, like cutting the pieces for the boxes themselves, sanding, assembling, and painting, I go to the shop.

But I have to be careful what I tell Little Man.

Once the shop was set up and ready for me to produce multiple boxes, I decided to spend most of one Saturday out there working. I left early. I kissed Caroline goodbye, and as I walked out the door I patted Little Man on the head just like I do every time I leave the house and said, "'Bye, Little Man. Daddy gotta go to the shop."

I walked out.

No sooner had I walked into the shop but my cell phone rang. It was Caroline.

"This isn't going to work," she said, obviously frustrated.

"Why not? What's the matter?" I asked.

"It's Little Man. Ever since you left he's been pawing at the garage door and crying. Didn't you tell him you were leaving?"

"Of course I did."

"Well, what did you tell him?"

"I said I was going to the shop. I always say goodbye to him before I leave, especially every day when I go to work."

"He doesn't do this during the week," she pointed out. "What do you tell him then?"

I sighed and said, "I tell him I'm going to work."

"All right then. From now on, no matter where you're going, tell him you're going to work. Got it? *Work*."

"Yes, General."

From that day on, I did as Caroline ordered, and Little Man hasn't cried for me since. Good grief. Sometimes he's like a human toddler. Only more spoiled.

※   ※   ※

As time passed, I continued to monitor Little Man's glucose levels. I followed the same steps as before, reducing his insulin dosage one unit at a time, until he finally reached a point where his urine output was too high for too long. When that occurred at four units of insulin twice a day, I bumped him back up to five units twice a day, kept him at that level for a while, and his urine output went back down.

I took him to the vet for a curve, and they concurred I had found the correct, long-term dosage. His weight was back down to a more reasonable eighteen pounds. At that weight he looked skinny to me. But he was happy, healthy, and spoiled rotten.

※   ※   ※

After basic military training, Brandon and his bride had moved to Biloxi, Mississippi, for some advanced training before they moved on to their first, permanent assignment in Rapid City, South Dakota. Then in April 2011, about nineteen months after their wedding, we became grandparents.

As soon as the doctors said it was safe to travel, which was about thirty days after he was born, we got a visit from our grandson, Emmett. Brandon, his wife, and Emmett stayed in Alabama for a few days, and Caroline and I took turns holding Emmett for hours at a time. But the real reason for the trip to Alabama so soon after birth was for a very special purpose: we wanted to take a photograph. Not just any photograph, but a photograph with five generations of Emmett's relatives in it.

Maw Maw was over ninety years old by that time but still going strong. Brandon and I took Emmett down to see her. My mother, or "Granny," as Brandon and her other grandchildren call her, met us there. We took pictures, which included Emmett, his father, his grandfather, his great-grandmother, and his great-great-grandmother all in the same photograph.

Awesome.

Five Generations.

Left to right: Mama (Emmett's great-grandmother), Jonathon (Emmett's uncle), Maw Maw (Emmett's great-great-grandmother), Emmett, me (Emmett's grandfather), and Brandon (Emmett's father).

CHAPTER 14 –
THE SPACE SHUTTLE

Just a couple of weeks after we met Emmett for the first time, I got another letter in the mail from NASA. Rex was assigned to STS-135 aboard *Atlantis*. That was the very last space shuttle mission before the fleet was permanently retired. The launch was scheduled for early July and we were invited. That time, there was no turning down the invitation.

In anticipation of witnessing a launch in person for the very first time, I realized I would soon have everything I needed to complete the frame project with all the mission patches Rex sent me over the years. The photograph of Rex on a spacewalk would of course be included, but I had another idea—to include in-space photos of each of the four of our classmates who flew aboard a space shuttle. I downloaded some free photos from a NASA website and sent them out for autographs. In no time, they trickled back in.

As the launch date approached and we made plans for the trip, I turned to Little Man one day and said, "C'mon, Little Man. Let's go upstairs and look at some NASA stuff."

We went upstairs to our room. I pulled out the patches, the picture of Rex, and the class photo of our TPS class. I arranged everything on the floor the way I wanted them placed in the frame, and I realized I needed to remember to make room for placards to identify each astronaut. I spread everything out a little more and was fairly satisfied with the arrangement.

I turned to Little Man and said, "What do you think, Little Man?"

He was right there the whole time, but when he heard his name, he walked a little closer and sniffed at everything. Surprisingly, he avoided stepping on pictures and seemed more interested in sniffing the patches. He walked around the arrangement a few times and finally stopped off to one side.

I studied everything for a few minutes, but wasn't completely happy with it. I rearranged a couple things, then rearranged them again, and finally settled on what I thought would look very nice. Still, something didn't seem quite right.

I said, "I don't know, Little Man. It's like there's something missing."

I looked around to make sure I had everything, which I did, and said, "Everything I have is right here, though. Hmmm…"

Little Man walked over and paused, then walked all the way around one time and stopped at the very top, directly in the center. Then he turned and looked at me without a sound.

That's when it hit me.

"Oh my God, Little Man! You just gave me a great idea!"

I grabbed my cell and called Bloomer. By that time, he was retired from NASA but had flown three space shuttle missions, including one to the Russian Space Station, *Mir*. I had all three of his patches.

I explained what I wanted to do and asked him, "How hard would it be to get my hands on a little something that one of you guys actually flew into space that I could include in the frame?"

Clearly, I knew the best thing to get was a TPS Class 92A patch, our class patch. But as I found out from Bloomer, what I asked was HUGE! NASA had very strict rules regarding these things. Each astronaut was allowed a very limited number of small items to take with them into space, and these were normally designated for family members or commercial sponsors.

And no, Bloomer did not fly one of our patches. The hunt was on!

The next person I called was Digger. Duane "Digger" Carey and I were teammates on our final test project at TPS. He too had gone on to become an astronaut.

When I reached Digger about my idea for the frame, he was astonished that no one had thought to fly one of our class patches into space.

He said, "You *have* to get a patch to Rex, and you have to do it *now*! And I want pictures of this thing when you're finished!"

It was twelve days before the launch of STS-135.

I got in touch with Rex and told him what I wanted to do.

He said, "It's going to be hard to get a patch on board this late, but if you're willing to try, go ahead and overnight one to me."

So thirty-four dollars and seventeen hours later the patch was on his doorstep—eleven days before launch.

Two days later, I got an email from Rex.

He said, "I got it, Spayney. I will get it on board (by hook or by crook)."

That was the last I heard about the patch, until ...

A week before the launch I realized I had a problem. It was obvious I couldn't take Little Man along since there was no way I could be sure to be in the hotel room at the specific times in which to give him his insulin injections. Boarding him again was also out of the question since there was every possibility we would be gone for several days. I pondered what to do.

Then Caroline suggested, "Why not let Matt do it?"

Matt was fifteen at the time, so I thought it was worth a try. I taught him how to feed and give Little Man his injections, and since Lauren would be around as well once she came down from Knoxville to stay with Matt, I explained to her the importance of not letting Matt slip in his duties.

I watched Matt take care of Little Man for a few days and was confident he would be fine. Caroline and I were going it alone this time, and soon we were ready to hit the road.

We were about to witness history.

Kennedy Space Center, or KSC, is about seven hundred miles from Huntsville. We left early one morning and made the trip in one very long day. After we arrived, we checked in with the NASA representative responsible for communicating with all the astronauts' guests.

Even more special was that Rex arranged for us to attend the night viewing at dusk the night before launch. Of the tens of thousands of people there, not to mention the additional nine hundred thousand or so in the area, only about two hundred got to attend the night viewing. We got within about two hundred yards of the launch pad, right in the middle of the most prolific mosquito breeding grounds in the entire world. Even the NASA folks were handing out mosquito repellant. I thought those mosquitoes were going to pick me up and carry me away.

Jonny and Caroline with Space Shuttle Atlantis in the background.

While at the night viewing, I got a neat surprise. CJ walked over to shake my hand.

By the time STS-135 was scheduled to fly, CJ had four shuttle missions under his belt and was in training to become a crew member aboard the International Space Station. As it turned out, he was scheduled to fly the weather observation aircraft the day of the launch. It was great seeing him again.

CHAPTER 14 – THE SPACE SHUTTLE

After the night viewing, we got back to our roach motel at about eleven-thirty in the evening, but were up at two in the morning to check the schedule. Everything was still a "go" even though there was a seventy-percent chance of a weather delay, so we loaded up and headed back to KSC. We arrived at about 3:30 AM and the parking lot was already practically full. After waiting in line for hours to catch a NASA bus to the causeway, we finally arrived and put out our chairs at about 8:00 AM—three-and-a-half hours before launch. The date was July 8, 2011.

We had been there for a couple of hours when I noticed there was a man close to us at the causeway with a radio. He was picking up airborne transmissions to NASA regarding the weather. I heard a familiar voice over the radio and knew it was CJ. NASA was not convinced the weather was good enough for launch, and CJ was frustrated.

At one point, he said something to the effect of, "Look, I don't see the problem. There's plenty of blue sky up here. Let's light her up!"

That's CJ.

Finally, we heard the countdown at T minus 10 seconds. The place went berserk. We heard the "Liftoff!" call over the loudspeaker and got a fabulous once-in-a-lifetime view of the launch of the Space Shuttle *Atlantis*. Being there in person allowed me the opportunity to notice something about the launch I had never seen in video or photographs—the plume was blowtorch bright and very hard to look at without sunglasses.

Atlantis was almost to the clouds before we heard any sound at all from the launch. When she punched through the clouds, the crowd cheered, but then became oddly quiet for just a second or two. Then, through a tiny hole in the clouds, we saw *Atlantis* on her trek into space. The crowd went nuts all over again. Many cried. It was an awesome feeling.

When we got back home, I tried to keep track of some of the activities whenever the *Atlantis* crew was shown on television. I was able to see video of Rex floating around many times, but I regretted not asking him to do one more thing while he was in space.

Before the launch, I meant to tell Rex, merely as a joke since the shuttle can't really loop in space, at least not in the same sense that an aircraft can loop in the atmosphere, to be sure and "loop it." I completely forgot to mention it.

But during each mission after the *Columbia* disaster, NASA required that a maneuver be performed by the crew as the shuttle approached the space station to allow observation of the bottom of the shuttle for any damage which might have occurred during launch. As *Atlantis* neared the space station for docking for the very last time, the crew did exactly that. They pulled up on the nose of the shuttle so that it did a complete back flip—just like a loop.

When I saw that on television, I simply couldn't believe it. I ran around the house yelling, "Come quick! Come quick! They're doing a loop! They're doing a loop! Loop it, Rex! Loop it!"

I'm sure Caroline considered sending me to an insane asylum.

In my heart, it was "mission accomplished."

A week to the day after *Atlantis* landed back on earth, I couldn't stand it anymore. I emailed Rex and asked, "So, did you get that patch on board?"

My thoughts were that, even if he did manage to get it on board, it was likely just stashed away in a cargo container somewhere so he could say, "Yes, it flew."

I figured that would be about all there was to it, and that would have been good enough.

But two days later I got a short response from Rex via email which read, "Here's proof!"

It included an attachment.

The attachment was a photograph taken from inside *Atlantis* looking out through a window on the flight deck. Through the window to the left is the blackness of space. To the right is the Earth, and in the center is part of the space station. And there, floating in the weightless environment in front of *Atlantis'* window, is the patch.

That was an awesome thing Rex did.

The patch for USAF Test Pilot School Class 92A floating on the flight deck of Atlantis. Atlantis is docked
and in orbit with the International Space Station.
Photo courtesy of Astronaut Rex J. Walheim.

A few days later, Rex emailed me to let me know the entire crew of *Atlantis* would be visiting Redstone Arsenal in the coming weeks. I knew he would bring the patch with him during the visit. In the meantime, something else rather extraordinary occurred.

My first day back at work after the launch, before I knew whether Rex had flown the patch, I sent an email to everyone in the building where I worked. I included copies of photographs I took while Caroline and I were there. Redstone has a huge NASA presence, and many folks are still there from the early days of the shuttle program. I thought they would like to hear about my experience at KSC.

The response I received was overwhelming. I received hundreds of emails from people thanking me for sharing. Some just said, "Thanks." Others included their own similar stories.

I didn't mention the patch.

After Rex sent the photo of the patch and I knew it had actually been in space, I decided to send another email. This time, I told everyone about the patch and my frame project and included a copy of the photo of the patch in space. Again, the responses came. In fact, one woman, Jana, was so moved by my story she felt compelled to do something very special.

In her response to my second email, she wrote to me and shared her own space-related story. During a visit to a local antique shop, she found and bought a small, silver, lapel pin. It was Snoopy from *Peanuts* wearing a space helmet. She bought it for a dollar and wore it to work every day for about three months.

One day, a co-worker stopped her in the hallway and asked her about her little Snoopy pin.

"Is that a Silver Snoopy?" he asked.

"Well, I think it's silver, and it's Snoopy. Isn't it cute?" she responded.

He then explained to her that what she thought was a just a cheap, silver, lapel pin was actually a very special item known as a Silver Snoopy. Silver Snoopy pins were flown into space and presented by astronauts to NASA employees who went "above and beyond" in support of flight safety and mission success. The first such pins were flown during the Apollo space program and every space mission after that. The one she found was the real deal.

Once she realized its significance, she decided she could no longer wear it since, in her words, "I didn't earn it."

She contacted NASA in an attempt to find and return it to the original recipient. NASA told her they had no ability to track that particular Silver Snoopy since the pins weren't marked with anything to identify a recipient. As far as NASA was concerned, it belonged to her.

She stuck it in a box where it remained for the next ten years or so.

Then, along came my emails.

When she read my emails, she decided I should have it for inclusion in my frame project. She wrote to tell me about it and asked if I would take her "homeless Snoopy" and finally "give it a good home."

I was floored and understandably honored by her generosity. I did a little research and found that Silver Snoopy pins are quite valuable to collectors, even without supporting documentation. I pointed all this out to her, but she still wanted me to have it, on the condition that I never sell it and use it only for my project. I countered with a request of my own: that she allow me to include her name in the frame and indicate the Snoopy was donated by her.

We both agreed to the conditions and met for lunch one day. She gave me the Snoopy, and I showed her Rex's spacewalk photo and all the mission patches of my TPS classmates.

We both felt there was more to do.

After several days of more research, we made a startling discovery. Based on the markings on the back of the Silver Snoopy she found, we were able to narrow the possibilities as to when it was actually flown in space. Our research revealed it was likely flown on either Apollo 7 or Apollo 8. If it was flown on Apollo 7, then it was in the first batch of Silver Snoopy pins ever flown in space. If it was flown on Apollo 8, then it orbited the Moon!

About a week after my lunch date with Jana, Rex and the rest of the crew of the last space shuttle mission arrived at Marshall Space Flight Center on Redstone Arsenal. I was there already. I walked around inside the small museum while I waited. I brought the Silver Snoopy Jana gave me to show Rex and the rest of the crew.

When I saw him walk in, I called out, "Rex!"

"Spayney!"

We gave each other a hug. He immediately reached into a pocket of his blue NASA flight suit, pulled out a sandwich bag with the patch inside, and handed it to me.

"Here ya go! I have to do some PR stuff and sign autographs, but don't go anywhere. Stay and have supper with us and we'll talk afterwards."

"Will do," I said as he walked off.

After a video presentation of the last launch and the mission highlights, I stood at the back of the line for an autographed crew photo. Once everyone else had passed through the line, I met the rest of the crew and showed them the Silver Snoopy. Then we headed over to a different building for dinner and more presentations by the crew.

At dinner, we talked at length about space flight and reminisced about our time at TPS. I brought along a couple of photos of the patch in space and Rex signed them for me. I also told Rex about Jana and the Silver Snoopy. In appreciation, Rex sent Jana a package a few weeks later. Inside were an autographed crew photo, a mission patch, and a personal thank you note from Rex. Jana cried. And I made a new friend.

That night after dinner with Rex, I showed the rest of the family the patch that had actually been in space. I couldn't wait to get the frame completed.

But of course, I had to show it to Little Man first.

I said, "Come on, Little Man, let's go upstairs. I got something to show you."

We headed upstairs. Little Man went straight to his pillowcase on the recliner, and I pulled out all the patches and photos for the frame. I placed everything on the floor as I had before, only this time I put the flown patch in its place at the top center of everything else, just where Little Man stood when he gave me the idea in the first place.

Little Man on his pillowcase in our recliner.

CHAPTER 14 – THE SPACE SHUTTLE

"Check this out, Little Man. It's been in space on the space shuttle!"

At the mention of his name, Little Man jumped down from the recliner and walked around sniffing the patches. When he got to the flown patch, he stopped. He seemed genuinely interested in this new patch and sniffed at it for quite a bit longer. He stopped sniffing and stepped over to a different patch, sniffed at it briefly, then returned to the flown patch and continued his sniffing.

"What is it, Little Man? What do you smell?"

I reached down, picked up the patch, and sniffed it myself.

"Hmm, I don't smell anything."

Little Man stretched his neck toward me and the patch. It certainly captured his interest. I reached down to put it back in its place, and Little Man followed it all the way to the floor with his nose. He sniffed and sniffed again. He definitely smelled something.

That's when it suddenly hit me.

"Oh my gosh, Little Man! Do you smell the space shuttle?"

I snatched the patch off the floor and tried and tried to see if I could smell anything. Nothing. I put it back down, and Little Man sniffed at it again.

I just sighed and said, "I wish I could smell it, Little Man."

It occurred to me I never asked Rex how the space shuttle smells. He's flown aboard it three times, so he should know.

Apparently, Little Man knows, too.

Several days later, after measuring, figuring, and measuring and figuring some more, I took the plans for the frame to the Arts & Crafts Center on base. I ordered museum quality Plexiglas, matting and filler, and had one of the guys in the woodshop design and build the actual frame.

In short order, everything was ready for pickup. I planned to place all the items on the matting myself—with Little Man's help of course.

It took us a full day to get it just right, but we finally mounted everything in the frame and completed the project. It's huge. It's about three feet wide and almost as tall as Mama at just under five feet in height. I took lots of pictures and emailed them out to several people, including some folks in the building where I work, but especially to every 92A classmate I could find. Digger would have come after me if I hadn't.

I'm still surprised at how nice it turned out, and I never dreamed I would have two items in it that have actually been in space—the patch and the Silver Snoopy—one from the early days of space exploration and one from the very last shuttle mission, and all in the same frame. But Rex didn't fly the patch into space for me. He did it for our entire class, Class 92A. I'll eventually donate the whole thing to the Test Pilot School in their honor.

But not until I enjoy it for a while first!

The finished project. The patch that flew in space aboard Atlantis is at the top center.

CHAPTER 15 –
COCOA

In mid-July, just days after we returned home from the launch, Caroline was at work and called me to share something interesting.

"You need to stop by here on the way home this afternoon," she said.

"Why? What's going on?" I asked.

"There's a cute little kitten, a stray. It keeps running in and out of the service area. It's starving and nobody can seem to catch it."

Oh brother. Just what we need. "All right. I'll see if I can swing by for a few minutes," I said and hung up.

That afternoon after work, I headed to Harley to check out the kitten. Caroline and I walked around the building a couple of times, but never saw it.

That was that, or so I thought.

On Saturday, just a day or two later, Caroline came home with a new, furry little bundle.

"What have you done?" I asked.

"Well my boss said it couldn't stay there as a shop cat and it wouldn't stop crying and I didn't want it to starve and isn't she cute?" she said in a single breath as she stuffed the little thing in my face.

I had to admit, she was a cute little thing, probably about eight weeks old and a Tortoiseshell, or "Tortie," as they are sometimes called. Torties are typically dark brown with some light brown or tan highlights in their fur. This one had something funny going on with her tail, however. She had an inch-long bald patch all the way around the middle of her tail. I couldn't tell if she had been attacked or what, but she didn't seem to be in any pain, or even to notice for that matter.

Cocoa the day after we got her. Note the fur missing from her tail.

We didn't want to upset the other cats, especially Zoe or Boo, so we decided to keep her in our master bathroom for a few days. Little Man was not a concern. He's never intimidated by another cat. He's the king.

I wanted to name her Haley since she was found at a Harley place. Simply remove the "r" from "Harley" and what's left would be a nice, feminine name for a female cat. I was overruled. Everyone else wanted to name her Cocoa, so Cocoa she became.

Monday morning I dropped Cocoa at the vet's office on my way to work. I knew she was going to need her first round of shots and likely had ear mites and possibly worms as most strays do. They called a little while later to fill me in.

CHAPTER 15 – COCOA

"Well, little Cocoa has worms and ear mites, so we de-wormed her and treated her for the mites. She's also had her first round of shots. Otherwise, she seems perfectly healthy," the technician said.

"What about that bald spot on her tail?" I asked.

"The doctor didn't say anything about that other than that her fur will likely grow back soon. She might have had a run-in with another cat somewhere along the way. I think she's fine."

"Okay. I'll drop by on my way home to pick her up," I said and hung up.

When I got her home that evening, we decided to keep her in our bathroom for a few more days until the other cats became accustomed to her scent. Under supervision, we let her walk around the house for about thirty minutes only once. The other cats sniffed and hissed a little, but there was no physical contact.

A couple of days later, I became concerned. The bald spot on Cocoa's tail had grown larger. I suspected mange, so I took her back to the vet to be tested. It took a couple more days for the results.

"Well, it's not the mange," the doctor said when she called.

"What else could it be? I've had lots of cats and I've never seen this before," I said.

"Well, it's possible it's from the ear mites."

"Ear mites? On her tail?" I asked, surprised.

"Yes. I've seen this kind of thing before, especially with a large infestation like she had. Give her a few more days. Her fur should grow back just fine."

A full week went by. By then, most of the fur on her tail had thinned out. Something funny was going on. I called the vet again. The doctor came on the line.

"There is another possibility," she said. "It could be ringworm."

I knew absolutely nothing about ringworm, but at that point, I wasn't overly concerned. I imagined a few pills would take care of the problem.

"How do we find out?" I asked.

"Bring her back in and we'll test her. It may take a couple days for the results to come back. Let's just hope it's not ringworm."

Uh-oh. "Why not?"

"Because ringworm is especially difficult to treat and cure, and it's expensive. The test is over one hundred dollars. Let's just wait for the results. In the meantime, don't let her near the other cats."

At that point, I still had no real understanding of what was at stake. I paid for the test, kept Cocoa isolated, and waited.

The day the doctor called me back with the results, it had been two weeks since Caroline brought her home for the first time. She had been in our bathroom every minute since, except for that one thirty minute outing and the occasional trip to the vet.

"It's ringworm," the doctor said.

"Okay ... so ... what now?" I asked.

During that phone call, I received more of an education on ringworm than I ever wanted. And I was not happy.

Ringworm is not actually because of a worm. It's a fungus. It's very similar to athlete's foot. Treatment is intense. Our lives were about to change for a while.

The first step was to bathe Cocoa with a specially medicated shampoo twice a week. In addition to the bathing, there were some pills we gave her daily. By the end of the next couple of weeks, nothing changed. There was no improvement. I called the vet.

"Looks like we're going to have to take more drastic measures," the doctor said.

"What does that mean?" I asked.

"We can give her lime-sulfur dips. Since the shampoo and meds aren't working, we'll need to dip her twice a week for about six weeks, then test her again."

"So, I'm going to need to drop her off twice a week for six weeks?"

"Yes, unless you want to try doing this at home. But I have to tell you, lime-sulfur dip is not pleasant. It smells like rotten eggs. Once the cat is dipped, she has to be left alone to drip dry, not dried off with a towel. And this stuff stains everything. It can stain clothes, walls, even jewelry. But it's the go-to method for getting rid of ringworm."

"How much does it cost?"

"Fifty dollars per dip."

"You gotta be kidding."

"There's more," she warned. "Ringworm is extremely contagious, and we recommend at least six weeks of treatments before testing her again. But even if she tests negative, we need two, consecutive, negative results to consider her ringworm-free."

The first thing I thought about after hearing that little bit of news was Little Man.

"What about Little Man? He's a diabetic, you know. What if he gets it?" I asked.

"Ringworm can certainly have a negative impact on a diabetic. If it gets bad enough, well, I've seen some diabetics have a particularly rough time with it. Some have had to be put down."

The decision was just made for us. Even though some quick math revealed this was going to be expensive, I didn't think we had much choice. We needed to knock this stuff out before Little Man or any of the other cats came down with ringworm. Keeping Cocoa separate from the other cats was a must.

We were in for a very long fight.

A day or so after Cocoa's first lime-sulfur treatment, Matt came to us with his own problem. He had spots all over his forearms. He had held Cocoa more than anyone else, and I assumed there must be a connection. I mentioned this to the vet when I dropped Cocoa off for her second treatment.

"Uh-oh," the doctor said.

"What?" I asked.

"Matt may have contracted ringworm from Cocoa. If he has it, you and your wife probably do, too. The other cats are next."

"Please tell me there's a happy ending," I said.

"Treatment for you guys is no big deal. It's hard to get rid of, but there are medications and creams that seem to work well. But treating cats is a different matter. I recommend that all four cats be given lime-sulfur treatments, just in case."

Things were getting worse and worse. Even if we were heartless enough to simply get rid of Cocoa, there was every possibility we would still be stuck with the ringworm. In fact, one or two days later, both Caroline and I found spots on each other that we suspected were ringworm.

Our situation at home was obviously spinning out of control. The veterinarian we were seeing seemed to be professional and competent, but at the same time seemed to have no problem at all with hitting us with suggestions resulting in vet bills in the thousands of dollars. As if Cocoa wasn't enough, all three of the other cats were due for annual check-ups and shots.

The clincher was the veterinarian's behavior when I picked up Cocoa after her second lime-sulfur treatment. She handed her to me at arm's length, wrapped in a towel, and acted as though Cocoa had the black plague.

We needed a different veterinarian.

As I drove home from work one afternoon a couple of days later, I contemplated what to do about Cocoa and our ringworm problem, and I passed a new sign. It was on a building I had seen many times before, but I just never paid much attention to it. That day, I slowed to take a closer look.

The sign was for Catisfaction Cat Clinic. The clinic was fairly new and hadn't been in business all that long. I decided to stop and check them out.

I liked it the moment I walked in. It was a cat-only facility. It seemed fresh and new, and the staff seemed genuinely friendly.

The first thing I said was, "Does your veterinarian make house calls?"

I figured it would be much easier to have her come to us rather than trying to haul four cats back and forth in the car, including one with ringworm.

"As a matter of fact, she does. When would you like her to come by?"

"Yesterday," I said.

I explained a little about the situation. Luckily, the doctor had an opening for the next day right about the time I normally arrived home from work. I scheduled the visit and headed home.

The next day, right on time, the doorbell rang. It was Dr. Stephanie Gandy and one of her technicians.

"Hi! Come on in!" I said as I opened the door.

We started with introductions, then walked into the kitchen. For some reason, I felt it necessary to say something.

"All right. If you're going to be our vet, there's something you need to know. Little Man is my little boy."

I just wanted to throw that out there. Neither of us had any idea those words would one day come back to haunt her, but for the time being, she just brushed it off.

She said, "I understand you've got a ringworm problem."

"Yes, we do," I said. I also noticed she had something in her hands.

"What's that?" I asked.

"It's a black light."

"What's that for?"

"Let me see the cat with the ringworm and I'll show you."

We walked through the house to our master bathroom where the little culprit was staying. Dr. Gandy picked her up and gave her a quick look.

"Hmm, could be. I need a very dark room," she said.

I led her to the powder room just outside our bedroom door. With the light off, it's pitch-black in there. Dr. Gandy, the technician, Cocoa, and I crammed into the tiny room.

"Turn the light off," she said.

I turned off the light, and Dr. Gandy turned on the black light and held it close to Cocoa's tail. Cocoa glowed like a light stick in several places, and not just on her tail.

"Yep. That's ringworm," she said. "See the area here, and here, and here? When it glows bluish-green under a black light, that's ringworm."

"Wait just a minute!" I exclaimed. "You mean to tell me I just spent over a hundred dollars for another vet to run a test to tell me it's ringworm, and all they had to do was hit her with a black light?"

"Well, not quite," Dr. Gandy said. "There are three different strains of ringworm. Only one of them glows like this under a black light. But it just so happens that the strain that is most common in cats is also the one that glows."

Still, I didn't buy it. The other vet could have very easily hit Cocoa with a black light on the very first day. That would have saved us an unbelievable amount of trouble—and money. Instead, we had Cocoa in the house for two full weeks before we had any knowledge of the ringworm, which gave it plenty of time to spread all over. I made the decision right then and there. Dr. Gandy was our new veterinarian.

"How are you treating her right now?" she asked.

I explained about the shampoo and that she had been given two lime-sulfur dips. She could see we were already keeping Cocoa isolated.

"Let's keep on like that for a while. Here, keep my light for the time being. Use it to check on her progress over the next few days. Under the circumstances, I think you ought to plan on doing the treatments yourselves to keep costs down. We can order bottles of the lime-sulfur treatment, and we can also get the shampoo. In the meantime, I understand you have other cats needing shots and checkups. We brought a scale and some vaccines. Let's have a look," she said.

"Okay," I responded, and then had an idea. "Will that light make ringworm glow on a human?"

"Yes."

"Check this spot right here on my neck."

A quick illumination with the black light revealed that I too had ringworm. Dr. Gandy said, "I think you guys have a fight on your hands."

That was an understatement.

Within about an hour, all the other cats were weighed, checked, and given necessary shots. We thanked Dr. Gandy and promised to keep her updated on Cocoa's progress. We also gave her the name and number of our old vet so she could have all the cats' records transferred to her office.

As soon as she left, I hit Matt with the black light. The spots on his arms were definitely ringworm, but it was confined. He didn't have it anywhere else. Still, as a precaution, we limited our contact with the other cats hoping to spare them.

We felt a little better since we had a plan to keep costs down. But as we were about to learn, the adventure was just beginning.

Even before Cocoa's next shampoo and treatment were due, I noticed an irritation on Zoe's face, just above her left eye. I grabbed Dr. Gandy's black light, picked up Zoe, carried her into the powder room, and turned off the light. I turned the black light on and held it down to Zoe's face. There it was, that horrible bluish-green glow. It was confined to the one spot, and it wasn't very large, but it was there.

I had an immediate, sickening feeling. *Oh no. Little Man.*

I dropped Zoe on the floor and ran out of the powder room.

"Little Man!" I called to him.

He came out from under the dining room table. Plop. Stretch. Yawn.

I picked him up and headed to the powder room. I looked him over with the bathroom light still on, but found nothing like what I saw on Zoe. I turned out the light, turned the black light on, and started at Little Man's tail. Dr. Gandy warned me about the black light. It illuminates every little piece of lint or dust and makes things appear horribly messy. The trick is to know the difference between the things that glow blue or white from the things that glow bluish-green— ringworm. Under the black light, Little Man appeared covered with lint. In fact, I held it against my arm and saw the same thing, so I wasn't concerned.

As I ran the light all over his body and up to his face and head, I found no ringworm. But just as I was thinking that Little Man had been spared, I found it. He had a couple of tiny spots on the underside of his ear.

The only one of the cats who never showed any sign of ringworm was Boo.

As soon as Caroline walked in the door after she got home from work, I hit her with the news. Then, she hit me with her own.

She had noticed several spots on her own body. Using the black light, we found about eight spots of ringworm on Caroline and another one on me.

I called Dr. Gandy.

"You're going to have to treat all four of the cats," she said, "and if it's spreading like this, I'll give you some topical medication to use in between baths and dips. It's not as good as the lime-sulfur treatment, but hopefully it will keep the spreading to a minimum. I'll also give you some oral medication to give Cocoa that should help."

My all-time favorite cartoon character has always been Bugs Bunny. Of all the things he said during his comedic exploits, there is one thing he occasionally said which I thought stood above everything else. It just happened to fit our situation perfectly: "*Of course you know this means war.*"

Bugs got it right. It was all-out war on ringworm.

🐾   🐾   🐾

The twice a week schedule meant two baths and two dips for each cat with the baths done the day before the dips. We decided to give baths on Tuesdays and Saturdays and dips on Wednesdays and Sundays. We planned to apply the topical medication Dr. Gandy gave us every off day. Sounded simple enough. Looking back, our naiveté was record-breaking.

On the first Saturday of our do-it-yourself efforts, I headed to the hardware store for a five-gallon bucket. Little Cocoa certainly didn't need anything that large, but Little Man and Boo barely fit. Our plan was to submerge each cat, being careful not to let water get into their eyes and ears, while at the same time trying to stay away from claws.

Surprisingly, the first set of baths went off fairly well. The medicated shampoo required that each cat be completely wet before being lathered up, but also that at least ten minutes should pass before being rinsed. It took about an hour and fifteen minutes to bathe the four of them. They hated it of course, but they tolerated it without causing too much blood loss—ours, not theirs.

On Sunday it was time for the first of the at-home lime-sulfur dips. I already had a bottle in its concentrated form from Dr. Gandy, and according to the directions, there was a specific amount to be mixed with every gallon of water used. Heeding the advice of our earlier veterinarian, Caroline and I stripped to our underwear, removed all our jewelry, and placed some old towels on the floor next to the bathtub. Our plan was to have Matt bring us each cat, one at a time. After dipping each cat, we would then put them in the shower next to the bathtub to let them drip dry. They didn't have to be dipped into the solution for very long, just long enough so they were soaked to the skin. Lime-sulfur does kill ringworm as long as it's allowed access to the spores. We could use the same mixture for all four cats since any spores which might fall off would be in direct contact with the mixture, killing them.

CHAPTER 15 – COCOA

We decided to start with the largest cat, Little Man, then Boo, Zoe, and finally the tiny little culprit herself, Cocoa.

We were ready.

I put three gallons of warm water into the bucket. I poured a couple of ounces per gallon of water of the concentrated mixture in a measuring cup and poured it into the bucket.

The smell hit us instantly.

Caroline said, "Oh my God," and covered her mouth with her hands. Her eyes began to tear up.

"Don't tell me," I said, "don't tell me. That smells like, um, essence of um, essence of … yes. Essence of poo. Yeah, that's what it smells like."

I stuck my hand in the bucket and mixed everything up. It was gross.

"Matt! Bring Little Man to us!" I called to Matt.

Caroline opened the sliding door to the bathroom and took Little Man from Matt, then she handed him to me and closed the door again. Caroline and I both got into the tub, stood next to the bucket, and submerged Little Man up to his shoulders in the solution.

Little Man was wild-eyed and cried a couple times, but otherwise seemed to tolerate the wetness and the stench fairly well. I stuck my hand in the solution and rubbed him all over to make sure he was soaked to the skin. Then I took an old washcloth, soaked it in the solution, and dabbed him around his head and face, and paid particular attention to his ears where I saw the spots of ringworm under the black light. Once that was done, I pulled him out of the bucket, placed him in the shower, and closed the door. He immediately shook and splattered the solution all over the inside of the shower. He wasn't happy, but he was fine and didn't make much of a fuss.

One down, three to go.

Boo was next.

"Matt! Bring us Boo!" I called to Matt.

Caroline opened the door, took Boo from Matt's hands, and closed the door. I had already stepped back into the tub, so Caroline handed Boo to me, then stepped in herself.

As I lowered Boo toward the solution, all hell broke loose.

Boo wanted nothing to do with that putrid smelling stuff. She grabbed the ridge of the mouth of the bucket with her hind claws and fought like crazy to get away from my grip.

"Help me!" I said to Caroline as she grabbed at Boo's hind legs.

Boo began to kick at the bucket and tried to regain her grip, but instead she splashed the lime-sulfur solution all over the three of us.

"Grab her legs! Grab her legs!" I said to Caroline.

We managed to get Boo's bottom half down into the solution, but she still kicked and clawed and screeched. Lime-sulfur solution went everywhere.

"Aw, for heaven's sake!" I said as Boo fought for her life. By that time, I had stuff dripping down my face into my left eye, but I couldn't release my grip on Boo to wipe it away.

"Hold her down!" I said to Caroline.

Caroline put her hands on Boo's shoulders to hold her in the solution as best she could while I rubbed her all over. I grabbed the washcloth and dabbed at her face, head, and ears. Boo screamed, kicked, and splashed the whole time.

Satisfied Boo was soaked to the skin, I said, "As soon as I get Boo over there, open the shower door."

I pulled Boo out of the bucket, stepped out of the tub, and walked the few steps to the shower door.

"Watch out for Little Man! "I said, too late.

Little Man made his escape and ran straight to the bathroom door leaving a trail of lime-sulfur dip all over the floor.

I threw Boo into the shower, slammed the glass door, and said, "Grab Little Man!"

Caroline picked up Little Man and handed him to me.

"Open the shower," I said. "Watch out for Boo!"

Boo tried to make her own escape, but Caroline managed to block her exit. I dropped Little Man on the shower floor and closed the door. Little Man gave me a look that said, *I'm gonna get you for this,* while Boo tried to shake the stuff off her body. I reached to my face with the back of my wrist to wipe the lime-sulfur stuff out of my eyes.

I took a deep breath, sighed, and said, "Two down, two to go."

Suddenly, I heard somebody hacking up a fur ball.

I looked through the shower glass door, but it didn't look to me like the sound was coming from either one of the cats.

That was because it wasn't one of the cats. It was Caroline.

"I can't … *hack* … do this … *hack* … anymore! I gotta … *hack* … get out of here … *hack*," she said and ran out of the bathroom.

Bewildered, I just stood there for a minute. I looked around the room. Lime-sulfur solution was everywhere. My underwear was stained a brownish-yellow color in several places. Spots of the solution were splattered on my eyeglasses and dripping down my nose. I had no idea when it happened, but there were claw marks on my arms and a few drops of blood running down my hands.

"What am I supposed to do now?" I asked aloud to no one.

I just stood there for a few seconds.

Finally, I yelled, "MAAAAATT! Strip to your underwear and get in here! NOW!"

I could only imagine the look on his face when he heard that, but he came running anyway.

When he got to the bathroom door, I said, "Tell your Mom to bring us Zoe."

Although Zoe was much smaller than either Little Man or Boo, she was as strong as an ox. Her dipping experience was only slightly less violent than Boo's and served to make certain that Matt was as covered in lime-sulfur solution as I was. But within about ten minutes, we had three of the four cats shaking and crying behind the glass shower door.

Lastly, it was Cocoa's turn. The poor little thing put up practically no resistance whatsoever. We submerged that tiny little baby into the remains of the solution up to her neck. She had the most pitiful, fully dilated eyes I had ever seen. My heart just melted. Matt held her in place while I stuck my hand back down into the bucket and rubbed her all over. I dabbed her little face with the soaked washcloth, then lifted her out of the solution and walked her over to the shower door.

By that time, the other cats had had enough. Before I could get to the door, Little Man heaved himself against the door and it flew wide open. All three ran out and left trails of the solution all over the floor.

I sighed and said, "Screw it. Let's just let 'em run around in here."

We never tried to put them in the shower again.

I put Cocoa on the towel next to the tub and turned her loose. She shook a little bit and gingerly walked around the room, shivering. Poor thing.

I sent Matt upstairs to rinse off while I stayed downstairs to clean up the mess as best I could. Within minutes, the cats were dry enough to let Little Man, Zoe, and Boo out of the bathroom. Cocoa had to stay put. I stepped on the towel on the floor and slid it around with my feet to sop up the wet spots on the tiled floor. I put Cocoa in the shower to keep her out of the way while I got down on my hands and knees to scrub the floor, then I let Cocoa out and jumped in the shower myself.

And to think we went through that only about fifty more times.

Days turned into weeks, and it didn't take long for the cats to associate being carried into the bathroom with the marvelous experience of being soaked in lime-sulfur solution. Boo was always the most challenging.

She developed a most peculiar habit. As soon as Caroline picked her up and headed to the bathroom where Matt and I waited, Boo urinated all over Caroline and left a trail of urine all through the house right up to the bathroom door.

But one day Caroline made an interesting discovery.

After she took Boo into her arms but before she walked her to the bathroom, Caroline simply placed her hand over Boo's eyes. It seemed to do the trick ... until she handed her to Matt.

As Matt stood outside the bathtub while I dripped next to the bucket after we had dipped Little Man, Matt stood just inside the bathroom door with his arms outstretched. Caroline came around the corner with her hand over Boo's eyes, handed Boo over to Matt, and removed her hand.

Boo immediately urinated all over Matt forming a puddle of urine at his feet. I will never forget the look on Matt's face. His face quickly became devoid of all expression. He very slowly just turned his head toward me, held Boo in his outstretched arms in an attempt to keep from getting urine all over himself, tilted his head to one side, and stared me down.

Oh yeah, his fun meter was *pegged*.

After several weeks and what seemed like a million dip sessions, Little Man and Zoe were ringworm-free. But Caroline, Matt, and I still had it, and poor Cocoa was still a light stick.

I went online to see if anyone else had been through the horror we were experiencing only to find even more fantastic news. Ringworm spores can survive in a climate-controlled environment, like an air-conditioned and heated home, *for up to two years*. The article I found suggested such things as having the entire house cleaned with anti-fungal cleaners, including all the carpet, rugs, hardwood floors, drapes, upholstery, even the walls and baseboards and anywhere else a cat might normally rub. But more than that, there was a recommendation to use anti-fungal fabric spray on bed linen and to keep a towel outside the entrance of the bathroom where Cocoa was kept. We were to keep a spray bottle with bleach on the counter near the door in the bathroom and spray the towel before stepping out of the room. This was to prevent us from tracking any spores outside the bathroom.

We were having the time of our lives.

I called Dr. Gandy and told her about Cocoa.

"Bring her in and we'll shave her fur. It may be that the lime-sulfur solution isn't getting enough access to the spores on her skin."

I took her to Catisfaction.

Dr. Gandy sedated Cocoa, then grabbed the clippers and shaved off all her fur, even from her tail, and as much as she could get off her face and head.

We got a shock.

About half of Cocoa's little body was covered with ringworm. The worst part was her tail and backside, but she had it on her belly, under her "arm pits," on her face and head, on her legs—seemingly everywhere.

"Good grief," Dr. Gandy said. "This poor thing's in bad shape."

We just looked at her for a couple minutes. It was obvious our current regimen wasn't working. Dr. Gandy suggested we switch from the generic, oral medication we were currently giving her to the major trade-name brand.

Then she said, "Refresh my memory. What do the directions say on the bottle of lime-sulfur concentration?"

"I think it says to use two ounces of mixture for every gallon of water," I responded.

"Double it."

Based on our latest "intel," we made plans to have the house cleaned from top to bottom, as soon as we got rid of the ringworm on our own bodies, and instituted some new procedures in the house. We put a towel on the floor outside the bathroom door, bought some spray with bleach and some anti-fungal fabric spray, and even went so far as to sleep in separate beds to keep from spreading the ringworm back and forth. We found some different topical stuff for our own ringworm spots, and also doubled the amount of concentration for Cocoa's dips.

Finally, after a few more weeks of giving it the good fight, we were able to rid ourselves of any trace of ringworm. Next we had to get the house cleaned.

We scheduled three different crews to come clean the house. One company, the one responsible for the carpets, rugs, drapes, and upholstery, declined. The day after they came to the house to give us an estimate they called and claimed that one of their men had come down with ringworm as a result of being in the house.

"That's ridiculous," I said. "It takes at least ten days for any symptoms to show, and you guys were just here yesterday." *Bunch of scaredy-cats.*

We finally found a company willing to tackle the job, another to do the general house cleaning—to include walls and baseboards—and another to clean out all the ductwork and ventilation systems. We planned the effort to happen over three consecutive days when Cocoa had to go back to Catisfaction for another clipping so she would be out of the way.

All the rugs were sent out for cleaning. When the rugs came back, we put them in the storage room upstairs, which left the hardwood floors bare. After the drapes were cleaned, they were left to hang on the curtain rods but folded up away from the floor on coat hangers to keep them out of reach of the other cats, just in case. The only carpeted areas in our house are upstairs and in our bedroom, so once they were cleaned we limited the other cats' exposure to those rooms. The house was clean, but seemed very open since the windows were uncovered without any curtains, blinds, or shades.

But Cocoa still had ringworm. We had hoped she would be ringworm-free by Christmas with the problem behind us, but no dice. The ringworm simply would not go away.

Winter was especially hard on Cocoa. Even though we kept the heat on constantly, the poor thing shivered after every clipping. She looked absolutely pitiful. We left extra towels on the floor so she would have something soft to sleep on, but most of the time we found her under them instead of on top. Poor baby.

"It could be her immune system," Dr. Gandy said. "She contracted the ringworm at a very young age. Let's just give her time."

So we kept on fighting. A few more weeks, a couple more clippings, another gallon or two of lime-sulfur dip. We washed our hands so much during that time our skin was constantly raw. As Cocoa grew, she resisted a little more when it came time for a bath or a dip. But for the most part, she was resigned to her life of ringworm treatments. Those eyes. I'll never forget those huge, sorrowful eyes. They made me want to hug her even more.

Finally, in early March 2012, I could find no evidence of ringworm anywhere on Cocoa. But we still needed to have cultures taken and two consecutive, negative, test results.

The first one came back negative. We were pumped.

"Not so fast," Dr. Gandy said. "Let's wait ten days and then take another one. If that one is negative, she's negative."

Ten days later we took her in for the last culture.

A few days later Dr. Gandy called and said, "Check your Facebook page."

She had placed a cartoon on my page. It was a picture of a worm answering the telephone.

"*Hello?*" the worm asked.

"*Is this Mr. Ringworm?*" a voice on the other end of the line said.

"*Yes.*"

Finally, the voice on the other end gave the message we had been waiting for: "*The Payne Family has kicked your butt.*"

At long last we could breathe a sigh of relief. It had been eight months—eight long months for Cocoa locked in a bathroom——not to mention gallons of lime-sulfur dip, tube after tube of creams and ointments for all of us, cleaning crews, anti-fungal sprays, and towels, which by that time were little more than rotted threads of material after so much bleach was sprayed on them for so long.

As for the money, well, we gave Cocoa a new, informal nickname. It's a Harley thing. Our bikes have designations consisting of strings of alphanumeric characters. For example, mine is an FXSTC. Caroline's is an FLSTSE2. Cocoa became our little FTDK—Five Thousand Dollar Kitty.

Once we got the news, we went straight to the bathroom to get Cocoa and give her a much long-overdue hug. We opened the bathroom door to find her standing right next to it. We stayed on our side of the doorway.

"It's okay, Cocoa. You can come out now," Caroline said.

"Come on, baby girl," I said.

She answered with an indecisive trill. She took a step toward the door, then stopped, sniffed, and backed up a couple of steps.

That was too much. We both reached in and snatched her up off the floor and loved all over her. She was about ten months old by that time but had never been allowed outside the bathroom other than the occasional trip to see Dr. Gandy and one thirty-minute exploration eight months earlier.

Finally, she could live a normal life.

We didn't have a set date, but Dr. Gandy suggested that she, her husband Chris, Caroline, and I get together for a celebratory dinner at some point. We were going to celebrate, "No more ringworm!"

It wasn't long before we thought we had another problem. Cocoa started to display some "tortitude" for which Torties are infamous. I had to have a little talk with her.

"Look here, little girly," I said as I held her up to look into her eyes one day. "We spent a ton of time and money on you. You need to straighten your little self out."

Apparently, she listened and understood. In no time she became the sweetest thing ever. Every night at bedtime, she simply has to spend some time cuddling with us under the covers. First, she'll paw at the bedspread. That's the signal. We have to lift the bedspread so she can get between it and the top sheet. Then she'll crawl in and paw at my hip. After pawing for a minute or so, she'll curl up and purr for hours.

I love it all.

Cocoa—ringworm free. Note her tail now!

CHAPTER 16 –
WORKING AT CATISFACTION

In early April 2012, just a couple weeks after Cocoa's release from her prison, Caroline and I took a trip to South Dakota for our grandson Emmett's first birthday party. As before, Lauren stayed with Matt and the cats, and by that time Matt had become a pro at giving Little Man his insulin. Feeding the cats was like working at a zoo. Little Man ate his special food for diabetics, so he ate in the kitchen. Zoe and Boo were shut up in the laundry room while they ate so Little Man couldn't get to their food, and little Cocoa wouldn't eat anywhere except our bathroom, so she was shut in there again, but only at feeding times. It was like being on a cattle drive with cats instead of cattle.

When we arrived at Brandon's home in South Dakota, I was surprised to see an old friend: Sunshine! Brandon took Sunshine from his Mom and brought her to live with him and his family. I snatched her up off the floor to give her a bear hug and got a shock. Something was terribly wrong with Sunshine. She was literally a bag of bones, which was quite a change from her usual, pudgy self.

I told Brandon, "You get that baby to the vet as soon as we leave to go back to Alabama, got it?"

"Yes, Dad," he said.

"How long has she been like this?"

"I don't know. We've had her for a few months now. I guess it all just happened kind of slowly."

"Is she eating?"

"She eats constantly."

I had no idea what was going on. I just knew Sunshine needed help.

While we were in South Dakota, we all took a trip to Mount Rushmore and took turns carrying Emmett around the park. Before we headed back to the base, we decided to eat dinner at a small restaurant there on the mountain that was known for extraordinarily good food. We spent the whole time playing with Emmett. We threw a blanket over his head, then heard him giggle and pull it off again, over and over again. He's such a cool little guy.

It was dark by the time we left the restaurant. In an attempt to get home quicker, someone suggested we take a different route back to the base. Essentially, that meant going through the mountains instead of around them, and it was a route Brandon had never taken before. It would shave about twenty minutes off our return trip, so we decided to give it a try.

Brandon and his family drove their car while Caroline and I followed in our rental. In no time, we were hopelessly lost deep in the Black Hills. There were no houses, no buildings, no lights, and no cell phone reception. There was just the two-lane road and the stars to keep us company. We just followed Brandon.

Suddenly, as we rounded a curve I saw Brandon hit the brakes and jerk his car to the left side of the road in an attempt to go around something. Once he was out of the way, I saw what it was. At first I thought it was a billboard sign or something that had fallen in the road, except there were no signs or anything else out there in the middle of nowhere. Instead, it was the biggest buffalo in the world. It had to have been the biggest one ever. That thing looked as big as my pickup truck. It was just standing there in the middle of the road. We missed it by about a foot, and I had to look up to see its eyes as we passed by. We talked about that for days.

We made it back to the base about an hour-and-a half later than if we had gone the way Brandon already knew. Chalk up a lesson learned.

We had a great time at Emmett's party. He had two cakes, one for everyone to eat and a smaller one for Emmett to enjoy for pictures—any way he wanted. We expected him to just dive in and make a mess, but he didn't. Instead, Brandon took Emmett's little hands and smashed them down into the cake hoping Emmett would take the hint. He didn't. Instead, his lip started quivering and he burst into tears. But when it came time to open presents, he perked right back up.

🐾   🐾   🐾

We hadn't been home for very long at all when Brandon called with the news. Sunshine had hyperthyroidism. I called Dr. Gandy.

"Weight loss is a classic sign of hyperthyroidism," she said.

"What can be done about it?" I asked.

"There are pills she can take, but they don't cure the disease, they only mask the signs. Personally, I recommend radioiodine. It's expensive, but it's one shot and she's cured. If you can get her down here, I can do it."

As it turns out, Dr. Gandy is one of only a handful of veterinarians licensed to provide radioiodine treatment, and Catisfaction is the only clinic in Alabama offering it. The shot itself is no big deal, except that it costs over a thousand dollars. The real challenge comes after the shot. Sunshine would have to be isolated from other cats for two weeks, and her urine and feces would have to be collected and stored for thirty days before being thrown out since she, and her waste products, would be considered radioactive.

Sometimes I think I'm living life in a B-rated movie.

I explained the options to Brandon. He opted for the pills for Sunshine, mostly because of the money, but also because he couldn't find a single veterinarian in the entire state of South Dakota who was licensed to provide radioiodine treatment. Sunshine took the pills, but she didn't seem to get any better. I called Dr. Gandy again.

"Is there any way you can get her down here?" she asked.

"I suppose we could put her on an airplane," I suggested.

"I don't recommend that. For the trip down here, that would be okay. But for the return trip, she'll be slightly radioactive following treatment, and that may cause problems with airline security."

Oh brother. Here we go.

I called Brandon a couple days later to tell him I was driving up there.

"If you're going to do that, I need to warn you about something," Brandon said.

"What's that?"

"Sunshine screams the whole time she's in a car. It's gonna drive you crazy."

"That's another sign of the disease," Dr. Gandy said. "I can give you some pills to give her that might help calm her down. Just make sure you give her each pill at least forty minutes before she has a clue she's going to be put in the car."

A few days later, I hit the road for the 1,400 mile drive to Rapid City.

I stayed a couple of days for a short visit. I played with Emmett, loved on Sunshine, and relaxed. Late one morning, I gave Sunshine a pill, waited forty minutes, threw her in the car, and left.

The pill didn't faze her, not one little bit. I had driven about three hundred miles when my cell phone rang. It was Caroline.

"Hello ... *meow*," I said.

"Is that Sunshine?" she asked.

"Yep ... *meow*."

"How long has she been doing that?"

"Well ... *meow* ... let's see ... *meow*. I've been ... *meow* ... on the road for ... *meow* ... about three hundred miles ... *meow* ... and she's been doing this ... *meow* ... for about ... *meow* ... three hundred miles ... *meow*."

"Good grief," Caroline said and laughed. "You and your cats. Remember, it was your choice to do this."

"I know ... *meow*. I'll talk ... *meow* ... to you later ... *meow*."

Another chuckle. "Okay. 'Bye."

"'Bye ... *meow*," we said, and hung up.

That was the longest 1,400 miles *ever*. When I got back home, I took the screaming thing straight to Dr. Gandy. Sunshine got her shot the next day, and the two-week countdown began. Rather than bring her home for that two weeks, I decided to have Dr. Gandy board her in a special room set aside just for cats who have received radioiodine treatments.

Sunshine screamed for the entire two weeks. I went to visit her about every other day. The only time she was quiet was when I was there with her. On each visit I was allowed to take her to an examination room and sit with her for a few minutes. I was allowed to pet her, but I couldn't hold her for more than a minute or two. She was still considered radioactive.

On one of my visits, I walked into the clinic to visit Sunshine and I could hear her screaming from the back of the clinic. The receptionist was on the phone and already knew why I was there, so she just pointed to an examination room. Just a few feet beyond the room was a door with "Radioactive" signs all over it. I stepped over to it and called to Sunshine, "How's my little Sunshine doing?"

Dr. Gandy poked her head out from the lab. She was cleaning cages.

She said, "Her name is not Sunshine. It's Rain Cloud. She's driving us crazy. You sure you don't want to take her home, like, right now?"

"Oh no. She's all yours, for the time being," I said.

"This is the most vocal kitty I've ever seen in my life," Dr. Gandy grumbled as she went to get Sunshine.

"By the way, why are you the one cleaning cages? Don't you have technicians to do that?" I asked.

"We're a little short on help right now."

"Really?" I said, and immediately thought of Matt. "You know, Matt just turned sixteen and is looking for a job."

"Oh yeah? How is he with animals?"

"He gives Little Man his insulin injections whenever I'm not around."

"Well," she said as she reached for a job application, "have him fill this out and bring it in. I'd like to talk to him."

Within the next week, Sunshine was at home with us and Matt was a Boarding Technician at Catisfaction Cat Clinic working part time. He was responsible for cleaning kennels and some other tasks like washing food bowls and towels. He seemed to enjoy it.

With five cats in the house, things were hectic. In no time at all, Sunshine gained weight and got back to her old self, which included sleeping on my chest with her nose right up next to my chin. Rotten.

Sunshine.

One afternoon after work I dropped by the clinic to pick up some food for Little Man. Dr. Gandy heard me from her office in the back.

"Hey," she called out, "how's Sunshine and life with a house full of cats?"

I walked back to her office. She had paperwork all over her desk. She looked a little frazzled.

"Actually, things are just fine. We still need to have that celebratory dinner, by the way," I said.

Then in a more serious tone, I asked, "How are things around here?"

She sighed, started to speak, then paused. She took another breath and said, "You know, things could be better."

"What's wrong?"

She began to confide in me a little. "Having my own clinic has always been a dream of mine. Being a veterinarian is the easy part, and I think I'm pretty good at it. But one thing they don't teach you very well in vet school is how to run the business part. There is just not enough time in the day to be a full-time vet, a full-time practice manager, and a full-time wife and mom. I'm getting tired."

"I know exactly who you need to talk to," I said with a smile.

"Who?" she asked.

"Caroline. You need to talk to Caroline. She's been doing this kind of stuff her whole life. She has a bachelor's degree in business administration with a minor in marketing. She was even a practice manager for an MD several years ago."

"No kidding! Sounds like I need to talk to her."

"Why don't the four of us get together for that dinner and talk about it?" I suggested.

We set a date.

Toward the end of May, Dr. Gandy and her husband, Chris, and Caroline and I met for dinner at a restaurant in town. We got a booth and sat down. A waiter came over to introduce himself and take our drink order. Chris and I ordered wine. Dr. Gandy and Caroline ordered margaritas.

"We're celebrating," I said.

"Fantastic!" the waiter said. "What are we celebrating?"

Chris spoke up and said, "No more ri …"

CRASH!

Just at that instant, someone in the kitchen dropped a tray full of plates. It startled all of us, but it startled the waiter the most. It was either that, or it was what he thought Chris was about to say. Maybe it was both.

He turned back to the table, took a couple of involuntary steps backward, and asked, "So, we're celebrating no more … rehab?"

We all went with it.

"That's right! No more rehab! Get those drinks for us, won't you please?" a couple of us said in unison.

When the waiter left, we all burst into laughter, but we kept the gag going. That waiter treated us very well the entire night, and we almost shut the place down. Chris and I talked about engineering stuff since we're both engineers, and Dr. Gandy and Caroline talked about Catisfaction stuff. We had a really good time.

A few days later, Caroline became the new, part-time practice manager at Catisfaction Cat Clinic. Bless her heart. That meant she had to work seven days a week, five at Harley and two at Catisfaction. Between us, we essentially worked four jobs since I was full-time on the Arsenal and spent weekends on our little side business building and selling action figure display boxes. If we counted Matt, the three of us worked five jobs. We were one busy family.

Caroline did have one condition for taking the job, and it was something to which Dr. Gandy had no objection. She wanted a few days off for us to ride to the Biltmore Estate in North Carolina during the first week of June for our anniversary.

The day we were scheduled to ride to North Carolina it was pouring rain. At about three hundred and fifty miles one-way, it was the longest trip we had ever taken on our bikes. But we were determined to do that rather than ride in a "cage." We packed the night before, got up early, and looked outside to see rain, rain, and more rain. Undeterred, we decided to don our rain gear.

On my way to the garage, Little Man tried to follow me.

I patted him on the head and said, "Daddy gotta go work for a few days, okay Little Man? You be good boy for Matt and Lauren while I'm gone."

He just blinked and wandered off. He understood.

I reached into my saddlebag and grabbed my rain pants first. I started to pull them over my riding boots and jeans, but just as I was about to get my right leg all the way through the leg of my rain pants, the seam split from the crotch all the way to the ankle. Unfazed, I simply did what any engineer would do. I grabbed the only thing I had available—bright blue duct tape.

Rip, slap, rip, slap, rip, slap, rip, slap—done.

Caroline walked into the garage right about that time.

"What do you think you're doing?" she asked.

"I'm getting ready to go," I said, matter-of-factly.

"You're not riding around with duct tape on your pants! You look like a hillbilly. How redneck can you get?"

"At least I'll be a dry one. What else am I supposed to do?"

She gave me an eye-roll and seemed to just let it go. We finished getting everything on, turned on the communication devices attached to the sides of our helmets, and took off.

It rained on us for two hundred and fifty miles without letting up. Eventually, the device on my helmet simply died. I guess the rain was too much for it. Caroline's worked fine, so she listened to music via the radio function on her device. I rode in silence with nothing but the hum of the engine between my knees and the sound of the wind against my helmet. Even in the rain, it was a great ride.

A little after mid-day, we rode through some beautiful country in the Nantahala National Forest. It was about lunchtime, so we looked for a place to eat. There wasn't much of anything where we were, but soon we came across what appeared to be a campsite with a restaurant near the road. We were tired, wet, cold, and hungry, so we stopped.

We ate some of the best food we had ever eaten. We sat outdoors under a covered area and watched the ducks swim by on the river by the restaurant. After lunch, the rain eased to little more than an occasional sprinkle, but we kept our rain gear on just in case. Soon we were on the road again.

The last one hundred miles or so was relatively uneventful. About five miles from our destination, Caroline signaled that she wanted to pull over at a gas station. I thought stopping to fill up was a good idea.

That wasn't what she had in mind.

I pulled up to the pump first since I was "leading," and Caroline parked right behind me. I shut off my engine, stepped off my bike toward the pump, and reached for the handle.

Without warning, Caroline came up behind me, spun me around, lifted my rain jacket up to my waist, and tugged at my rain pants. She jerked me around like I was a ragdoll.

"You … (tug) … are not … (tug) … walking into … (tug) … a five-star resort … (tug) … with duct tape … (tug) … on your pants … (tug)!"

On the other side of the pump, a man was filling his own bike with gas. I still had my helmet on, but my visor was up. He could see me, and our eyes met. I gave him an eye-roll and just shook my head. He smiled and shook his head right back. He understood.

We had a great time at the Biltmore House. The first thing we did after we checked into our room at the hotel was ride over to the House. We pulled in front of the House, very near a NO PARKING sign, parked, and asked a kind gentleman to take our picture. It's one of our favorite pictures, and of course, it's on Facebook.

Jonny and Caroline in front of the Biltmore House in Asheville, North Carolina.

The few days we spent there were fantastic. We went on several different tours of the House. We bought tickets to a wine-tasting event where there were glasses of several wines to sample along with a different flavor of chocolate candy with each glass. We rode around the grounds and around town a little bit, and had a great time. It didn't rain again the whole time we were there or for the ride home. We definitely plan to do that again sometime.

It was during that trip when we realized something about ourselves and about bikers in general. If we had taken that trip in a car just four years earlier and had stopped at a gas station where a biker was filling his tank, we probably would have steered clear and picked a different pump. We might have even passed the station altogether and sought another one. But since we have been riding, we have met some of the nicest people, most of them complete strangers, and all because of a shared desire for freedom on the open road in the open air.

HOOAH!

Back home, things got back to normal, and by "back to normal" I mean everything, including Caroline's habit of calling me whenever something needed to be fixed at Harley. With her new position as practice manager for the vet, that apparently included Catisfaction also.

Caroline worked at the clinic on Mondays and Thursdays. The rest of the time, she worked at the Harley store. One Saturday she asked me to run by the clinic to see Dr. Gandy and get a list of things that needed to be done. Matt happened to be working there that morning since the boarded cats need care every single day even though the clinic was closed for business. We arrived together at about 8:00 AM.

Dr. Gandy was sitting at the receptionist's desk when we walked in. We talked about this and that when an idea struck her.

"You know, one of the things I'd like to have eventually is some sort of a hole in the wall between this desk and the lab on the other side. Right now, whenever we have medication for a client's cat, we have to walk all the way around to hand it to the receptionist. What do y'all think?"

"I think it sounds like a good idea," I said.

Nobody said anything for a minute or two.

Then Matt said, "How about a doggie-, I mean, a kitty-door?"

"Hey! That's a great idea, Matt. I'll see about getting one," she said.

"You need to be careful," I said. "Most of the ones I've seen are for doors. I don't think I've ever seen one wide enough for a wall, but I'm sure they're out there somewhere."

"Good point," Dr. Gandy said. "Here's my card."

Uh-oh. "When do you want it done?" I asked.

"Right now."

Oh boy. "Okie-dokie. Be back in a few," I said as I started toward the door.

"Take my number, just in case," she said as I typed her number into my cell phone.

As I drove around looking for a kitty-door wide enough to be installed in a wall, I had only one thought: *Oh, no. Now there are two of them. Caroline and Stephanie are just alike.*

I resigned myself to the fact that I was going to be a busy man.

I didn't find anything at the hardware store, but I did find one at a pet store. It was more expensive than I expected, so I called Stephanie to get the okay.

"Sure, go ahead," she said. "And while you're out, see if you can find a few more of those little baskets I hang on the kennel doors in the lab."

"Will do."

I bought the kitty-door with Stephanie's card, drove back to the hardware store for the baskets, and then went straight to the clinic.

It took the rest of the day, but I managed to cut a hole in the wall, barely missing a conduit with electric power cords running through it, mount the kitty-door, and even install a small basket under the opening on the receptionist's side of the wall. Stephanie thought it was perfect.

As the weeks went by, I was called on to do various things at one place or another. One weekend I had to go to Harley to repair the leg of a display table. The next weekend I wound up at Catisfaction working on several doors that didn't close properly. After that I was back at the Harley place hanging mirrored items for sale.

Good grief. Those girls kept me busy.

🐾   🐾   🐾

When I wasn't at Harley or Catisfaction on my "off" days, I worked on my action figure display boxes at the shop or with Little Man in the garage. Sales were fair, but not great. The problem was I had to build them all by hand, and one at a time. They took an incredible amount of work. I charged as little as I could for them, and it may have been too much, but it couldn't be helped. I made practically nothing on them, especially if I considered the amount of work involved. I just hoped that maybe a toy company would pick them up and buy the idea from me. Time will tell, I suppose.

Our busy schedules meant something else, too. It meant nothing got done at home. But Caroline had a plan. Labor Day was just around the corner. Both Harley and Catisfaction would be closed on that day, and I would be off work as well since it was a federal holiday, so Caroline had a long list of things she wanted done.

CHAPTER 17

LABOR DAY – THE FIRST DAY

Monday, September 3, 2012

Labor Day started out like any other day with both of us off work, with honey-do's galore! Lucky me.

I got up at my usual time and fed all the cats. Caroline awoke early and felt a little sickly, so we just cuddled on the couch in the living room for a while until she felt better. Matt arose shortly thereafter, and after some pigs-in-blankets (sausages wrapped in biscuits) for breakfast, the work began. We moved some old chairs out to the street for the weekly yard debris pickup, but less than thirty minutes later a woman came and rang the doorbell. Caroline answered the door.

"Are you giving away these chairs?" the woman asked.

"We certainly are." Caroline noticed she was a young mother, and continued, "We also have an old crib you're welcome to have, but you may need to make more than one trip."

"Well, I guess I'll have my husband come and get the rest. Thank you very much!"

Off she went after she stuffed the two chairs in her SUV.

About fifteen minutes later, a young man came to the door. "I guess you've already seen my wife."

My first impression of this man was that he seemed a little put out for having to come get this stuff his wife thought they could use, but I just brushed away the feeling.

"Yep," I replied, "she said you would be heading this way pretty soon. We'll need some help getting it down from upstairs."

He helped us load the pieces into his truck. Surprisingly, Little Man never once tried to run out the front door. He just lay under the dining room table and "supervised." He's such a good boy.

Little Man under the dining room table with his legs crossed. He lies like this all the time.

When we finished, the young man noticed some loose shingles on our roof and handed me his card. He was in the business of fixing such things.

He said, "I noticed those shingles. Tell you what. Since you gave us all this stuff, I'll come by sometime later this week and take care of it for you."

"I appreciate that!" I said, and my earlier impression of him changed.

He thanked me again for the furniture and drove off.

Once the old items were out of the way, Matt and I were given the "opportunity" to move some remaining things around. Of course, it didn't matter that we had already moved some things from upstairs to downstairs and some things from downstairs to upstairs only a few days earlier. Apparently, that was just *practice* until we were told what we really wanted to do.

After a few hours of lifting and moving and "discussing," the job was done … for the time being. Caroline wanted to go shopping for some things for her Barbie Room. I was happy to see her go since that meant I could get some things done in the garage. As soon as she pulled out, Little Man and I headed for the garage.

1:30 PM

"Come on, Little Man. Let's go to the garage." He beat me there.

I walked over to my workbench with Little Man hot on my heels. He promptly plopped down and rolled over my feet, then spread out on the mat on the floor. I bent down and gave him his usual rubdown.

"Somebody sure is rotten," I said as I rubbed him and scratched his chin. He loved every second of it. He simply purred in response.

I stood up and pulled pieces of wood out for my action figure gun racks. I worked on them for a little while, then decided to run out to the mailbox to check the mail. As I walked back around to the garage side of the house, I heard Little Man. He cried, louder than usual, and it sounded as though he was pacing me as he walked along the garage doors on the inside. When I came back inside, Little Man was right there close to the door and was licking his lips like he had just eaten something.

"Little Man, what did you get into?" I asked. He just licked a little more and wandered off. I thought he probably found a piece of Ginger's dog food on the floor, as he had several times before, and thought nothing of it. Then I went back to the workbench.

About an hour later, we went back into the house. I needed to get some usual chores done in preparation for work the next day. I went to the refrigerator and pulled some things out for my lunches for the week, and after I cut up some tomatoes and chopped up some celery, I was soon on to the next chore. I cleaned the litter pans, made coffee for the next day, and was just about ready to take my shower. I looked for Little Man to make sure he wasn't still in the garage. I found him just wandering around the house.

4:00 PM

The concern began. Little Man licked his lips again, and this time I noticed he was drooling heavily, almost foaming at the mouth. He also seemed very agitated. Not angry, just restless. He also cried to me a couple of times.

"*Something's wrong, Daddy*," he meowed. Then, a little louder, "*Something's WRONG!*"

"Little Man, what did you eat?" I headed to the kitchen and got a paper towel to wipe his mouth. On the way, I noticed some spots of drool in various places on the floor. It was just clear liquid, and not very messy, but unusual nonetheless. I wiped Little Man's mouth and cleaned up the drool. When I finished, I called for him.

"Little Man! Are you okay?" I walked around the house looking for him. When I found him, my concern grew.

He stood in the middle of the living room with his head turned to the right, like he was stalking his tail. Then he walked around in a tight circle, but in slow motion. He expressed a low growl, and there was more drool and foam on his mouth. I grabbed more paper towels and cleaned him up. He seemed to settle down a bit, so I went to the bedroom, sat down, and took my shoes off to get ready to jump in the shower. Little Man followed me in there.

As I sat in the chair, I looked at him. He didn't make a sound, but I just had a feeling. He seemed better, but not quite right. I considered it for a while since it was a holiday, then decided.

Something is just not right, I thought, *and after all, this is Little Man we're talking about.*

I picked up my cell phone and called Dr. Gandy. I got her voice mail.

"Hey, it's Jonny. I'm really sorry to bother you on Labor Day, but I think I have a little problem and I'm not sure what to do about it. Little Man is acting very strangely. He's drooling a lot, growling at nothing, and walking around in slow motion like he's chasing his tail. It's really weird. If you get a chance, please give me call. Bye." I hung up the phone.

Just a few minutes later, Dr. Gandy called me back. "Hey. Got your message. So, what's going on?"

"Well, I don't know what to think," I said. "I've never seen this before. I'm looking at him right now, and he seems okay, sort of, but he's acting strangely, too."

"As it turns out, I'm going to be over that way later on today. Keep an eye on him, and if things get worse, let me know and we'll get together and have a look."

"Okay, thanks," I said, "and I'm sorry to bother you on a holiday."

"No problem," she said. "Have a good rest of the day and we'll talk later. Bye."

"Bye," I replied, and hung up.

I decided to go ahead and take my shower, and I hoped Little Man had simply eaten something that upset his stomach. I expected to find vomit somewhere on the floor by the time I got out of the shower.

After my shower, I shaved, dressed, and then looked for Little Man. On my way through the living room, I found a very large puddle of vomit on the floor about the size of a dinner plate. It was just clear liquid, no foam, bubbles, or anything else. I wasn't overly concerned by that and started cleaning it up. As I was wiping the floor, Little Man walked in the living room.

He was obviously more agitated, and a long line of drool dripped from his mouth. I grabbed another paper towel and wiped his face. I walked to the kitchen to throw the paper towel away. Little Man followed me in there. Then something even more strange happened.

He was standing right in front of the refrigerator. He turned to his right, as though looking at his tail again, and growled. Then he started walking around in a circle, slowly, chasing his tail, when suddenly he growled louder. Then in a jerky motion, he spun around very quickly and fell to the floor. He didn't get back up. I decided.

I ran upstairs, grabbed his travel kennel out of storage, and ran back down the stairs. I picked him up and put him in the kennel, then headed for the door and set the alarm. I put Little Man in the front seat next to me, backed out of the driveway, and grabbed my cell phone. I called Dr. Gandy. She answered.

"Hey, it's Jonny. I'm on my way to the clinic. I don't know what's going on here but Little Man just jerked around really fast, fell over, and wouldn't get back up."

"Okay. We'll meet you there."

6:30 PM

By the time we got to the clinic, Dr. Gandy was there and met Little Man and me at the door. We took him to the lab, got him out of his kennel, and placed him on an examination table. Dr. Gandy inserted an IV into a vein on his left front leg and started him on a fluid drip, then took some blood and his temperature. His temperature was about 104 degrees, a little higher than normal, which is 102.5. Something really strange was happening to him, but we had no clue as to what it could be. As Dr. Gandy did all that, I explained what I saw that afternoon. Then we put Little Man in one of the hospital kennels and decided to watch him for a while. He was agitated, but seemed to be okay. By that time it was about 7:00 PM.

She said, "Okay. It's about seven o'clock now and Patton hasn't had supper yet, so Chris and I will take him to go get something to eat. Little Man should be fine here for a while until we get back, then we'll decide what to do. If he's not any better, you may need to take him to the ER at the emergency vet clinic so they can monitor him all night."

"Works for me," I said. "Just let me know when you're on the way back and I'll meet you here."

"Fine. See you in a bit." She locked the door behind us and we both left.

At around 8:00 PM, I went back to the clinic even though Dr. Gandy had not yet called. I wanted to be there when she got back. It wasn't but five minutes later when she called to say, "On the way."

"I just got here myself," I said. "See you when you get here."

8:15 PM

As soon as Dr. Gandy arrived, we walked into the clinic together. We were shocked at what we saw.

There was urine all over Little Man's kennel. His IV line was a tangled knot. He was moving his head back and forth with a slight jerky motion, and his eyes were dilated to the point that he looked blind. I didn't know what to think.

I turned to look at Dr. Gandy and said, "He's going to have to go the emergency vet clinic, isn't he." It was not really a question since we both knew it was true.

"Yes. Let me get them on the phone. The closest one is out past your house, about thirty minutes away."

She walked around the table in the center of the room, picked up the phone, and dialed the number. They answered.

She said, "Hello. This is Dr. Gandy over at Catisfaction. I'm about to send a cat your way. He's my practice manager's cat, a ten-year-old male, domestic shorthair, and he's exhibiting...UH-OH!"

At that instant, as I listened and looked at Dr. Gandy as she explained the situation to the emergency vet clinic, I heard Little Man. I turned in his direction and got the shock of my life.

Little Man went into a full-blown seizure. He was like a superball. His involuntary muscle contractions made him slam himself against all four walls of his kennel. It sounded like someone was swinging a baseball bat around inside of it. The seizure was the worst thing I had ever seen.

Dr. Gandy dropped the phone without bothering to hang up. Then she ran around the room, opened and slammed cabinet doors and drawers and collected a syringe, a needle, and some medication to use in an attempt to stop Little Man's seizure.

As I watched Little Man jerk and writhe, I wanted nothing more at that moment than for God to take whatever it was that had gotten into Little Man and give it to me instead.

As I looked at him for a few more seconds, everything suddenly slowed down. It seemed as though time itself came to a screeching halt, and in a flash, Little Man was gone.

But he wasn't really gone, just … replaced. I no longer saw Little Man. I saw a tiny, little kitten with wispy, gray fur.

The voice in my head screamed, "*NOOOOO!*"

And just as suddenly, time sped back up. Another flash and I once again saw my Little Man. The seizure was a bad one.

It was all I could do to keep myself from going right through that grated metal kennel door. But all I could do was to yell, "HOLD ON, LITTLE MAN! HOLD ON!"

After about twenty seconds of bouncing around uncontrollably, Little Man suddenly threw his head back, drew his front paws up under his chin, and went completely stiff as every muscle in his body contracted. Then, after what seemed like an eternity, he relaxed.

Dr. Gandy jerked opened the door to his kennel and injected some white medication, which I later learned was Propofol, directly into his IV.

Then she turned to me and said, "Okay. I'm going to leave this syringe in his IV so you can… " She paused and then continued, "No, I'm going to go with you. There's no way you'll be able to inject this if he seizes again while you're driving. Where's his kennel?"

"It's over here," I said, and reached to pick it up. We took the top and the door off, placed a couple of towels in the bottom half that remained, and placed Little Man on the towels. He was awake, but completely limp.

"Let's go," she said.

I headed for the door. Dr. Gandy carried Little Man in his kennel and was right on my heels. Chris and her son Patton were behind us as we headed out the door.

I opened the passenger door for Dr. Gandy, ran around to the other side, and jumped in. She climbed in, set Little Man on her lap, and said, "All right."

Then, obviously concerned about his temperature, she continued, "Let's crank up the A/C and get going."

"No A/C," I said. "It hasn't worked for years. I'll roll the windows down."

"I guess that'll have to do," she said as I backed out of the parking lot. "Wait! I left my cell phone on the counter in the lab," she said as Chris was locking the clinic door.

She looked in his direction and yelled out the window, "Chris! Can you get my cell phone for me?"

Then, after a quick look down at Little Man, she yelled at him, "Forget it!"

Then she turned to me and said, "We have to go. We have to go NOW!" We took off.

I hit the interstate just up the road from the clinic and headed in the direction of the veterinary ER. Once on the interstate, I pushed that quad-cab diesel truck of mine right to the limit. As someone who actually reads owners' manuals, I was aware of a warning in my manual which states, "Never exceed 85 MPH." This is because the tires on the truck, although very good tires, are primarily for towing rather than speed. When I looked at the speedometer, I realized I was at almost ninety-miles-per-hour.

The first thing that popped into my head was, *Slow your ass down, Spayney. You're flying outside the envelope again.*

I slowed down—a little. After all, Little Man needed care *right then.*

A couple of miles down the highway, Dr. Gandy realized she had not yet put her seatbelt on and reached to wrap it around herself. She said, "I guess I better put this on in case we get pulled over."

"I'll turn the flashers on, too. I just hope everybody stays out of my way," I said.

Then I asked, "Where are we going?"

Funny how I had not asked before. I just assumed Dr. Gandy knew where we were going.

She said, "Crap! I don't really know. I've only been there once myself. I didn't get a chance to ask directions before Little Man had his seizure."

"I'll call Caroline and have her give us directions," I said. We had to yell at each over the roar of the diesel engine and the wind as it blew through the cab.

I whipped out my phone and dialed the number only to see the battery signal flashing at me.

"I don't believe this!" I yelled over the roar.

"What is it?" Dr. Gandy asked.

"My battery is dying! Tell Caroline to talk fast!" I yelled as I handed her the phone.

I couldn't hear a word of the conversation. The engine was screaming, the wind was blowing, and Dr. Gandy's hair was whipped around her face as she tried to talk to Caroline and get directions. Every so often, she tapped Little Man on his face to make him blink just to make sure he was still with us.

"HANG IN THERE, LITTLE MAN!" was all I could yell.

Before we got directions, the battery on my cell phone died. With no other options, I decided to stop and ask directions at a gas station. I whipped into the parking lot, parked the truck, and ran inside. The clerk was foreign and could barely speak English. All I knew was the vet ER was off Beltline Road in Decatur, Alabama.

I asked, "Do you know how to get to Beltline Road?"

The clerk merely shook her head, "No."

"I don't believe this," I said as I ran back to the truck.

This can't be happening.

Everything was going wrong, and there wasn't a thing I could do about it.

I jumped in the truck, tore down the road, and stopped again at a fast food place. "What's the phone number to the vet ER?" I asked Dr. Gandy as I got out. She handed me a piece of paper with the number on it. I ran inside.

Fortunately, the place was practically empty, and no one was at the counter.

I ran up to the counter and yelled, "I need to borrow the phone. It's an emergency!"

The manager walked over with a cordless phone and handed it to me. I dialed the number, got some quick directions, slammed the phone down, and ran to the door. "Thank you!" I yelled as I left.

Back in the truck, I got in and watched as Dr. Gandy, sweating to death herself, tapped and fanned Little Man's face again. He was still with us.

Dear God, please don't let Little Man's life end like this! I prayed as I cranked up the truck.

<u>9:30 PM</u>

Fortunately, we were just minutes away from the ER and found it without difficulty. We parked, got out, and ran to the door, which was locked because of the late hour and about that time, Chris pulled up next to us. I leaned on the door buzzer.

A technician came to the door, let us in, and escorted Dr. Gandy and Little Man to the back while I was asked to stay up front and fill out paperwork. Good grief.

The clerk handed me several forms, and one of them had three choices from which I was to choose. It was a Resuscitation Authorization Form.

The choices were:

Level 0: Do not resuscitate my pet.

Level 1: Normal resuscitation including CPR and drug therapy.

Level 2: All means necessary to save my pet including regular CPR, drug therapy, and emergency surgery if necessary.

The cost increased with each level, and in significant amounts, but the choice was easy. It's Little Man. Whatever it takes. I chose Level 2, signed the forms, threw them at the clerk, and followed her into a tiny exam room.

"The doctor will come see you as soon as he finishes looking over your pet. Please wait here," she said and smiled.

As *if*.

I waited about fifteen seconds, then walked through the door at the back of the room into the laboratory. Dr. Gandy was explaining the situation to the ER doctor, saw me enter, and motioned me over. "Tell the doctor what you saw today."

I walked toward where they stood and saw Little Man on an examination table. He was back on fluids and they had wet him down, covered him with wet washcloths, and had a fan blowing over him in a desperate attempt to cool him off. His temperature was now about 106 degrees, and everyone was concerned about brain damage. He was motionless, but seemed to respond to me when I spoke to him.

"Hey, Little Man. You okay?" I rubbed his head and he blinked at me. He obviously felt terrible. I told the story all over again.

When I finished, both Dr. Gandy and the ER doctor were at a loss as to what could have caused all this. But for now, Little Man seemed to be in good hands.

Dr. Gandy said, "I think we'll head back. Please keep me updated," she said to the ER staff. Then to me she said, "I'll talk to you tomorrow."

"Okay," I replied. As she was leaving, I reached over and held her arm, then said, "And hey, by the way, thank you."

She smiled and said, "No problem at all." Then she left.

When she got in her car with Chris, who had followed us there, the first thing she said was, "I almost wish I hadn't mentioned Little Man's diabetes."

"Why not?" Chris asked.

"Because it's going to be very easy for them to conclude this is just a hypoglycemic episode, but something tells me that's not it."

Still in the clinic, I talked a little more with the ER doctor, and reminded him that Little Man was a diabetic. He checked Little Man's blood glucose with a glucometer. It was 27. The normal range is between 70 and 150. Below 40 is considered hypoglycemic.

He said, "I'm going to add some glucose to his fluid bag to get his levels back up. Beyond that, we're just going to monitor him and keep on with supportive care. Why don't you go try to get some sleep and call us in the morning? I'll be here until about seven in the morning."

Another temperature check revealed Little Man's temperature had come back down to a reasonable level, so they dried him off, moved him to a rollaway kennel that closely resembled a bed, covered him with a little blanket, and settled him in for the night. I walked over toward him.

"Nite-nite Little Man. Daddy'll be back in the morning, okay?" I said as I rubbed his head one more time and left.

I was so upset when I left that I promptly took a wrong turn and was lost almost immediately. I couldn't call Caroline because my cell phone was dead. I finally backtracked and eventually found my way home. I arrived at about midnight, totally exhausted.

When I crawled in bed, Caroline asked, "How's Little Man?"

"You know," I said, "I really don't know. They got his temperature down, but nobody knows what caused all this. I'm going to call them first thing in the morning."

"Okay," she said, "I guess you better try and get some sleep. G'night."

"G'night," I replied.

Sleep. Yeah, right.

CHAPTER 18 –
THE ROLLER-COASTER RIDE

Tuesday – Day Two

As expected, I hardly slept at all. When my alarm went off at 5:15 AM, I was already awake. I got up, took a shower, shaved, dressed, and then headed to the kitchen to feed the other cats. While they ate, I made my lunch for the day. I moved by rote, acting purely out of habit. My mind was a complete mess. I was scared to death and could barely think at all.

At about 5:45 AM, just before the time when I usually leave for work, I reached in my pocket, grabbed my cell phone, and flipped it open. My hands were shaking so badly I could barely dial the number to the ER. I had no idea what to expect. I didn't know if Little Man was alive or dead.

The phone rang a couple of times and a technician answered. I got straight to the point.

"Hello. This is Jonny Payne, Little Man's Daddy. How is he?" I asked, and held my breath.

"Actually, Little Man is doing well. He's standing up, and he urinated a little while ago. We think he just had a hypoglycemic episode last night, which can certainly cause seizures, but he seems to be okay now," she said.

I could breathe again. "That's great news! I've been scared to death ever since I left last night! Is the doctor still there?" I asked.

"Yes. In fact, he'll be here for another hour or so."

"Okay. I'll head that way now so I can have a talk with him before he leaves."

"That will be fine. See you then," she said.

"Thank you. I'll see you shortly," I said, then hung up.

Wow. Little Man was okay. I couldn't wait to go get him. My mind was working again, and I remembered that only the bottom half of Little Man's kennel was at the ER and the rest was at Dr. Gandy's, so I went upstairs and grabbed another, slightly larger kennel. Then I ran to the bedroom, gave Caroline a kiss, and left.

I arrived at the ER at about 6:30 AM. They sent me back to the same little exam room where I waited so briefly the night before and told me the doctor would be with me shortly. He came in a few minutes later.

"Good morning," he said as we shook hands.

"Good morning," I replied. "So, what happened last night?"

"Well, it seems to me it was nothing more than a sudden hypoglycemic episode. His blood glucose got very low, and that will certainly lead to seizures and much worse if not treated quickly. But right now he's up and alert and seems to be fine. However, I recommend you take him back to your normal veterinarian for a checkup this morning."

"What about eating? Has he eaten yet?" I asked.

"No. When was the last time he had an insulin injection?"

"That would have been yesterday morning about 6:00 AM, his normal time," I said. "He got his usual five units after he ate."

Then I had a thought and said, "He hates going to the vet, and he rarely eats when he's there, so would it be okay if I take him home to feed him before I take him back to Dr. Gandy's office?"

"Sure. That should be fine. I'll take you up front so you can settle up with the clerk, then we'll bring Little Man out to you," he said.

"Works for me," I said. "Thanks for taking care of him last night."

"That's what we're here for," he said as we walked to the front desk.

After I paid the bill, they brought Little Man out in the larger kennel and handed me the bottom half of the other one from the night before.

"Hey, Little Man. How are you doing this morning?" I asked as I stuck my fingers through the kennel door. He sniffed and rubbed against my fingers, and seemed to be better. I thanked the ER staff once again and headed out the door. We were back on the road in no time.

When we got home, I took Little Man, still in the kennel, straight to the laundry room in case he needed to use the litter pan. I opened the door but he didn't come out right away, so I left him there and stepped into the kitchen to open a can of food for him. When I walked back into the laundry room, I put his dish down in front of the door of the kennel hoping to coax him out. He finally came out, but my hopes sunk.

He didn't just come out, he ran out, or rather, *jumped* out with very jerky motions. He made no attempt to eat. He turned to his right, growled, then with more jerky motions, went right back into his kennel. I grabbed my cell phone out of my pocket and called Dr. Gandy. She answered.

"Hey, it's me," I said in a voice that told her something was wrong.

"What's the matter?" she asked.

I tried to summarize as quickly as I could. "Well, I called the ER this morning. They said they think Little Man had a hypoglycemic episode last night but that he's fine now. They told me to take him to you this morning, just for a follow-up. He hasn't eaten yet, so I asked if I could bring him home to feed him before heading out to your place since he never wants to eat when he's at the vet. I just tried to feed him. He ran out of his kennel, growled, then ran back in, without eating. And now he's ..." I looked at him in the kennel and could see the same agitated head motions from the day before, "... he's jerking his head back and forth again. I think we're right back where we started. *WHAT THE HELL IS GOING ON HERE?*" I wasn't just scared. I was *pissed*. About that time, Caroline walked up behind me.

"Do you have any glucose you can give him, and quickly?" Dr. Gandy asked.

"Yes, I think so." I jerked the cabinet door open and dug around until I found some Instaglucose I had for emergencies just like this. It's a reddish paste in a toothpaste-like container, high in glucose, that's used strictly for first-aid treatment of a hypoglycemic episode if Little Man's glucose levels ever bottom out after an insulin injection.

"Found it!" I yelled into the phone.

"Okay. Take a glob of it on your finger and rub it onto his gums, then get him to the clinic. I'm on my way now."

"Will do. I'll get him there as fast as I can," I said, then hung up the phone.

Caroline grabbed the paste from my hands, ripped the cap off, and squirted some on my finger. Then as best I could, I smeared it on Little Man's gums but got some of it on the outside of his mouth. If he didn't look bad before, now he looked like he had blood all over his face. I closed the door to the kennel, grabbed it off the floor, and headed for the door, yelling to Caroline on the way, "Gotta get Little Man to the clinic—*NOW!*"

The clinic is only about ten minutes away, but I did it in less. I could see Little Man through the slits in the side of the kennel and could tell he was getting worse.

"Hold on, Little Man, we're gonna get you taken care of real quick!" I said to him as I slowed to make the last U-turn in front of the clinic. By that time of the morning, it was rush hour, so I had to wait for a few cars to pass before I could complete the turn.

When I saw a break in traffic, I whipped the truck around, then heard Little Man. He went into another seizure right there in the kennel. Only this time he was in a much more confined space. Not good. Not good at all.

"NO! NO! HOLD ON, LITTLE MAN! HOLD ON! WE'RE JUST ABOUT THERE!" I screamed as I jerked the truck into the parking lot at Catisfaction.

I jumped out of the truck, ran around to the other side, opened the door, and grabbed the kennel. I slammed the truck door behind me, then burst into the clinic and headed straight for the lab.

"He's seizing!" I yelled to Tabatha, one of the veterinary technicians. She was standing right next to the examination table in the center of the laboratory and was on the phone with Dr. Gandy.

"Jonny just got here and Little Man's having another seizure," she said into the phone. Then, "Okay. We'll see you in a minute." She hung up.

"Dr. Gandy's pulling in the parking lot right now," she said to me.

"All right. I'm going to get him out of the kennel," I said as I opened the kennel door. I reached in and pulled Little Man out. His seizure had stopped, but there were other problems. He couldn't stand up. Just then, Dr. Gandy walked in.

"I thought you said the ER said he was fine?" she said.

"They did! So how can this be happening all over again?" I asked.

"I have no idea, but let's have a look," she said.

I stepped out of the way to let her and Tabatha do their thing. Sure, I had no fear at Jump School. Sure, I was relatively calm when Moe and I were flopping around in that CF-18. Sure, I had "confidence under stress" when Caroline stalled my 'Cuda in the middle of six lanes of traffic. But *this* was *Little Man!* I was a basket case.

Dr. Gandy injected more Propofol to prevent another seizure, then began to take more blood and check his temperature and whatever else veterinarians do. She prepared a very large syringe full of charcoal looking stuff and was just about to insert a tube down his throat through which to inject it into his stomach.

"What's that?" I asked.

"Well, I'm thinking there's some kind of toxin in his system that is causing all this. This stuff will absorb any of it that remains in his digestive system. He should just poop it out later," she explained.

After she gave him the charcoal stuff, Little Man seemed calm, but certainly not well. At least he was in good hands.

"I think I better get to work," I said. "I'll call after a while to check on him."

"Okay. We'll keep you posted," Dr. Gandy said as I left.

I got to work at about 9:30 AM—late. I sipped on my coffee and looked over some emails, but realized there was no way I was going to be productive in any way. So, I surfed the internet.

A toxin, huh? I thought to myself. *Let's just see what I can find out*, and the search began.

But without more information, I didn't really know where to look.

At about 10:30 AM, I called the clinic to ask about Little Man. The receptionist answered.

Without introducing myself, I just said, "Hey, I'm just calling to see how Little Man is doing."

"Hold on. Let me get Dr. Gandy for you," was all she said. I was on hold for less than a minute when Dr. Gandy came to the phone. She knew it was me.

"Hey, it's Stephanie. I really don't know what's going on. But I've been looking over some of my medical literature and I think it's some sort of poison or toxin, maybe organophosphate poisoning."

"How in the world would something like that get ahold of him?" I asked.

"There are actually lots of things," she said. "Antifreeze, insecticides, household cleaning solutions, or even a Black Widow spider or a lizard, especially if he ate one. These are all certainly possibilities. Anything like that around that he could have gotten into?"

I racked my brain and tried to think of something, anything he could have eaten that would fit what she described.

"No, not really. How is he right now?" I asked.

"He has some paralysis in his back end and can't seem to stand up."

Oh boy. Not what I needed to hear. "Is he...?"

She knew what I was thinking and, thankfully, didn't let me finish my question.

"No, he's stable for now. At least I think he's stable. The medication I gave him settled him down so he's not showing signs of another impending seizure. I'm going to keep looking for clues. Are you coming back here when you get off work?"

"I'll be there about four-fifteen this afternoon." I said.

"Okay. Hopefully, I'll have something better to tell you by the time you get here. Bye."

"Bye," I said, and hung up.

The rest of the day went by at a snail's pace. I surfed the internet a little more hoping to find something to explain all this. I decided to see what I could find out about Black Widow bites.

Black Widows, it turns out, are extremely venomous. I found a list of signs to expect in a cat bitten by a Black Widow, and Little Man exhibited several, if not all of them. The toxin is neurological rather than local, which means it affects the nervous system as a whole, not just at the site of the bite. The bite itself is also easily recognizable. There are usually two puncture wounds, side by side, which make the bite look like a vampire bite. That was not something we had been able to find. But I was shocked to see an ominous warning at the bottom of one of the articles: *Usually fatal in cats.*

I felt the blood drain from my head. *Oh dear God, not Little Man.*

I sat there at my desk after reading that and prayed aloud, "God save Little Man!"

At 4:00 PM, I locked my office and headed to the parking lot. I couldn't wait to see my Little Man. As I told Dr. Gandy I would, I arrived at Catisfaction at about 4:15. She was busy with other clients, so the receptionist led me to the lab to see Little Man. I said hello to him and rubbed his head for a few minutes. I noticed he had not used his litter pan at all, and that worried me. But I was going to have to wait until Dr. Gandy had some time to talk, so I just wandered into the boarding area and looked at the cats boarded for overnight stays.

As I nervously walked around Catisfaction's incredibly nice boarding area, Meredith, one of the boarding technicians, walked over to me. She was a young woman who, when not at work at Catisfaction, worked with young girls with behavioral problems.

She asked, "Would you like to pet one of the cats?"

"No. Thanks. I'm just waiting to talk to Dr. Gandy about Little Man," I replied.

She could tell I was upset, and it was clear to me that she completely understood. In her quiet, soft-spoken way, she looked straight at me and said, "Dr. Gandy saved my cat's life. She can save yours, too." Then she turned and continued her daily duties.

I didn't realize it at the time, but that was probably the best thing anyone could have said to me at that moment. As the days went by, I would replay those words in my mind over and over again. They actually helped give me some peace. Whenever I had the slightest feeling I was losing hope, those words would come back to me. They gave me the strength to hang tough. Little Man deserved nothing less.

About thirty minutes later, I was standing near Little Man's kennel and Dr. Gandy walked over to talk to me. We sat on chairs around the examination table. She started the conversation.

"Okay. Based on the results from the blood I took, Little Man's liver enzymes are very high. His body is fighting whatever got into his system. He also has some paralysis in his back end. He can move his hind legs, but he can't stand. He doesn't seem to be able to urinate on his own and has a lot of blood in his urine. He hasn't pooped either. Also, his potassium is zero. I've never seen that before and I don't know what could cause that, but I added a potassium supplement to his fluid bag hoping that will bring his levels back up, and I checked his magnesium levels. On the good side, the dilation in his pupils is decreasing. I'm going to keep him on fluids, and I may need to insert a urinary catheter if he goes much longer without urinating. But I have a question for you."

"Shoot," I said.

"Are you absolutely certain he ate normally and got his insulin yesterday morning?"

"Yes," I answered. "In fact, around mid-day yesterday he was perfectly fine."

"If it was anybody else but you, I would question that. But I know you. I know how you are with your cats."

Then, she continued, "And I'll tell you something else. There's no way Little Man had a simple hypoglycemic episode to start all this. That does not explain his temperature. That doesn't explain why his liver enzymes are ten times higher than they should be. It doesn't explain the blood in his urine. And it doesn't explain his paralysis. And if I missed a simple case of hypoglycemia, I will shred my diploma and hang up my scrubs. I don't buy it. There's just no way. I think he's been poisoned or exposed to a toxin."

I had no idea how to respond to all that as I had no clue how that could have happened. For one thing, he's an indoor cat, and as for the garage, he's in there all the time and has never had a problem before. I just sat there for a minute before speaking again.

"How about eating? Has he eaten anything today?" I asked.

"No, not since he's been here. When does he normally eat and get his insulin injection?"

I answered, "About six and six every day. He's on half a can of wet food for diabetics, a tablespoon of dry food, and five units of insulin twice daily."

"Okay. He needs to be on as close to his normal schedule as possible. The problem is, we don't open until seven in the morning, and we close at six at night during the week. We're also closed on the weekends."

I thought about that for a couple of minutes. It certainly seemed to me that any attempt to move him again might result in another seizure. I was also concerned about his not wanting to eat whenever he's at the vet. But I thought that maybe if *I* were the one to feed him, he just might eat for me. If he's at Catisfaction, he's only ten minutes away and I can feed him every meal. If he were all the way out at the ER, getting there at every mealtime would be difficult and impossible at times. Besides, Dr. Gandy knew his history very well. The ER staff didn't.

I figured it wouldn't hurt to ask, so I said, "Over the past few years, he's gotten to the point where he simply won't eat whenever he's at the vet. But maybe he'll eat for me. Would it be possible for me to come see him for every meal and feed him myself?"

Although I was terrified I was about to lose Little Man, I think Dr. Gandy was more worried about *me* worrying about *him*. She could tell I wanted to be involved in as much of his care as possible.

She said, "Sure. You can come by anytime during normal business hours. And even though we're closed on weekends, someone is here at least twice a day to take care of the boarders at mealtimes. You can come by then, too."

"Fine by me. I can do that. I drive by here every day going to and from work anyway."

It really was no problem at all. Little Man has always been there for me. So by God, I was going to be there for him.

Then I realized there would be times when Little Man would be alone at the clinic. I asked, "Are we sure it's best to keep him here instead of at the ER?"

She answered, "I think we can give him great care right here. I'm usually here long after we close anyway, and I almost always have to come in on the weekends for one cat or another. If I'm here, you can drop by then, too, if you like. Don't worry. If I think he's getting to the point where he needs twenty-four hour care, I'll let you know."

Then I asked, "Is he going to pull through this?"

After a slight pause, she said, "I don't know. We'll just keep him on supportive care until we can figure out what got into him. Let's give him until the end of the week."

I did *not* want to hear that.

"What if we give him a dose of anti-venom?" I asked.

"No, we can't do that. For one thing, the anti-venom is extremely expensive. I don't know how much, but probably in the four- to five-thousand dollar range. And if all this is not from a Black Widow, there's no telling what the anti-venom would do to him."

She continued, "He's had food available all day and hasn't eaten anything, so don't worry about trying to feed him his supper. If he hasn't eaten by tomorrow morning I'll tube feed him."

"What about insulin? Should I keep him on his normal five units twice a day?" I asked.

"No, no, we're going to start him back up slowly, at two or three units, and only when he's eating again."

By that time, it was about five-thirty in the afternoon and I still hadn't fed the other cats at home, so I excused myself. I said goodbye to Little Man and patted him on the head.

I had been home for about an hour when my cell phone rang. I answered. It was Dr. Gandy.

"Hey, it's Stephanie. I wanted to ask you again about things that Little Man could have gotten into. Do you have any antifreeze in your garage?"

"Yes, I do," I answered, "but it's in a container with the cap on it and has other things on top of it. He couldn't get to it if he tried."

"Is it possible one of your cars is leaking?"

They wouldn't dare. Both of those cars are practically brand new, and I built the 'Cuda back up from scratch with all new parts. There's no way that car is leaking *anything*, especially after what I went through with the oil pan fiasco. I said, "I really don't think so, but I'll go have a look."

I kept the phone to my ear, went to the garage, and started crawling on the floor under both cars looking for any leaks.

"I'm on my hands and knees now, and I don't see anything under the cars or the motorcycles."

"What about insecticides, or cleaning solutions? Are there any signs of a half-eaten lizard or anything that you can see?"

I walked all over the garage, looking for anything that could even remotely explain what could have happened to Little Man. There was just nothing there.

"No. I do have some things like weed killer for the yard, but they're where they usually are and still covered in dust. The caps are still on them, too. And nothing seems disturbed. No lizards either, and except for a few little spider webs, no spiders."

"Wow," she said. "There has to be an explanation. I'll just have to keep looking. By the way, I have to be here later tonight anyway to check on another cat, so I'll check on Little Man too."

I said, "Okay. I'll come by later, too, so I'll see you then. Bye."

"Bye," she said, and we hung up.

I walked around in the garage for a few minutes more, then went into the house. As I thought about the call from Dr. Gandy, I walked all through the house looking for anything suspicious. As I walked through the dining room, I could see a few clumps of fur and a toy or two under the table, right where Little Man relaxes during the day when people are shuffling around.

I got down on my knees to look closer, but all I found out of the ordinary was a rather large piece of cat litter. I picked it up and threw it away.

I went to the clinic later that night as promised. Dr. Gandy was there checking on other cats and things, and Little Man showed no signs of more seizures, so I expected to be able to rest a little easier. Besides, I was exhausted. I said goodnight to Little Man and left for home.

Before I went to bed, there was something I had to do. Even as tired as I was, I was sure I wouldn't sleep well anyway.

I thought about the recording I made earlier of Little Man purring. I got on the computer and sent K-Naught an email. I told him what happened to Little Man and wanted to know if he still had the capability to download video from magnetic tape to a CD. I wanted a permanent recording of Little Man purring. My thoughts were that if the earlier recording wasn't any good, I would need to move fast to try and record another since I may not have another chance to make one if …

Wednesday – Day Three

I stopped by the clinic on my way to work and got there just before the clinic opened for business. After a technician let me in, I tried to feed Little Man. He was still the same, no better, but no worse, and he still had no appetite. I left a note for Dr. Gandy, pet him a little, and then left.

The first thing I did when I got to work was call our pest control company. I explained what happened to Little Man and that we thought a Black Widow might be to blame. Friday, only two days away, was my normal off day. I scheduled an appointment to meet one of their men at the house.

That afternoon after work, I arrived back at the clinic at about 4:15 PM. I went straight to the lab. Dr. Gandy was there, and with a flustered look. She hit me with the latest.

"Okay. I've been on the phone most of the day. There are three different veterinarians now all saying it must be poison. I've spoken with my mentor from Mississippi State and another vet up at Michigan State's toxicology lab. Like I said before, there's no way this was hypoglycemia. He still can't stand with his hind legs, and he can't urinate or defecate on his own. Based on the liver values, his liver is trashed. His bladder doesn't look like a bladder anymore. The ultrasound shows it looks like a glob of blood clots, and his blood has the look and consistency of two-percent milk. In fact, my machine can't read it anymore. I have to send it out to a different lab for analysis."

I could barely stand. I couldn't believe what I was hearing. I didn't know what to say. After catching my breath, I asked, "So, what do we do now?"

"We just keep on," she replied. "My mentor at State even said that since he's lasted this long, we shouldn't give up on him."

Finally, a tiny bit of good news. At least the vets involved weren't giving up, yet.

After a long pause, I asked, "How about eating?"

"I tube fed him today, and he tolerated it pretty well. I also gave him another syringe of activated charcoal, just in case."

Just then, I noticed Cody, a licensed veterinary technician, running his hand under some water in the sink in the lab. There was blood on his fingers.

"What happened?" I asked.

He said, "Little Man bit me while we were trying to give him his activated charcoal. I thought he was too sick to put up a fight. He wasn't."

Dr. Gandy said, "Yeah, he got him pretty good."

"Sorry about that," I said.

"Just an occupational hazard," Cody said.

That night before bed, just like the night before, Dr. Gandy was there with another patient, so I went to the clinic to see Little Man. Dr. Gandy had removed his IV catheter from one leg and placed a new one into the other, and she also put in a urinary catheter. To top it all off, Little Man was wearing one of those lampshade-shaped cones to prevent him from chewing at his IV. As bad as he looked, I was sure I felt worse. He was on one medication or another for various things, including something to help bring his liver enzymes back down.

Little Man was a sick little boy.

Thursday – Day Four

I went to the clinic as usual on my way to work. Little Man seemed only slightly better to me, but even then I couldn't be sure if it was just wishful thinking on my part or if he really was showing improvement. He still wouldn't eat for me, but Dr. Gandy was tube-feeding him as necessary, so I wasn't overly concerned. I loved on him a little, then left for work.

That day was a workday at Catisfaction for Caroline. When I got there after work, Caroline met me at the door. I could tell something was up.

"What is it?" I asked.

Caroline smiled nervously and said, "Let me get Stephanie."

A few minutes later, Dr. Gandy had a break in-between other clients, so the two of them met with me in the laboratory. They filled me in.

Not long before I arrived, Dr. Gandy and Cody were preparing to tube feed Little Man. They had him on the examination table in the center of the lab. Dr. Gandy was mixing his food with a tongue depressor to stuff it into the feeding syringe when Little Man seemed to show interest.

Pleasantly surprised, Dr. Gandy said to him, "Little Man, are you hungry?"

She held the tongue depressor up to his mouth. He sniffed and began to lick at the mush on the end.

"He wants to eat!" she said to the others in the room.

She took the tongue depressor, globbed up a little more food on the end, and held it to Little Man thinking he would continue to lick the gravy.

Without warning, Little Man bit at the end of the tongue depressor and snapped off a sliver about two inches long and swallowed it whole.

"Oh, no," Dr. Gandy said at the time, "I'm going to have to go get that."

But then she reconsidered. They let Little Man finish his meal on his own, and a few minutes later, I walked in. When she finished the story, we both looked at Little Man for a moment or two.

I asked, "So are you going to go in and get it?"

"No, I'm not."

"Why not?"

"Because I'm worried about dehiscence."

"What's that?"

"That's where the surgical site opens up."

She could tell I was confused, so she continued, "The problem is, his body is in no condition for that kind of surgery. Plus, he's had multiple steroid injections to help suppress his immune system while we figure out what's going on. He would survive the surgery itself, but then because of everything his body is going through right now, I'm afraid the sutures would open up. He would leak all kinds of nasty stuff into his body and he would be dead within a couple of weeks."

Great. Out of the frying pan and into the fire. "So what do we do now?" I asked.

"We just wait and see if it gives him any trouble. If it does, we go in anyway and hope for the best. If not, hopefully, he'll just pass it eventually. It's wood and very thin, so maybe it will go right through him without causing any damage."

Little Man still had both catheters and was unable to stand, urinate, or defecate on his own, but he seemed to enjoy being petted. I loved on him for a while and then left for home.

When I got home, I checked my email to find that K-Naught had responded to me. There was no problem with doing what I wanted.

He said, "Send it my way."

Friday – Day Five

It was my normal day off, but I went to the clinic at the normal time anyway. Little Man seemed to like attention, but after I fed him and gave him his medications, he growled at me when I tried to give him his insulin injection. I left a few minutes later to go back home to meet the pest control man.

He arrived at the house at about 8:00 AM. I told him everything that had happened.

"Well, if there are any Black Widows in here, we should be able to find some evidence," he said.

We looked all over the garage, but the man could find no evidence of Black Widows anywhere.

"Nice car," he said.

Then as we worked our way just about all the way around the garage, he stopped.

"Right there," he said, "if they're in here, that's where they'll be."

He pointed to a stack of bricks under the industrial sink. They were the kind of bricks with holes in the center.

"Those bricks are a Black Widow's most favorite place in the whole world," he said.

"Well, let's look," I said.

We pulled everything out from under the sink: work shoes, Matt's soccer ball, empty pots, everything. One by one, we looked at every single brick, about twenty of them. We found no evidence of Black Widows anywhere.

"Well, I suppose it could have been a straggler," he said, "but just in case, I'll powder up the garage in the places where Black Widows are most likely to hide. If they're hiding in here, they'll come out once this powder touches them."

We never saw a thing.

After he left, I was at a loss. While it wasn't impossible, a Black Widow bite was looking less likely. We just weren't getting anywhere.

I decided to seek some additional help.

I whipped out my cell phone and called Dr. Wagner's office in Nebraska. I thought that maybe she might have seen something like this before. A technician answered the phone.

"Hello," I said, "This is Jonny Payne. I'm calling from Alabama. Is Dr. Wagner available?"

"Who's calling, again?"

"Little Man's Daddy."

"Oh! How is Little Man?" she asked.

"You remember Little Man?" I asked in disbelief.

"Of course! Big, gray cat, right?"

Wow. It had been years since Little Man was there, and they still remembered him. I should have known. *Everybody* remembers Little Man. "That's him," I said.

"Well, how is he?"

I told her a little about what was going on and said I needed to talk to Dr. Wagner.

"Oh, my goodness! Well, Dr. Wagner isn't in the office today, but I can give you her email."

She gave me the address.

After we hung up, I went straight to my computer. I typed a high-priority email with the subject line, "Little Man is in a bad way, any advice?"

I explained everything to Dr. Wagner:

Dr. Wagner,

As of Labor Day, we believe Little Man was bitten by a Black Widow, or he got into something else, but he shows all the signs of some sort of neurological toxin like the stuff that comes in a dog's topical flea treatment (starts with an "O"). We have made extensive attempts to identify what it was to no avail. He exhibited seizures, spinning in slow circles, heavy drooling, agitation, and twitching, and although right now he can eat on his own, he can't stand, urinate, or defecate on his own. He has a urinary catheter also. We finally found a veterinarian down here that we trust completely. She is going out of her way to save him. We are proceeding with IV fluids, etc., and some other medications, but there are some other concerns.

Yesterday about 4:00 PM, I was not yet there at the clinic but the staff were very excited to see Little Man showing great interest in his food they were preparing to give him with a syringe, so they offered some to him on the end of the wooden tongue depressor being used to mix up his food. At first he just licked, but then without warning he bit off and swallowed a sliver of the tongue depressor. I'm told it's about 1/16" x 1-1/2" in size. The vet here is rightfully concerned about surgery to remove it given his current condition. She has cleaned his bowels (manually) the best she could, but his inability to even defecate has her worried.

Dr. Wagner, this vet is good. I have other reasons for believing she knows her stuff. Dedication is not a question at all. On Labor Day night, she left her husband and son (and her cell) at the clinic and jumped in my truck with me while we flew at over 85 MPH to a 24-hour emergency clinic. When we arrived, Little Man's temp was close to if not over 107 degrees F. They got it back down and him stabilized, but after he was discharged the next day he wound up right back in the same condition. Our new vet has taken over his care completely. Again, Little Man is in the best of care.

Anyway, what do you think of this sliver he swallowed, and what about his back-end problems (no standing, urinating, or defecating)? We, or rather, the vet, found some literature that describes Little Man's symptoms almost like he was the test case on which the article was based.

I'd love to hear any suggestions you might have. After all, this is Little Man we're talking about here, and I'm willing to do whatever it takes.

I signed my name and included my phone number. I was sure Dr. Wagner would get back to me within a couple of days.

A little while later, I decided to go to the grocery store to get some things, but stopped in at the clinic on the way. Dr. Gandy was in the process of manually cleaning out his bowels again since he was not defecating on his own. It was black from all the activated charcoal, but no stick. She did this and expressed his bladder regularly to prevent nerve damage.

"Wow, looks like you're having fun," I said.

She just looked at me.

"I'm going to run to the grocery store. I'll drop by a little later," I said and hit the door.

On the way, I dropped the tape of Little Man purring in the mail to K-Naught.

While I was still on my way to the grocery store, Caroline called. She said she needed to run some errands and stop by the clinic to check on some things and would look in on Little Man while she was there.

I made it through two aisles of the store when my cell phone rang. It was Caroline.

"Hello?" I said.

"Are you finished with groceries?" she asked. I could tell something was wrong.

"What?" I asked.

Silence.

"WHAT?" I asked again.

Caroline started crying. "I think you better get here."

"On my way," I said and hung up.

I swung the cart around and ran to the front of the store. I threw it at a clerk and said, "I'm sorry! I can't finish! I have an emergency!"

I hit the parking lot at a dead run. I jumped in my truck and tore out of the parking lot and onto the interstate going as fast as I dared.

"Please, Lord, just let me say goodbye," I prayed aloud. I was almost in tears.

I got to the clinic in about ten minutes. I jumped out of the truck, shoved the clinic door open, and ran to the lab.

Wrapped in a towel, Little Man was in Caroline's arms. He looked cozy and didn't appear to be in any pain. He was shaking a little, but I couldn't tell if he felt cold or if it was just because of everything that was going on. Caroline was still crying, but managed to tell me a little about what happened.

She had arrived at the clinic just as Dr. Gandy and Cody were cleaning Little Man after his manual enema. They put him back in his clean kennel to let him recover from the gas used to sedate him. A few minutes later, Caroline walked by the kennel and saw Little Man struggling. Something was in his mouth.

"Cody!" Caroline called. "There's something in Little Man's mouth!"

Cody came over to take a look. He grabbed Little Man out of the kennel. Little Man had accidentally caught a corner of the blue piddle pad on which he was lying with a tooth, and some of it had been ripped off and was stuck in his mouth.

Cody immediately placed Little Man on the examination table and tried to pry his mouth open.

"Don't hurt him!" Caroline said.

Cody turned to her and said, "Caroline, I *have* to get it out!"

After a few minutes, Cody managed to get Little Man's mouth open to find he had almost swallowed a four-inch long strip of his piddle pad. When it was over, Cody wrapped Little Man in a blanket and handed him to Caroline. She had been holding him since then, right up until I arrived.

I realized he was okay, and I felt a little better. Caroline handed him to me.

When Dr. Gandy had a chance to talk, she shared some disturbing news. "I'm very concerned about brain damage. It seems to me Little Man doesn't quite know what he's doing. Remember, his temperature was a little above a hundred and six degrees when we took him to the ER Monday night. I just wish I could see some sign of conscious alertness from him."

That scared me to death. The "end of the week," which I hoped was Sunday in Dr. Gandy's mind, was fast approaching. Even though I thought I saw little signs of improvement here and there, I desperately needed Dr. Gandy to see something, too. He was eating on his own, but little else. I knew what she was saying, and I was none too happy about it.

I put Little Man back in his kennel after we replaced his piddle pad with a towel and loved on him for a few minutes. Then Caroline and I left for home and lunch.

After lunch, Caroline left to continue her errands, and I headed back to the clinic. Little Man was eating on his own when I arrived, but seemed to be falling asleep in his bowl. I offered him more, but he didn't eat. I patted him on the head and told him I loved him. I stood there and looked at him with his catheters sticking out, essentially unable to use his back end at all, and wanted to scream. After a few more minutes, I went back home.

When I walked into the house, I made it as far as Little Man's food bowl. It was right where he had left it after eating Monday morning before everything happened. I sat down on the floor with my back against the kitchen cabinets directly across from the bowl. I was a wreck. Thankfully, I had the house to myself.

I just stared straight ahead. My mind took over, and all kinds of thoughts swirled around in my head.

This can't be happening. It just can't. Not to Little Man. Nothing makes sense. Nothing at all. I could understand if he was hit by a car. Or attacked by a dog. Or if something in the garage fell on him. Or even if he had cancer. But this, this is just not right. How could Little Man be fine at mid-day, then at death's door just hours later, and with no discernible cause? I know he has to go sometime, but not now. It's just not time for him to go.

It just can't be. Little Man has GOT to pull through. He just has to. I will NOT sit back and watch another innocent animal die, especially not Little Man, without a very good reason!

Suddenly, I didn't feel very well. I was breathing in short, shallow breaths. It was coming, and there was nothing I could do to stop it.

I slammed my head back against the cabinet, clenched my fists, and gritted my teeth. I strained and tightened every muscle in my body. I took a deep breath and held it.

It happened anyway.

"NNNNNNNNNNNNNOOOOOOOOOOOOOOOOOOOOOOOOO!!!!!" I screamed at the top of my lungs, emptying them with one long scream.

I took a deep breath, relaxed, and let my head fall forward. I rested my arms on my knees, laced my fingers together, and watched a couple of tears fall on the floor.

I sat there like that for a minute or two, and then leaned my head back against the cabinet.

I looked straight up and prayed, loudly, "God save Little Man!"

I sat there for a couple of minutes more, then got up. I needed to do something, anything, so I decided to go check and see if I had any purchases for my display boxes.

I headed upstairs.

When I got to our room, I walked in, took about two steps, and stopped cold. I saw Little Man's pillowcase in our recliner, just where he left it. I closed my eyes and took a deep breath. So many things are in there that I once thought were oh, so important. Yet, I couldn't even look at them.

Well, zippity-do-da, I thought. *None of this helps now.*

I turned and walked out in disgust. I didn't go back into our room for several days.

I went back to the clinic about five-thirty that evening to feed Little Man and give him his insulin injection and other meds. His appetite seemed normal. Still, he couldn't seem to do anything else. He seemed to enjoy attention, so I smiled the whole time. But I hated seeing him in the kennel that way. I decided to just sit with him for a few minutes before closing time. I pulled up a chair, sat down, and reached in and pet him some more. He seemed to like it and purred a little in response.

After a few minutes, I said, "Little Man, I need to talk to you for a minute."

My voice was quivering a little, but I couldn't help it. He looked up at me and blinked.

I said, softly, "Little Man, I just want to say thank you. I want to thank you for sharing your life with me. You are such a sweet boy. I'll love you forever."

I stood up, leaned over into the kennel, and kissed him on the top of his head. I said goodbye to the clinic staff and left.

It had been one heck of a day.

Saturday – Day Six

The clinic was closed for business, but Matt had to go take care of some boarders. With Dr. Gandy's permission, I went in with Matt during his shift.

Little Man seemed happy to see me and cried. He was lying in urine and feces, but seemed otherwise comfortable. I cleaned him up a little and replaced the towel in his kennel, then fed him. He ate his normal meal, so I gave him his insulin. I loved on him for a few minutes and left to go back home. Ever since all this started, I had barely seen Caroline. She was scheduled to go to work at the Harley place soon, so I went home to have some coffee with her.

After Caroline left for work, I went back to the clinic. Cody was already there helping Matt with some of the usual chores. Dr. Gandy arrived soon afterward, and at about 9:00 AM, Dr. Gandy and I started to clean Little Man. She walked over to the washing tables in the back, and I reached in and picked up Little Man. He was filthy.

I carried him to the back and laid him on one of the grated, metal, washing tables, and noticed I had feces all over my hands. He had been lying in it. Dr. Gandy began to wipe him off, and I stepped over to a sink to wash my hands.

Just as I finished, Dr. Gandy said, "Check this out."

I looked over and Little Man was trying very hard to get off the table. He was using his hind legs by stretching them out, but he still couldn't stand. It was good to see he was trying.

"Good boy, Little Man!" I called over to him.

I dried my hands and stepped toward a box of rubber gloves hanging on the wall like the ones Dr. Gandy was wearing.

Suddenly, Little Man shoved himself and almost managed to get off the table. I happened to be right at his head when it happened. I reached out, caught him, and held him by the shoulders while Dr. Gandy turned on the water and began to clean him up.

As she washed him, she said, "You know, he does seem to be able to use his hind legs a little better. I just wish he would show some sign of alertness, like he knows what he's doing. If he could poop and pee on his own…"

I heard a sharp, little growl and felt a clamp. Little Man bit me. Hard.

"He's got my finger!"

"Hold on!" Dr. Gandy said.

I looked down. Little Man bit the middle finger on my left hand. My whole fingertip, down to the first joint, was in his mouth. The pain was excruciating, and I was bleeding. Little Man wouldn't, or couldn't, let go.

I reached over with my right hand and tried to help get his mouth open. We got him to open up slightly, but all that did was allow him to also bite the middle finger of my right hand and rearrange the finger he had in his mouth so he had a better grip on it.

After struggling for a minute or so, Dr. Gandy yelled, "Cody! I need you back here, NOW!"

Cody came in, saw what was happening, and handed Dr. Gandy one thing after another to use to try and get Little Man to open his mouth. Nothing worked. Everything seemed to make him clamp down harder.

Finally, after what seemed like about three or four minutes, Dr. Gandy managed to pry open Little Man's mouth with a hairbrush handle.

I pulled my finger out and took a look at it. I had eight punctures in my finger, including two in the fingernail. Blood oozed out of several holes at the same time, and there was evidence that at least one tooth had gone all the way through.

Cody grabbed some blue liquid, used especially for cat bites, poured it in a bowl, and filled the bowl with water.

Dr. Gandy said, "Don't cover the wound. Just let it bleed. Stick your fingers in that solution and soak them for a while. You're going to need to go to the ER at the hospital."

Cody put the bowl on a different washing table, and I stuck my fingers in the solution. Within seconds, the water was black.

I looked at Little Man and thought, *Well, I guess we're blood brothers now.*

I had just become the second member of the Little Man Bite Club.

I stood there for a few minutes while Dr. Gandy struggled with Little Man. She grabbed the gas mask and tried to sedate him while at the same time trying to hold him down.

I started feeling very strange. I tingled all over. My knees were buckling, and I was sinking very slowly toward the floor. I got down on my knees with my fingers still in the water, but it didn't help. I thought I recognized the symptoms.

When I was in the Air Force on flight status, I completed altitude chamber training on a regular basis. Part of the training involved being intentionally subjected to hypoxia, or a lack of oxygen. Everyone reacts differently. The purpose is to be able to recognize your own symptoms so that if it ever happens in flight, proper steps can be taken to avoid it. Initially, that's what I thought was happening.

I said, "If I didn't know better, I'd think I was hypoxic. Was I holding my breath or something?"

"Didn't notice," Dr. Gandy said as she continued to struggle with Little Man.

"I don't feel so good. I think I better get on the floor."

"Be my guest," Dr. Gandy said.

I took the bowl and placed it on the floor, then lay down next to it with my fingers still in the water.

I soon realized I was wrong about the hypoxia—I was going into shock. But after about ten minutes, I felt better.

Dr. Gandy said, "If you're through with your little nap down there, I could use some help."

I laughed, got up, and carried my bowl over to Little Man's table. He was sedated, but Dr. Gandy needed some help with the mask so she could finish cleaning him up.

As I stood there with the bitten fingers of both hands still in the water, I held the mask on Little Man with a couple of spare fingers and asked, "So, you were saying?"

"Scratch that," she said.

Clearly, Little Man was not himself. After he was all cleaned and squared away, I left to go see a doctor about the bite.

When I got to the ER, the doctor took x-rays because he was concerned about the joint. The x-rays looked fine, so he wrote me a prescription for an antibiotic.

I went straight home after seeing the doctor. I felt terrible, but not because of my finger. I was worried about Little Man.

I called Brandon and told him what happened. He felt my pain and understood completely. He knew just what to say.

"Dad, you know that movie where a girl is getting married, and she's in the beauty shop in the chair, and has some kind of episode?"

"Yeah, I think I know that movie," I said.

"Well, right after that, after she gives her mother a hard time, she comes out of it, and tells her mother over and over again that she's sorry. Remember that?"

"Yep."

"Well, if Little Man could talk, I'm sure that's what he would tell you right now."

That actually made me feel better.

At about 6:00 PM, another technician was there to take care of the boarders, so I went back to the clinic. Little Man was still clean, and I didn't smell any urine or feces. He acted a little more like his usual self. He purred when

I pet him and seemed definitely interested in eating. Dr. Gandy had removed his IV and urinary catheters, so he wasn't on continuous fluids anymore. She was going to be giving him fluids under his skin subcutaneously, or "SQ fluids," as a transition before going home—*if* he eventually urinated on his own.

To change things up a little, I put him on a towel on the floor to feed him. I thought it would be easier to give him his insulin injection that way. I put his food bowl down just out of reach, and to my surprise, he crawled a few inches on all fours, without actually standing up, to reach his bowl. He ate normally, so I gave him his injection, and then just sat with him on the floor for a little while.

He began to look around a few minutes later, and then cried.

"Little Man, do you need to potty?"

I put his litter box on the floor next to him. He crawled to it and sniffed, but didn't act like he needed to go. He grabbed a piece of the litter in his mouth, but before I could do or say anything, he spat it right back out.

I decided to test him.

I took my glasses off and laid them on the floor right next to him. I wanted to see if he would bite at them. I thought this might let me know if he was alert enough to know what he was doing. Thankfully, he made no attempt to bite them.

I picked my glasses off the floor, and with the earpiece, I gently rubbed the tip of his nose. He stretched his nose toward them, but only to give them a sniff. Again, he made no attempt to bite.

Feeling a little better about things, I put him and his litter pan back in his kennel. I loved on him a little bit more, then left for home.

Shortly after I got home, Caroline arrived home from work. She asked about Little Man. I filled her in on the details of the day, including my little visit to the hospital.

"Good grief, Jonny. He sent you into shock?"

"I think so," I said.

"How is he now?"

I told her about my last visit with him, including the attempt to get him to use the litter pan. Then she had a thought.

"Why don't you take one of the litter pans from here? He's used to the clay litter. Maybe he'll be more inclined to try to go if it's his normal litter."

I thought that was a great idea.

The next time I visited Little Man I did just that. When I put him on the floor near his litter pan, he made several attempts to stand up to get to it. I had to help him. I picked him up and put him in the litter since the walls of his pan from home were much higher than the walls of the disposable litter pans used at the clinic.

He scratched clumsily at the litter and spun around several times. It was obvious he felt the need to go. He finally settled into a position where he felt comfortable making the attempt.

With herculean effort, he strained and strained and strained. I could see the muscles on his back contract, and he wiggled his tail violently. But all he could do was squeeze out a couple of teaspoons of urine.

I praised him big-time. But at the same time, I felt sorry for him. I would have given anything to take his place. I was sure he still needed to urinate, but there wasn't anything I could do about it.

I left him in the pan to rest for a few minutes, then picked him up and put him back in his kennel. He settled down and seemed comfortable, but tired. I loved on him for a minute or so, then left.

Sunday – Day Seven

Sunday morning, I went to the clinic while Matt cleaned kennels. There were spots of feces on the towel in Little Man's kennel, but no urine. I offered Little Man his litter pan, but he made no attempt to go. I fed him and gave him his insulin, then gave him some fresh water. He was very thirsty.

I waited a few minutes, then tried the litter pan again. Just as he had the day before, he strained and strained, but managed to force out very little urine. I put him back in his kennel and left. I wanted to spend a little time with Caroline before she headed off to work at Harley.

After Caroline left for work, I went back to the clinic. There were an unusually large number of boarders there, so I knew Matt and another technician would be busy for quite a while. Although I was feeling a little better about it being "the end of the week," I wanted more time with Little Man, just in case. Dr. Gandy was due to arrive at some point, and I wanted to be there.

He seemed comfortable when I walked in, and he cried when he saw me. I grabbed a clean towel from under a storage cabinet and wrapped him in it. I picked him up and cradled him. He closed his eyes and seemed very relaxed.

We walked around in the clinic, and I gently rocked him as we walked. There's a couch in the boarding area right next to floor-to-ceiling windows, and after we walked around and talked to several of the other cats, I sat down with my back to the window overlooking the street outside so Little Man could gaze out there every now and then.

I held him until I couldn't feel my arms.

Just moments before Dr. Gandy arrived, I put him back in his kennel. I left the door open and pulled a chair up next to it. I just sat there with him and petted him until I heard Dr. Gandy come in.

I got up and met her at the door. In a way, it was the moment of truth. I prayed a little silent prayer, and we walked to the lab.

As soon as Little Man saw Dr. Gandy, he lifted his head straight up in the air, looked her right in the eyes, and cried.

"Well, somebody sure seems a lot better than the last time I saw him," Dr. Gandy said, and smiled.

Little Man cried again, and Dr. Gandy reached in and gave him a scratch. He stretched his neck wanting more. His eyes were clear, and he certainly seemed "alert" to me.

Dr. Gandy seemed to agree.

"All right," she said, "let's see if we can get some urine out of him. Come here. I'm going to show you how to do this."

We took Little Man out of his kennel and put him in his own litter pan from home. As before, he strained and strained, but couldn't go.

Dr. Gandy said, "Put your hand right here."

She moved my hand to Little Man's side and placed her hand on top of mine.

"Can you feel that?" she asked.

Suddenly, his bladder moved because of our attempts to locate it.

"Was that it that just moved?" I asked.

"That's it," she said. "Now whenever you think he needs to go, just press right there from both sides and it will help him go."

As we pressed, Little Man emptied his bladder. That was good, but we still had concerns that he couldn't do it on his own.

"Let's give him a shave," Dr. Gandy said.

We took him to the back of the clinic to one of the washing tables, laid him on top, and sedated him. Then Dr. Gandy grabbed the clippers and began to cut off his fur.

This was for two reasons. First, it would make things much easier on us to keep Little Man clean since he obviously couldn't do it himself. Second, we were looking for a bite mark.

We clipped Little Man all over, from his neck to the base of his tail. On the left side of his neck, we found a red spot about the size of a quarter.

"Hmm," Dr. Gandy said, "that might be something."

I could see it, too, but I didn't see what I understood a Black Widow bite to look like: two tiny punctures close together. Besides, from what I read over the last few days, the bite of a Black Widow should disappear within a couple days. If he had been bitten, it happened almost a week earlier.

"I don't know," she said.

"Could that be a bruise? Maybe he did that when he had that seizure in his kennel on Tuesday morning," I said.

"I don't think it's a bruise, but I really don't know what it could be," she said.

After being shaved, Little Man got a good bath. When that was done, we put him in his kennel to wake up from the sedation. A few minutes later, he started moving around a bit, obviously still very groggy.

Dr. Gandy said, "Okay, we're going to start some physical therapy. I'm concerned about his inability to stand up on his own. He needs to be reminded of where his hind legs are."

She disappeared around the corner and returned a minute later with a big, blue, rubber ball.

"You gotta be kidding," I said, and laughed. If anyone had told me that one day I would be giving a cat physical therapy, I would have told them they were smokin' dope.

"Drape him over the ball on his belly, like this," she said as she held him on top of the ball.

"Now what you want to do is rock him back and forth and side to side, very gently, just so he can feel his feet touch the floor. You want to rock him just far enough so that he has to push against his own weight, like this."

She demonstrated while I watched. Little Man growled and hissed a little bit and obviously hated it. But he did it.

"How often do we need to do that?" I asked.

"Three times a day for about five or ten minutes each time. This will help build strength in his hind legs."

When I visited that evening, I saw more improvement. When I put him on the floor to feed him, he tried many times to get up on all four legs and walk. But try as he may, he just couldn't seem to get his hind legs to cooperate. He looked like a baby deer trying to walk on ice.

Back in the litter pan, he made no attempt to go, but instead seemed more interested in the lid to the litter pan which lay nearby. He crawled over to it, got underneath, and then pawed at the clips used to hold it in place. It seemed to me he was actually in a playful mood.

During a break in the action, I felt for his bladder and it didn't seem to be very large, but I was still concerned that he couldn't go on his own. At least there was improvement in his demeanor. I grabbed the ball and draped him over it for a quick therapy session. As before, he hated it, but he did it.

I put him back in his kennel and he seemed happy to be there. I gave him a pat, told everyone goodbye, and left.

Monday – Day Eight

When I arrived at the clinic on my way to work, I learned that Dr. Gandy had reinserted his urinary catheter at some point during the night. As she did at other times, she did not attach a bag to the catheter. This was to avoid the possibility of yet another line getting all tangled up. As a result, Little Man's towel was soaked in urine, and it was orange in color. Still no bowel movement. I put him on the floor and got a neat little surprise. He didn't stand, but he actually put weight on all four legs. Then he rolled over to one side and started grooming himself. After I fed him and gave him his insulin and meds, we spent some time on the ball. It certainly seemed to me the physical therapy was having a positive effect, and I felt better about his progress. That allowed me to have a better day at work than any day the week before.

When I arrived after work at about four-fifteen, Dr. Gandy met me at the door with a package.

"I need you to run right now and overnight this. It's a sample of every bodily fluid I could get out of him. It's for the toxicology lab at Michigan State."

"Will do. Be back in a few," I said and left.

When I got back to the clinic after mailing the package, Dr. Gandy sat me down and we talked about Little Man's status. Her biggest concerns were his inability to urinate and defecate. At least he was getting better at trying to stand and was doing a fair job of keeping himself clean.

Tuesday – Day Nine

I didn't sleep very well on Monday night. On Tuesday morning as I passed through the garage on my way out the door, I decided to look around … again. I'd looked around several times before, but we needed to find something, anything, which could explain all this and lead us to better treatment. We wanted and needed a diagnosis. We were treating only the clinical signs as they appeared and giving him supportive care. There had to be an answer. Maybe it might even help with his bladder problem.

I walked all around the garage. I looked under the cars again. I looked under the motorcycles again. I looked in the corners. I looked at the cleaning supplies, still undisturbed and dusty. There were still no signs of Black Widows, and no dead or partially eaten lizards. Nothing.

I stood in the middle of the garage, dumbfounded.

As I looked over the top of the 'Cuda, I noticed my sign: *Think Outside the Pan*.

Hmm, I thought, *maybe that's just what I need to do.*

I stopped at Catisfaction again on my way to work and saw even more improvement in Little Man while he was eating his breakfast. He actually got up and squatted on all fours to eat. He still didn't stand up, but he was trying.

On my lunch break at work, I checked my personal email account. Dr. Wagner had responded to the email I sent right before the weekend.

She explained that she had never dealt with a bite like what we suspected, so she wasn't sure how to handle that. She also said the signs of organophosphate poisoning usually go away after a couple of days, but also that every animal reacts differently. She pointed out that it could still be something else and suggested we test Little Man for toxoplasmosis.

I went online and started checking out some things, including toxoplasmosis. While I was looking around online, I thought again about my sign hanging in the garage.

"Think Outside the Pan," ... *whatever that means,* I thought.

As I thought about it some more, I realized that maybe we needed to come at things from a different angle. Maybe we should look for some things that *aren't* normally in the house that could cause Little Man to show these signs.

I typed in some things and read some articles. I was looking for any substance that might cause seizures in cats.

Then I found something very interesting.

About three years earlier, someone sent a question to one of those *Ask a Vet* websites. I read the answer provided by a veterinarian, and...

Oh my God...

It was all there. There were thirteen signs listed, and as far as I could tell, Little Man had the first ten. The drooling, the pupil dilation, the seizures, everything. The only signs Little Man didn't show were the last three listed: coma, cardiac arrest, and respiratory arrest. Or put another way ... death.

CHAPTER 18 – THE ROLLER-COASTER RIDE

The question someone had asked was, *What happens if a cat ingests crack cocaine?*

Crack cocaine? I thought. *How in the world would Little Man get hold of something like that? There's nothing like that in our house, and no one else...*

It hit me. There *was* someone else in our house on that very day. I didn't think for a minute he had done so intentionally, but he *could* have dropped something accidentally.

I read more of the answer and saw that the onset of signs should be expected to occur within an hour or two. Even that fit.

Wait a minute, Jonny, I thought. *Isn't this a bit of a stretch?*

Then something else came to mind, something Spock said in one of those *Star Trek* episodes Little Man and I watch all the time. It's something that just happens to be true ..."*When you eliminate the impossible, whatever remains, however improbable, must be the truth.*"

I called Catisfaction and left Dr. Gandy a message: "Please make sure the toxicology lab tests for illegal drugs. I'll explain later."

As I looked into it a little more, I found that many of these drugs are detectable in the body for a maximum of only about eight days. The samples Dr. Gandy sent to Michigan State were taken on the afternoon of the seventh day. I thought it was a long shot, but just maybe, if something were there, it would show up on the report.

I decided to call my brother, Jason—the one with over fifteen years of law enforcement experience. I had a question for him.

"Hey, it's Jonny. Got a minute?"

"Shoot," he said.

I explained everything that had happened with Little Man, and then asked, "What does crack cocaine look like?"

"Wow," he said. "Well, the best way to describe it would be that it looks like a piece of pea gravel, like what you see on the side of the road."

"Pea gravel, huh?"

As he explained a little more about crack, I remembered something else. I interrupted him and asked, "Hey, could it be mistaken for a piece of cat litter?"

He said, "Um, well, yeah. I guess it could."

"Thanks. Gotta go," I said and hung up.

I called the county sheriff's office and asked to speak to the sheriff. When he came on the line, I explained a little about Little Man, that we suspected poisoning, and that I wanted to know if he knew anything about the man who was in our house that day.

"With what you've told me so far, there is no case against him," he said.

"I can understand that," I said, "but I'm not interested in any sort of prosecution right now. I'd just like to find out the cause of all these problems because it may help us treat Little Man."

"Do you have his name?"

"Yes, I do."

After I gave the sheriff the name and phone number from the card the man gave me before he left the house that day, he said, "I'll check with my narcotics folks and see if they know anything. I'll get back to you."

When I went to Catisfaction that afternoon after work, Dr. Gandy gave me a little more good news. Little Man's liver enzymes were coming back down.

"Fantastic!" I said, "Now I have some stuff for you."

I told her what I discovered about the possibility of a narcotic causing all of this. She looked at me like I was out of my mind.

"I know. I know," I said, "but I don't think we can rule it out. According to the answer from that veterinarian on line, Little Man has just about every sign."

"But he has every sign of a Black Widow bite," she said.

"Okay, well how about this?" I went on. "I contacted Dr. Wagner, Little Man's vet in Nebraska, and told her what was going on. Have you considered toxoplasmosis?"

"I don't think that's it," she said. "That's something you get from an infected mouse."

Oh brother. Here we go again.

I replied, "A couple months back, Little Man brought me two mice he caught in the garage."

Dr. Gandy looked at me with a look that said, *Why didn't you tell me that before?*

Then she sighed and said, "All right. Let's get a sample."

Tabatha and Cody were both there that day, and Dr. Gandy called them over to hold Little Man while she prepared to take a blood sample.

When Tabatha opened the door to Little Man's kennel, he started kitty-cussing. She picked up a towel, threw it over Little Man, and quickly grabbed him out of his kennel. The towels on which he rested tumbled onto the floor.

She placed him on the examination table in the center of the lab, and Little Man was not happy about it at all. Cody came over and grabbed a handful of Little Man's fur on the back of his neck while Tabatha draped another towel over him, then helped Dr. Gandy get control of Little Man's hind legs. He might not have been able to stand up at that point, but kicking was no problem at all.

Little Man was giving us the *what for*.

Dr. Gandy said, "All right, Jonny. Your job is to take a ballpoint pen and tap him on the head with it. It's to draw his attention away from us and onto the pen. It's just until I can get a sample."

I took a pen and started tapping, and Little Man went off on us.

"Don't you stick me! NOOOO!! Don't you stick me!"

Poke.

"OOOOHHHH, YOU STUCK ME!! YOU STUCK ME!! OHHH, I'M GONNA KILL YOU, AND YOU, AND YOU, AND YOU!! AND THEN WHEN YOU'RE ALL DEAD, I'M GONNA EAT YOUR EYEBALLS!!"

Looking back, I think that was actually a good sign. Little Man couldn't even stand up on his own, but he wasn't going down without a fight.

Dr. Gandy got a sample, but said, "Wow. I think the next time we have to do that we'll just sedate him."

Cody and Tabatha let go of their holds on Little Man and left him to rest on the examination table. When he settled down, we all noticed it. He was on his side. His eyes were closed. His legs were stretched out. And he looked completely and utterly content.

We just looked at him for a minute, then Tabatha reached over to pick up the towels that fell out of the kennel when she moved him to the examination table. Under the towels we found the biggest pile of feces I had ever seen. It looked like Great Dane poop.

Tabatha said, "Good grief, that came out of Little Man? No wonder he looks so comfortable over there!"

We all looked back at Little Man. He looked as comfortable as ever.

"Hey!" I said. "I wonder if the stick is in there somewhere!"

Cody grabbed a tongue depressor, walked over to the pile, and started chopping it up in little pieces. It was a remarkable sight. The entire staff at Catisfaction Cat Clinic walked over to see if Cody could find the stick. It looked like a football huddle in the middle of "the big game."

Nothing was there.

I got a package in the mail that afternoon. It was from K-Naught. I ripped it open and found a CD inside, along with the original tape I sent to him a few days earlier. He found a nice, long, uninterrupted stretch of Little Man purring, made multiple copies, and then strung the copies together for over an hour's worth of purring.

I put it in a CD player and listened to it for the first time since I recorded it over a year earlier.

It was Little Man all right. But it sounded like a lion.

CHAPTER 19 –
ROAD TO RECOVERY?

The next couple of days were relatively uneventful, but each day there were signs of slight improvement. One day Little Man stood up on all fours and walked a couple of steps before lying back down. The next day he walked a couple more steps, then sat with his front legs straight down in front of him. In fact, I grew concerned that he might actually jump out of his kennel and hurt himself. Apparently, his physical therapy sessions helped greatly, and now at least he could defecate on his own. But he still couldn't urinate without a catheter.

Thursday – Day Eleven

For the first time since everything began, Little Man stood up and walked to the kennel door when I arrived at the clinic to feed him. I praised and petted him, and after breakfast he spent a little more time on the ball. Afterward, I offered the litter pan again. As before, he strained and strained, but couldn't seem to go. I attempted to help him as Dr. Gandy taught me, but I didn't think I was doing any good.

During the day, Dr. Gandy checked Little Man's bladder again, and she could tell he still couldn't urinate. She shared her concern when I walked in the door after work.

She said, "I'm really concerned about his inability to urinate. I know you're trying to be cautiously optimistic, but the reality is we may have to face the possibility of having to put down an otherwise healthy cat because he's lost all bladder control."

I was speechless. Just as I had begun to think he might actually pull through, another setback.

She continued, "Here's what I want to do. First, I want you to understand what the bladder is. It's like the bulb of a turkey baster. There's the bulb part, and there's the neck. I want to try three different drugs. One is to increase the muscle tone in the bulb part. Another one is to relax one of the two muscle types in the neck part. The third is to relax the other type of muscle in the neck. Hopefully, one of these will restore his bladder control."

"Have you ever seen this problem in cats before?" I asked.

"Yes," she said.

"How did they turn out?"

She just shook her head.

Again, I couldn't believe that after everything Little Man had been through, he might be stopped cold by something like his bladder.

"When do we start?" I asked.

"Right now," she said. "I'll reinsert his catheter tomorrow and leave it in for a while to let the drugs begin to take effect, and then we'll take it back out and see how he does."

When I stepped outside, I could barely think. Surely, Little Man's suffering, his fighting spirit, and his progress wouldn't be for naught. As I pulled out of the parking lot at Catisfaction, I stared straight ahead, took a deep breath, and said aloud, again, "God save Little Man!"

Over the next few days, Little Man showed even more signs of improvement. He could stand, walk, and at one point even stood on his hind legs with his front paws on my waist in anticipation of being fed. But he had developed another little problem. He was very grouchy at times. And he still couldn't urinate.

CHAPTER 19 – ROAD TO RECOVERY?

By the end of the second week, we got the results of both the toxicology report and the toxoplasmosis test. Everything was negative. There simply was no sign of anything wrong. Of course, there was the possibility that whatever it was had been flushed out of his system enough to be undetectable by the time the samples were taken.

The good news was that he was still with us.

Monday – Day Fifteen

When I arrived at the clinic on Monday morning, I was very happy to see Little Man standing in his kennel. Except for the occasional grouchiness, he was just like his old self. Even his appetite seemed to be an issue no longer even though it had been such a problem in the past whenever he was away from home.

All he had to do was urinate.

I went on to work, and Dr. Gandy removed Little Man's urinary catheter. It was the moment of truth.

I waited until after lunch to call. At about 1:00 PM, two weeks to the day after Little Man's ordeal began, I got the news: Little Man urinated! And all by himself!

I smiled the rest of the day. I never thought I would be so happy to hear about a cat, my Little Man, using the litter pan.

The corner had finally been turned.

As usual, I drove straight to the clinic after work. I walked right up to Little Man and gave him a great big smooch.

The staff were still allowing me to help with Little Man's treatments, so at suppertime, I let him out of his kennel. We found a vacant examination room where he could roam around a little, and he took off. He wandered all around the room, sniffed at this and sniffed at that, and I had to chase him down to get him to eat his supper. As I prepared it, he stood on his hind legs again and put his paws on the edge of the table.

Then he looked at me and meowed, *"Feed me, Daddy!"*

Tuesday – Day Sixteen

Little Man was restless. I didn't suppose anyone could have blamed him. He'd been locked up in a 24 x 24 metal box for over two weeks, and he wrecked his kennel. There were feces and litter everywhere—and a good clump of urine in his litter pan. Such a good boy!

That afternoon we made a remarkable and totally unexpected discovery.

Before everything began on Labor Day, Little Man received five units of insulin twice a day. Based on his blood glucose readings since then, we had to reduce his dosage little by little. He was down to only one unit twice a day.

It appeared Little Man's diabetes was going into remission.

Wednesday – Day Seventeen

I walked into the clinic after work. It was obviously a slow day, one of those very rare occasions. I stepped around the corner to the lab to find Little Man comfortably on the floor. Cody sat on the floor a few feet from Little Man, legs crossed, with his back up against the hospital kennels. A couple of the other technicians milled around in there also.

When Cody saw me enter, he looked up at me and said, "I was just telling Little Man how I never thought I would see today."

"Today?" I asked.

"The day he would be going home."

He got up off the floor and handed me a copy of Little Man's discharge instructions!

I smiled and said to Little Man, "Hey, Little Man! You ready to go home?"

But Dr. Gandy still had one concern—that dreadful tongue depressor sliver Little Man swallowed over a week earlier. Before I could take him home, she wanted to make one more check. She administered barium and then took some x-rays. She couldn't see the sliver, but neither did she see any evidence it was causing any problems.

We took Little Man back to the lab to gather his things and get him into his kennel for the much-anticipated trip home. One of the things Dr. Gandy wanted me to do at home was give him fluids under the skin, so she taught me how to do that and gave me a box of needles, a box of syringes, and bag of fluid. She reminded me to never reuse a needle but to always replace a used one with a new one. When she stepped out to finalize the bill, Cody remained to help me get Little Man ready to go.

As we gathered Little Man's things, Cody said, "You know … I have to say … if it had been any other cat, or any other vet I've ever worked for, Little Man would have been put down by that first Friday."

"And now he's going home," I said.

"And now he's going home," Cody said.

I took Little Man home!

I set him up in our room upstairs, isolated from the other cats since I still needed to monitor his urine output. His discharge instructions included information on how to wean him off each of the three "bladder drugs" one at a time so we could determine which one of them was working.

Once he was all settled with his water bowl, litter pan, and a nice, comfy blanket to lie on, the first thing Little Man did was curl up in a ball, roll his head upside down, go to sleep, and snore.

Home from the hospital.

I was on my knees petting Little Man just after he went to sleep when I realized something quite remarkable. At that moment, I realized I had been given an incredible gift. It's something everyone wants, or will want, at some time in their lives. I had wanted it at least twice already. One time was when Pop died. Another was when Daddy died. I didn't get it either of those times.

Everyone on earth usually finds themselves wishing for the same thing after the death of a loved one—to see them just one more time.

As I loved on Little Man just moments after bringing him home, I realized the one thing I wanted more than anything else during his terrible ordeal was for him to come home and be well ... just one more time.

And here he was.

One week after I brought Little Man home, I arrived home from work and began my usual chores. The first thing was to check on Little Man.

I went up to our room and he met me at the door. As usual, the room was in shambles. Litter was everywhere. Even his toys were strewn about. I didn't mind at all. That's what vacuum cleaners are for.

The last thing I usually did during my afternoon cleanup sessions was to scoop the litter pan. I grabbed a plastic grocery bag and the scooper and starting sifting out the clumps of urine and feces when the scooper caught on something.

With the edge of the scooper, I fished around until I could see what it was.

Sure enough, there it was. I ran downstairs and grabbed a paper towel, then ran back upstairs and picked it up. Then I took it over to a sink and washed if off.

It was just as I imagined after Dr. Gandy and a couple of the other people present at the time said it would be. It was almost two inches long, about one-fourth of an inch wide at one end, and narrowed to a point at the other. Thankfully, Little Man had swallowed the blunt end first, rather than the sharp end. It had passed all the way through and was still intact.

I grabbed my cell phone and sent a text to Dr. Gandy: "Well slap my ass and call me giddy! Little Man passed the stick!"

I waited anxiously for Dr. Gandy to text me back.

I waited for two hours and received no texts. Then out of the blue my cell phone rang. It was Dr. Gandy.

"You've got to be kidding me!" she said.

"Nope. I'm holding it in my hand right now," I said.

"Well, take a picture of that thing and put it on Facebook! I want to see it!"

I did exactly that.

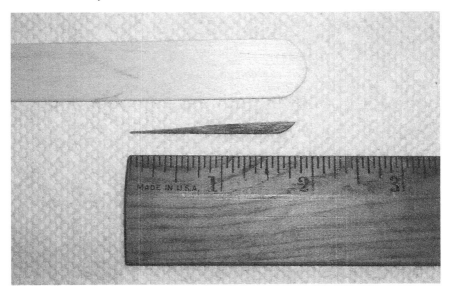

The infamous tongue depressor sliver.

Brandon called right after I spoke with Dr. Gandy.

When I told him what had happened, he said, "Dad, do you mean to tell me your cat eats Black Widows and poops out wooden sticks?"

"Um, well, um, I never thought about it quite like that. But yeah, I guess that's about it. And don't forget he sends grown men to the emergency room."

"Good grief, Dad."

"Yeah. I'm starting to think Little Man's mama used to hang around with a mountain lion or something."

CHAPTER 20 –

MORE GOOD NEWS...AND ANOTHER SCARE

A few days after I brought Little Man home, I ran out of one of the three bladder drugs, Bethanechol. I had a refill if necessary, but it was the first one to run out, so Dr. Gandy suggested I try to keep him off it to see what would happen.

Within only a day or two, I saw Little Man run to the litter pan, turn around in circles, and then get out. He repeated this a few times without urinating. I already knew what to do. I ran to get a refill and started him right back on it. In no time, he was able to urinate again with no problem.

A couple days later, another of his bladder drugs, Phenoxybenzamine, ran out. This time, however, there were no changes in urination. One down, two to go. That was also the last day Matt and I had to give Little Man fluids under his skin. I'm sure he was happy about that.

Days later, the third bladder drug, Diazepam, ran out. Again, there was no change in urination. But something else was going on. Little Man was down to only half a unit of insulin twice daily. Apparently, whatever happened on Labor Day must have jump-started his pancreas because we definitely saw indications his diabetes was going into remission.

Finally, on October 9, I gave Little Man his last dose of Bethanechol and reduced his insulin yet again. He was down to one-fourth of a unit of insulin twice daily. It was rather difficult to do. There was no device designed to give such a small dose, so I had to do the best I could with his normal syringes.

The following weekend, Dr. Gandy wanted me to do a glucose curve on Little Man. I already had my own glucometer and just needed to get a few more test strips, and on Saturday morning, I started collecting the data. I collected a blood sample from Little Man's ear every two hours beginning at 6:00 AM. He was still getting 0.25 units of insulin twice a day.

At 10:00 AM that Saturday, I thought I saw a disturbing trend. Little Man's blood glucose had dropped to 70 from 94 at 6:00 AM, and according to the trend, it was headed even lower. I knew that 70 is the bottom threshold of what is considered normal, so I gave him a few crunchies just to help keep his glucose level from getting too low.

By the end of the day, his levels were back up, but only in the 90s.

And then I had a thought.

I decided to do another curve on Sunday—without insulin. So he got no insulin Saturday night.

Sunday morning I started as before. The first reading was 137. By noon, it had dropped to 99. At the end of the day, it was back up to 127. Perfect.

The engineer in me reared his head, and I prepared some beautiful curves worthy of inclusion in a medical journal. I prepared one for Saturday's results *with* insulin, and one for Sunday's results *without* insulin. They were complete with headings, labels for the axes, and even notes. Since Caroline was scheduled to work at Catisfaction on Monday, I gave them to her to give to Dr. Gandy.

I think that was the first time Dr. Gandy called me an "enginerd." She and Caroline both got a huge kick out of my curve charts.

Dr. Gandy said to Caroline, "Good grief. All I wanted were the numbers!"

I also got a bit of wrist slap. It was too soon to take Little Man completely off the insulin. Dr. Gandy had me continue giving it to him.

On Veteran's Day in November, a Monday, Little Man had done so well over the last few weeks that Dr. Gandy thought it was time to clean his teeth.

He had eaten so much canned food that, even though we really didn't have much choice about what to feed him, his teeth badly needed a cleaning. I took him in that morning and Caroline brought him home after work.

As soon as he saw me after I returned home, he did it again—plop, stretch, yawn—and got a whole bunch of Daddy-lovin'. He was doing great.

Two days later, on Wednesday evening, we were in the middle of our normal feeding routine. I gave him half his supper while I drew up a syringe with 0.25 units of insulin, which I planned to give him with the second half of his meal.

Suddenly, I thought I heard him playing with one of his toys on the other side of the bar in the kitchen. I basically ignored it and knew he would come running when I put the rest of his supper in his bowl on the floor. I continued to draw up his syringe, but the noise didn't stop. I walked around the bar and stopped dead in my tracks.

Little Man was having another seizure. It was nothing like the bad one he had on Labor Day, but the fact that he had another seizure at all was puzzling to say the least.

I grabbed my cell and called Dr. Gandy. Her line was busy. I called the number to the clinic. No answer. Everybody was busy with other clients.

Finally, I texted Dr. Gandy, "Little Man is having another seizure! What do I do?"

She immediately texted back, "Glucose on gums and bring him in."

Little Man and I arrived at the clinic moments later.

A quick check of his blood glucose showed his levels were fine. We had no idea what was happening. The only minor concern with his blood work showed his potassium was a little low, but that wouldn't cause seizures.

Dr. Gandy started Little Man on Phenobarbital, an anti-convulsive medication. It would take a couple of days to build up in his system, but in the meantime, she gave me some emergency medication to give him if his seizures continued. If that didn't work well enough, I was to take him back to the emergency vet clinic.

Around bedtime that night, he had another seizure. I gave him his emergency medication and he seemed to settle down.

Then at three-thirty the next morning, he had another one. That was enough to convince me he needed more help than I could provide at home. I gave him his emergency medication and loaded him up. We arrived at the ER about thirty minutes later.

The ER staff inserted a catheter into one of Little Man's his front legs and placed him on a fluid drip. He was there only that morning and up until about noon. By that time, the Phenobarbital had begun to take effect, and he had no more seizures. The ER doctor suggested I take him to Dr. Gandy before taking him home, and Dr. Gandy requested they leave the IV catheter in place, just in case.

When I arrived at Catisfaction, I met a relief veterinarian, Dr. Julie Tomlinson. She and Dr. Gandy met at vet school, and Dr. Tomlinson was pulling some duty at Catisfaction since Dr. Gandy had plans to leave the next day for a conference.

When Dr. Tomlinson walked into the lab, she was crying.

"What's the matter?" I asked.

She said, "I just had to do euthanasia. No matter how many you do, they never get easier."

Bless her heart. I don't know how much veterinarians make, but as far as I'm concerned, they're underpaid.

After a few minutes of chitchat, she checked Little Man.

"All right. I think he's ready to go home. Let's remove the catheter and he'll be ready to go," she said.

Unfortunately, the ER had used some tape to hold the catheter in place that was quite difficult to remove. We all knew Little Man wasn't going to like what had to be done. Someone suggested sedating him, but Dr. Tomlinson didn't like that idea.

"No. From what Dr. Gandy told me, Little Man has been sedated quite a bit lately already. I think I can get it off without too much trouble."

At first, Little Man seemed tolerant of the whole thing. But after a few tugs, he began to fight. With no other choice, Dr. Tomlinson snatched the tape off in one quick motion, but not fast enough for Little Man. He got her. Dr. Tomlinson became the third member of the Little Man Bite Club.

She grabbed some paper towels and held it to her fingers to stop the bleeding.

"You okay?" I asked.

"No worries. I have some stuff at home just for this purpose. I'll be fine."

What a trooper.

Just before I left, I asked Dr. Gandy about insulin. In all the excitement, I hadn't given him anything since the morning before. We did a quick check of his blood glucose—it was perfect. Dr. Gandy told me to just stop altogether.

Little Man's diabetes was in remission.

Still, we needed to find an answer. Seizures in dogs are apparently quite common, but seizures in cats are more rare. We were afraid whatever happened to Little Man on Labor Day might have caused some damage somewhere and that was what was causing more seizures.

After returning from her conference, Dr. Gandy spent several days inquiring on the phone. She finally decided the best thing to do was to take Little Man to her old stomping grounds at Mississippi State and have an MRI, or magnetic resonant image, done on his head to check for any brain abnormalities. She also wanted an ultrasound done on his belly to check for any growths or adrenal tumors in his midsection.

On November 28, Little Man and I hit the road to Starkville, Mississippi.

We arrived at about 11:00 AM at the Mississippi State College of Veterinary Medicine. They were expecting us, so shortly after we arrived they took Little Man to the laboratory while I waited in an examination room. While he was still in the laboratory, Dr. Jill Manion, one of the residents, walked in and introduced herself.

We hit it off. I liked her immediately. We talked at length about Little Man and what he had been through. Dr. Gandy had done many tests, and she sent me with copies of all of Little Man's records, so there wasn't much left to do except the ultrasound and MRI. Dr. Manion suggested we wait until they completed the ultrasound before scheduling the MRI. I agreed.

That afternoon, they sedated Little Man and started the ultrasound.

I texted Dr. Gandy: "In ultrasound."

They did not find one single thing wrong anywhere. Dr. Manion came to give me the news.

The subject quickly changed to the MRI. We agreed to meet with a neurologist the next day, November 29, and to schedule the MRI for the morning of November 30.

Then I got a bit of a scare. Dr. Manion explained the procedure. The MRI was not a concern. However, the necessity of a cerebral spinal fluid tap, or CSF, was a possibility, and that carried with it some serious risks. Anything from brain damage, to hemorrhaging, to infection could result. While it doesn't happen often, it does happen.

As we talked, I was having a hard time deciding what to do. I knew we needed to do everything we could to find whatever was wrong with Little Man. But at the same time I didn't want to risk causing more problems, or worse, especially since he had done so well up to that point, and against terrible odds.

After the meeting with Dr. Manion, I texted Dr. Gandy: "Nothing found on ultrasound but need to talk."

I called a few minutes later and explained everything I learned. We talked for a few minutes, and then I said, "I'm having a little bit of a problem."

"What's the matter?" she asked.

In most cases, my objectivity is not an issue. In fact, most of the time I'm objective to the point I appear uncaring, and it's gotten me into trouble on more than one occasion, especially with family members. But with Little Man, things were different.

"Well," I began, "I'm finding it extremely difficult to be objective when it comes to Little Man."

"I already told them that," Dr. Gandy said.

"What do you think of this CSF thing?" I asked.

"I'm not a neurologist, so it's hard for me to say. I don't like the risks, that's for sure. Did Dr. Manion say who would do it if it comes to that?"

"No."

"If it's Dr. Shores, he's good. But still, I guess I'm of the opinion they'll probably find something on the MRI. If they do, that should explain his seizures.

If they don't, well, again, I'm not a neurologist so I'm not sure of the benefits of the CSF. Based on what we know so far, I'm not sure it's worth the risk. Why don't we just forego the CSF?"

"Works for me," I said. "I'll let you know how the meeting with the neurologist goes tomorrow."

Poor Dr. Gandy. I'm sure on her list of favorite "kitty purrents," I'm only about two or three from the bottom. I actually said that to her once. She said, "Yeah, but at least it's only intermittent."

I knew I drove her nuts at times, but I couldn't help it. I didn't speak up in time and an innocent kitten died a horrible death. I didn't ask the right questions and Kitty died. I didn't know to ask anything at all and Daddy's move to intensive care was unnecessarily delayed.

I was not about to let the same things happen to Little Man.

By contrast, Mama refused to listen to two doctors and Jeff still has his finger. That was a good call in my book.

So I decided to follow some advice I once heard, which is, "Ask every question, and then question everything."

In my view, Little Man deserved no less.

The next day, Dr. Manion introduced me to a resident neurologist, Dr. Simon Kornberg. He too had taken a look at Little Man and felt that an MRI would likely show something. But in no time, the CSF tap came up.

"I'm not sure I'm comfortable with that, based on what Dr. Manion said to me yesterday," I told him.

He said, "Everything she said is true. There are certainly risks. However, in most cases if something goes wrong it's because the doctors were forced to go in blind, without an MRI. In Little Man's case, we will have done an MRI. In effect, we'll have a complete road map. We'll know right where to insert the needle, and how far to go. The risks should be minimized a great deal with the knowledge the MRI provides."

Then I remembered what Dr. Gandy asked me when I talked to her the day before. I asked, "If it needs to be done, who will do it?"

"Dr. Shores will do it. He's done hundreds … thousands of them."

I still wasn't sure what to do. I knew I had to decide. But it's *Little Man.*

I turned to Dr. Manion and asked, "Will you be back there with them when all this is going on tomorrow?"

"If you want me to be there, I'll be there," she said.

"Good," I said.

I turned back to Dr. Kornberg and asked, "Can I wait and decide this tomorrow?"

"Yes, you certainly can. Just keep in mind one thing. If we're going to do it, we need to do it immediately after the MRI. We don't want to subject him to the anesthesia any longer than we have to, and we certainly don't want to have to put him under again later."

After Dr. Kornberg left, Dr. Manion remained for a while. I think she knew I was nervous.

"So, tell me a little more about Little Man. And by the way, he's anything but little."

We both laughed. It really did put me at ease.

I went through the whole thing, about how Little Man got his name, how he was with me at home, and how he became a mascot.

"Wait a minute!" she said. "I think I've seen a patch like that. It's a cat on a missile, right?"

"You gotta be kiddin' me!" I said. "You've seen a patch of Little Man on a missile?"

"I think so. My husband is in the Air Force, and he wears it on his shoulder."

"Well then, you need to go home tonight and tell your husband you know the *real* Little Man!"

As it turned out, it wasn't Little Man on the patch Dr. Manion's husband wore on his shoulder, but the possibility certainly helped relieve some tension at the time.

The next day, Little Man and I arrived right on time at the imaging center for his MRI. I texted Dr. Gandy every step of the way. By that time, I was sure what I said to her the very first time we met had begun to haunt her. Yes, I was certain she was fully aware that Little Man was "my little boy," and I was driving her crazy.

When they came to take Little Man to the back I texted: "About to put him under."

Then a few minutes later I texted: "Doing MRI."

After the MRI, Dr. Kornberg came out to see me. "The MRI showed no abnormalities whatsoever."

"You mean there's no brain damage that you can see?"

"Everything appears perfectly normal," he said.

I had a feeling. Sure enough, he said, "We'd like to do the CSF."

I hesitated.

He continued, "I know you're worried about it, but look at it this way. There's nothing else to check. So far, no test or procedure has found anything wrong with Little Man. But if there is an imbalance of some sort in the chemistry of his cerebral fluid, it could explain this sudden outbreak of seizures and point us to the proper treatment."

I decided. I decided to pass the buck.

"Is Dr. Manion back there?" I asked, then continued, "If she thinks it's a good thing to do, then all right."

"I'll be right back," and he disappeared.

About a minute later, he came back.

"Dr. Manion said she's comfortable doing it."

I took a deep breath and said, "Okay."

Then as he was leaving I said, maybe a little more forcefully than I intended, "Dr. Kornberg?"

He stopped and turned to look at me.

I said, "Y'all take care of my Little Man."

He smiled and disappeared around the corner.

I just sat there for a minute or two. I thought, *Surely Little Man won't be forced to come this far only to be hurt by some dangerously invasive medical procedure.*

I grabbed my cell and texted Dr. Gandy: "MRI normal. No abnormalities. Doing CSF tap."

I gazed skyward, took a deep breath, and prayed, "God save Little Man!"

A few minutes later, a man walked through the waiting room, clearly in a hurry to get to another appointment, and headed straight for the door. Just as he reached the door, he stopped and looked at me. I guess it was obvious I was Little Man's nervous Daddy.

He said, "Little Man did just fine. He's waking up now."

"Thank you!" I said.

Then he turned and walked out. I found out later that he was Dr. Shores—the doctor who did Little Man's MRI and CSF tap.

I grabbed my cell and called Caroline to share the news. She was working at Catisfaction that day, and at the time she didn't have texting capabilities. Apparently, Dr. Gandy had shared my texts with her.

"We've been laughing at your texts. Well, not at what you said, just that you were sending them for *everything*. You'd have thought a family member was undergoing a life-threatening procedure or something."

"He was," I said.

Then I called Mama. "Everything's fine, Mama. Little Man has been checked from his nose to the tip of his tail, and they can't find a thing wrong with him."

"Good!" she said, "Now take that baby home, keep him out of the vet's office, and leave him the hell alone for a while!"

"Um, yes, sir! Ma'am! Sir!"

"'Cause if you mistreat that baby any more, I'm comin' to get him—understand?"

I sighed, "Yes, Mama."

"There now. I have spake," she said.

We both laughed.

Dr. Kornberg brought Little Man out a few minutes later, still very groggy from the anesthesia. But I knew he was fine.

Dr. Kornberg said, "Well, Little Man is ready to head home. He'll most likely sleep most of the way."

"Thanks, Dr. Kornberg, and be sure to tell Dr. Manion I said thanks, too."

"I will," he said, "and by the way, we expect the results of the CSF tap in a few days. If the results are normal, and I'm starting to suspect they will be, I suppose we'll just have to consider Little Man's seizures as being of unknown origin. That happens sometimes. It's frustrating. But the very good news is that we've just eliminated all kinds of bad things. I think he's going to be just fine. Keep on with the Phenobarbital as Dr. Gandy prescribed."

I put Little Man, still in his kennel and obviously feeling no pain whatsoever, in the front seat of the car. Everything else went into the trunk or back seat. I got in the car and just sat still for a minute or two as I looked at Little Man and watched him breathe. I couldn't believe it was finally over.

I leaned back in the seat, gazed my eyes skyward once again, and said, "Thank you, Lord."

Little Man on a visit to see my mother shortly after his recovery.

🐾   🐾   🐾

Three months to the day after that horrible Labor Day, I was awakened at 3:30 AM to the sound of a loud crash followed by bangs, thumps, and thuds.

"Little Man's having another seizure!" I yelled over at Caroline.

I jumped out of bed, ran to the living room, and threw on the light. I couldn't see him, but I could hear him on the hardwood floor at the far end of the couch.

I turned to run to the kitchen to get his emergency medication, thinking about the trip I was about to take to the emergency vet clinic, when suddenly Little Man flew out from behind the couch. He was chasing a broken piece of a Christmas decoration.

Scared the crap out of me.

I took a deep breath and relaxed, then said, "Little Man, you're going to be the death of me yet."

I scratched him behind his ears and went back to bed.

🐾 🐾 🐾

Over the next several weeks, I was awakened many times in the middle of the night by more of the same noises. Each time I thought Little Man was having a seizure only to find him straddling a toy when I went to investigate.

Each time, he gave me a look that said, "*What? I'm not doin' nothin'.*"

But try as I may, I couldn't seem to catch him in the act.

Around March 2013, Little Man went in for some routine blood work. Everything looked fine. His potassium was once again in the normal range, and his diabetes was still in remission even though his blood glucose jumped up occasionally. But there was also one surprise. The level of Phenobarbital in his system was below what is considered a therapeutic level, and Dr. Gandy didn't think it was doing anything for him. At the time, I thought the Phenobarbital was making him grouchy, so with those two considerations in mind, Dr. Gandy had me discontinue giving him that drug.

He went a few weeks with no issues. Then in April, I noticed his blood glucose had risen, and this time it didn't come back down. It happened slowly, but it was increasing. Eventually, I had to give him insulin injections again, but at levels which were a fraction of what they were before Labor Day.

Then one Wednesday night in May I got up to investigate more of the same noises to find Little Man in the middle of another seizure. I gave him his emergency medication, and it seemed to work for a while, but he wound up back at the ER.

When I got to the ER, I met one of their new doctors, Dr. Travis Wagner. He took over Little Man's care while he was there. He went out of his way to ensure Little Man was comfortable and under good care. He called me regularly, when I wasn't right there holding Little Man, and once was around noon the day after he had already worked a twelve-hour overnight shift. I was impressed.

Dr. Gandy was aware of every step. She said, "At least we know now that he's going to have to have some kind of anti-convulsive for the rest of his life."

"I was thinking that myself," I said.

She said, "But this time I want to try something different, something better for long term use. I'm going to try Zonisamide. It has to be compounded. The trouble is, it's a holiday weekend, and the pharmacy probably won't be able to get any of it to us until Tuesday. He's going to have to stay at the ER until that time."

That meant several nights, and I was there for almost every feeding. I gave Little Man his insulin and plenty of Daddy-lovin'. What made this visit different from before was that he was having seizures every few hours and needed care around the clock, which is not something he could get at Catisfaction.

At the emergency vet clinic waiting on Little Man's compounded medication.

On Sunday afternoon, while Little Man was still in the hospital waiting on his medication, Caroline and I went for a ride on our Harleys. On the way back, we stopped at the ER so I could feed Little Man and check on him.

He had an IV catheter in his front leg. Dr. Wagner used some strong, short-term medication to keep his seizures under control until the compounded medication arrived. I stood at the door to his kennel, held Little Man, and rocked him back and forth. He seemed to enjoy it.

Just then, one of the technicians, Traci, walked in. As soon as Little Man and Traci saw each other, they both perked up. To my surprise, Little Man even seemed to stretch his hind legs in her direction.

She walked straight to us and said, "There's my little coffee mate," and she immediately started rubbing his feet. Little Man loved it.

I looked at her, confused, and asked, "Coffee mate?"

She never took her eyes off Little Man and said, "Every morning at about two o'clock we sit together and have coffee. Little Man sits in my lap while I rub his feet, and in between his toes … yes … everybody needs a little TLC sometimes … yes … don't they, Little Man?"

She continued to rub Little Man's toes for a while, and then said, "You know? I've never been a cat person, but Little Man is about to make me change my mind."

That definitely put me at ease. I felt secure knowing Little Man had a fantastic doctor and a caring technician in his corner while at the ER and away from Daddy.

Shortly thereafter, Little Man's new medication arrived at Catisfaction. I ran out there and picked it up, then headed to the ER. Dr. Gandy's instructions were that he needed to be on the new medication, and off the IV solution, for at least twenty-four hours with no seizure activity before he could come home.

When I spoke to Dr. Wagner about all that, he said, "Sounds like a good plan to me. I'll order the IV stopped a few hours after his first dose of Zonisamide. We'll monitor him closely. As long as everything goes as planned, and I think they will, you'll be taking him home tomorrow afternoon. By that time he'll have had at least three doses and should be fine."

Everything went well. I took Little Man home the following afternoon. The Zonisamide worked perfectly. In no time, he was back to his playful ways, but still had the grouchies on occasion.

Caroline had something to say about that.

"That's because he's got brain damage. He's a BDK: a brain-damaged kitty," she said, just to get on my nerves.

"Stop that!" I said.

"BDK! BDK! Come here, BDK!" she continued.

"I said stop that!"

Then to Little Man I said, petting him, "Him don't got no brain damage, no him don't."

"*Don't got no?* Is that what you just said? *Don't got no?* Good grief, Jonny, you've got a master's degree for Pete's sake. Why do you talk like that?" she asked.

I answered, matter-of-factly, "Little Man understands me."

More eye rolls.

CHAPTER 21 –
ALIVE AND WELL

One morning in June, my alarm went off at 5:10 AM as usual. I reached over and shut it off, and then leaned back to steal just one more minute of rest before starting the day. However, that's not what Little Man had in mind.

He walked over to my side, stood on his hind legs, put his paws up on the edge of the bed, looked me square in the face, and meowed, "*It's time!*"

Gotta love him.

One night that summer, I was awakened again in the wee hours of the morning by more bangs, thumps, and thuds. I got up to investigate as usual, just in case, but I was confident Little Man was probably not having a seizure. I was correct.

This time, I finally caught him in the act.

Instead of just walking straight into the living room, I moved as quietly as I could because I didn't want him to know I was there. I didn't have to turn on any lights since I had developed the habit of leaving a lamp on just for this purpose. I crept to the doorway and peeked around the corner.

Little Man stood in the middle of the rug on the floor in the living room. The rug was smaller than the living room, and all around the rug's edges were spaces about two to three feet wide of nothing but hardwood flooring all the way to the wall. There was a toy on the floor directly in front of him, but he wasn't looking at it.

Suddenly, Little Man raised his left front leg like a golf club and swatted the toy all the way across the floor. He took off after it at a dead run. When he reached the edge of the rug, he slid across the hardwood floor and banged into the wall. I realized that was the source of all those thumps and thuds.

The toy's trajectory had ended and it was just lying there—ready for the kill. Little Man attacked the toy with all his might. He grabbed it in his mouth and, lying on his side, held it between his legs and kicked and kicked until he was sure it was dead. After "killing" it, he rested for a moment, then got up, gingerly picked the toy up in his mouth, and walked slowly back to the center of the rug where he dropped it on the floor. But instead of swatting at it immediately, he simply stood over it and looked away, as though daring the toy to try to make a run for it.

Then without warning, he swung the golf club and started the process all over again.

I watched him do this a couple times, smiled, then turned to walk back to bed.

I stopped.

I stepped back a couple of steps and again peeked around the corner.

I watched Little Man play for a while longer and found myself looking at him with a sense of awe. He was on no medication other than his insulin and his anti-convulsive, a far cry from the dozen or so he took since that terrible Labor Day months earlier. I remembered something Dr. Gandy said, something that, as I watched Little Man play, seemed to make the scene just that much more remarkable.

In Dr. Gandy's own words, at his lowest point Little Man was, "circling the drain and could have died at any minute."

Yet, here he was, playing like there's no tomorrow. This little creature, tiny by human standards, had looked death square in the face. But with the help of God, an incredibly dedicated veterinarian, maybe a little help from me, and a whole lot of his own effort, my Little Man emerged victorious.

Wow. He sure is a mighty little thing.

🐾　　🐾　　🐾

One day while Little Man and I were in our room, I decided to go through some boxes in the closet. One box has several keepsakes in it, and as I pulled things out I came across Little Man's little stuffed cat toy with the superhero cape on it. Unfortunately, the full-sized cape I once had for him was long gone.

Little Man was on the floor right next to me. He sniffed at this and sniffed at that, and I reached over to pet him. As I did so, I thought about everything he had experienced and how he had put up such a mighty effort to pull through. I realized he needed a new cape; after all, he was a mascot and …

Yes. Things are different now. With everything that's happened over the last few years, it's as though Little Man were a real-life, no-kidding, superhero in his own right.

I pondered that for a while and considered some extraordinary things:

He's very protective; he defended Caroline against Tiger, and possibly even scared off an intruder.

He's always trying to warn us of trouble; he tried to let us know about the security system malfunction.

He displays almost human characteristics at times; he tried to let me know I was "doing it wrong" as I put stickers on Caroline's motorcycle.

He's certainly the king of all our cats.

And of course, most impressively, he fought death on several fronts—the poisoning, the tongue depressor sliver, and the issue with his bladder, not to mention the scary CSF tap—and won.

As I considered all of that, I knew what he needed. He needed a new cape, maybe even his own logo, and he needed a new, superhero name.

"What do you think, Little Man?" I asked him.

He looked up at me, and as he did so, the answer became clear. In fact, it was right there—on his forehead.

I looked at the "**M**" on his head and said, "That's it, Little Man! You're the *Mighty Little Man!*"

Now he has his own superhero name, his own cape, and even his own logo. I also had a miniature cape made to replace the one on his little stuffed cat toy.

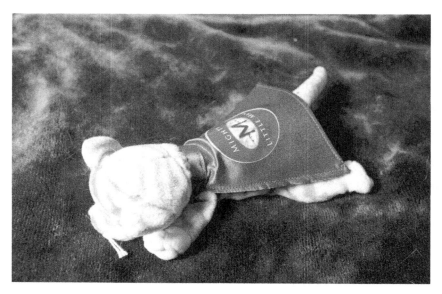

The Mighty Little Man cat toy. This is one of the original stuffed cats used by my military unit but with Little Man's new cape and logo.

But as awesome as all that sounds, there is something else even more amazing. Through all my fear and doubt, I prayed like I'd never prayed before, and God answered my prayers.

"The proof is in the pudding," as they say, and the proof is right here with me.

He's here because of only one truth.

God saved Little Man.

One evening, as Little Man and I cuddled in our recliner, we just relaxed and watched television. I sipped a shot glass of whiskey as I pet him. Little Man was on his pillowcase to my left. He faced away from me with his back along my waist and left thigh and his head at my knee. My left arm draped over him and rested on the seat between him and the arm of the recliner. All was well.

Suddenly, Little Man stretched and yawned, then reached out and wrapped both front legs around my left arm. He forcefully pulled my arm toward him, buried his face in my hand, and with a mighty squeeze pressed his nose into my palm. He held the squeeze for a few seconds, relaxed, and then gave my palm a little lick with his face still smashed into my hand. He took a deep breath and sighed.

It was as if he were trying to say, "*Thank you, Daddy*."

I could not help but smile.

I dared not even wiggle a finger on my left hand. I reached across both of us with my right hand and picked up the remote. I turned off the television and then placed the remote on the tiny end table at the left of the recliner.

The room was then almost completely dark, lit only by the tiny bulb in the small lamp on the end table. It was so quiet even the barely audible sound of the heat pump seemed deafening.

Now this, I thought, *this is peace.*

Like the peace of a heavy snowfall on a windless, winter day, where the sheer volume of flakes muffles all sound into silence, and the air itself appears frosty gray.

Like the peace of a warm, summer night spent in a rocking chair on the front porch of a house in the country, where the only light is from occasional "lightening bugs" which mimic the twinkle of the stars in a cloudless, black sky.

Ah, yes, the peace of a sleeping cat. Indeed, there is nothing on this earth more peaceful than a sleeping, purring cat.

I began to look around the room. Although everything was in shadow and barely visible, I knew what was there.

I started with the model train track going all the way around the room. It's mounted on shelving a mere foot from the ceiling. We run it during football games. Little Man even has his own, cat-sized, football jersey. After every score, we run a victory lap with the train and toot the horn. The image of Little Man's paw prints in the garage came to mind, and another smile came across my face.

To our left was the larger of two display cases containing my action figure collection, and next to that my framed diplomas and certificate from Jump School.

In front, the television Caroline bought for "us" is mounted on the wall above the cabinet that once held the GI Joe Jeep I thought Caroline destroyed. I put it back in its box months earlier for safekeeping. On the cabinet are the only two Barbie dolls I allowed in our room, and only because they're wearing *Star Trek* uniforms. On each side of the cabinet are two pictures: one of Pop to the left and one of Daddy to the right. God bless their souls.

On top of another cabinet to our right is a one-sixth scale mockup of the flag raising on the island of Iwo Jima during World War II, and directly above it is a shadow box with a vintage M-1 Garand rifle mounted inside, just like the one my step-grandfather carried as a paratrooper during the war. The smaller of the two display cases stands in the center of the wall between two cabinets and contains one of every color of my action figure display boxes, each one loaded to the gills with GI Joe accessories. To the right of the display case is another cabinet with some knickknacks on top, including an album with photos of the 'Cuda restoration from start to finish. Above that cabinet is another shadow box with Daddy's matching Winchester rifles. In the corners of the wall are two flags, Old Glory and the Alabama State Flag.

Behind us on the wall in the center is the shadow box with my wings and medals from my service in the US Air Force, and directly underneath that is a certificate of retirement signed by none other than President George W. Bush. Photos and plaques cover the remainder of the wall. There are graduation certificates, photos of Moe and me in "our" CF-18 aircraft, and going-away gifts from various people with whom I served over the years. There is also a model of the CF-18 on which Moe and I had our names painted. There are only two in existence. Moe has one. I have the other.

Lastly, I looked at the frame containing all the space shuttle mission patches Rex sent me. The patch he flew aboard *Atlantis* is at the top center. Below it are in-space photos of each of our astronaut classmates surrounding the photo of our TPS class. At the very bottom of the frame, beneath the photo of Rex on one of his spacewalks, is a plaque with the words I sent to Bloomer via email at liftoff the night of his first space flight.

Although I couldn't read the words on the plaque in the dimmed light of the room, I know them by heart even though I originally wrote them years earlier:

SPACE.

THAT PLACE WHEREIN LIES ALL THAT EXISTS. TO THOSE FORTUNATE FEW CHOSEN TO EXPLORE ITS VASTNESS— GO. GO TOWARD THE UNKNOWN, AND SEEK TO MAKE IT KNOWN. GO, SO THAT ONE DAY, OTHERS MAY FOLLOW. AND, ON OCCASION, FROM SOMEWHERE OUT THERE, PAUSE, GAZE IN HOME'S DIRECTION, AND REMEMBER. REMEMBER THOSE WHOSE THOUGHTS AND PRAYERS ACCOMPANY YOU. GIVE THEM A SMILE, AND PERHAPS, A WAVE. AND THEN, HAVING DONE SO, TURN BACK TOWARD THE HEAVENS. TURN BACK TOWARD THE UNKNOWN. TURN BACK TOWARD THE GREAT EXPANSE OF SPACE—

AND GO.

As I recited these words in my mind and looked at the picture of Rex, I noticed something about his picture I hadn't seen before. I couldn't believe that after all the time and effort spent designing and building that display, it had been there all along and right in front of me. I just never made the connection between the picture and the words.

Rex is smiling. And he's waving. It couldn't have turned out better if I had planned it that way.

I reached over with my right hand, picked up my shot glass, and turned my head to face the frame. I raised my glass and quietly toasted, "to those fortunate few."

I emptied the glass, put it back on the end table, and leaned back in our recliner. As I sat there a little longer enjoying the peace and quiet, I could feel the heat from Little Man next to my thigh. I gently stroked his fur with my right hand, and he purred in response. I smiled again.

Then I remembered a day from months earlier, the day I walked into this room while Little Man was in the hospital and at death's door. I remembered the hopelessness I felt, the powerless, desperate need to *do* something, *anything*, to help my Little Man. But all I could do was pray.

So pray I did.

Things suddenly fell into the proper perspective. In this room and on these walls are some of my most prized possessions and evidence of a lifetime's achievements. Yet, as I sat in "our" room reminiscing on the time Little Man and I spent together there over the last several years, I realized that the single, most important thing in the room to me—and the only thing that will be with me again one day after I'm gone—was right there next to me.

God had indeed answered my prayers.

I gazed up toward the ceiling. My eyes caught a glimpse of yet one more photograph I taped up there. It's a picture of Moe and me in "our" CF-18 as we were engaged in an air-to-air refueling operation. We were connected to a tanker aircraft via a refueling hose. The picture was taken from underneath us as we "*put out [our] hand[s] and touched the face of God.*"[1]

I closed my eyes and said, "Thank you, God."

I opened my eyes and leaned over to Little Man with my face as close to his as I could get without disturbing him. I looked at him for a moment, and then very quietly said, in barely even a whisper, "And thank you, Little Man. Thank *you*."

---

1 From the poem, *High Flight*, by John Gillespie Magee, Jr.

EPILOGUE

In March 2014, eighteen months after Little Man's terrible ordeal, my step-grandfather, Airborne, passed away. He was eighty-nine years old. Maw Maw, at ninety-five, is still here. She was with all of us at Airborne's military funeral. Soon after, what he did in the service of his country was a topic for discussion amongst all of us. To my surprise, I was given a tremendous honor. After they discussed things amongst themselves, Maw Maw, my uncle, my cousin Sonny, and my stepmother Jean, all decided that I, as the only family member of my generation to serve a career in the military, should receive Airborne's very special memorabilia. This included his original jump wings, his sterling silver identification bracelet that he wore in combat during the Battle of the Bulge, the United States Flag that was presented to Maw Maw at his funeral, and lastly, his Purple Heart. To say I was touched is the understatement of the century.

But we cannot dismiss the efforts of another family member during that war. Maw Maw also had a part to play, and I never knew about any of it until very recently.

She was a "Rosie the Riveter." She was one of the women who took jobs in factories building military weapons and equipment to free up the men so they could fight in the war overseas. Her job, however, did not involve "riveting." She was more involved in avionics: she built and installed instrumentation and other equipment in B-24, B-29, and most notably, P-38 aircraft.

In April of 1943, the US Navy intercepted and decoded Japanese messages in which the itinerary of Isoruku Yamamoto, the architect and commander-in-chief of the Japanese attack on Pearl Harbor, was spelled out in detail. President Roosevelt's orders were simple: "Get Yamamoto." A squadron of P-38 aircraft was assigned the task, and they were outfitted with additional equipment, some of which included larger weaponry: fifty-caliber machine guns.

On April 18, 1943, just as he was returning from an inspection tour which he had hoped would improve the morale of the Japanese after they experienced disaster at Guadalcanal, Yamamoto's flight was intercepted and shot down. They found him later, still in his seat. He had taken two rounds from a fifty-cal.

Maw Maw mounted the "Fifties" on those planes.

∴   ∴   ∴

Neither Caroline nor Matt are employed at Catisfaction Cat Clinic any longer. With her full-time job at the Harley place, Caroline could take only so much of working seven days a week. Matt lasted the longest and left not long before his high school graduation. I get calls every now and then from someone at Catisfaction asking if I can replace a doorknob or something, and I'm happy to do it. They know all they have to do is ask.

Of course, Dr. Gandy and her staff most certainly still provide veterinary care for our cats, so we see her regularly. In fact, during a routine check-up for Little Man just weeks before I sent this book to the publisher, Dr. Gandy's husband, Chris, snapped the only photograph I have of the three of us together:

Jonny, Little Man, and Dr. Gandy.

I recently gave Rex a call. I hadn't seen or spoken with him for some time, and I wanted to bring him up to speed on the status of this book. As we spoke, I remembered to tell him about Little Man's reaction when I showed him the patch after I brought it home, and I finally asked, "So, how *does* the space shuttle smell?"

Rex was not at all surprised at Little Man's interest in the patch. In fact, he told me the space shuttle *does* have a very distinctive smell. He said it smells like a "clean-room" in a hospital, which is at least partially due to the special soaps and cleaners used by the astronauts while in space. Apparently, everything aboard the shuttle that comes back from a mission in space has that same smell.

Wow. I guess Little Man really does know how the space shuttle smells!

As for Little Man, he is twelve years old now and going strong. I know that at some point he will pass on, and I hope my loved ones will understand something once he's gone: when they see me sitting quietly in thought during my retirement years, it's possible I will be thinking of any of a great number of things, from the good ol' days of flying, to driving the 'Cuda, to our wonderful honeymoon in Hawaii, or any of the many other incredible events of our lives. But mostly, I hope they understand that any silence on my part will never be because I purposely intend to ignore them. No. Most likely, I'll be thinking about Little Man.

But for now, I will just revel in the fact that he is still here. I am fully aware that I am tremendously blessed. I have a wonderful family, awesome friends, and incredible memories and experiences about which most people can only dream. And I thank God for all of it—and for every second of the blessing of Little Man.

Although we never determined with certainty the cause of Little Man's affliction on that dreadful Labor Day, we did find another clue.

About eight months after his ordeal, I was at the shop, I mean "work," building my action figure display boxes, when I realized my pistol permit was about to expire. I drove over to the sheriff's office to renew it. On the way, I remembered the sheriff had not contacted me since I called to share my suspicions, so I asked to see him while I was there.

He remembered our discussion from months earlier and did what he said he would do. He checked out the man who came to our home that dreadful day.

His exact words were, "Well, there's nothing we can do about it now, but he's a dope-head."

I found that very interesting. Though I never suggested that the man who came to the house that Labor Day intentionally poisoned Little Man, the news that he was a drug user seemed to add credibility to the possibility that he may have dropped something accidentally while he was in the house. Unfortunately, none of this came to light until long after the fact, and I never saw that man again since he never came back to take care of the shingles as he promised.

I must admit that it is possible the man had nothing to do with any of it. It is possible that what I found under the dining room table was just what I thought it was at the time: a piece of cat litter. It is possible it was a Black Widow, just as Dr. Gandy originally suggested.

However, it is not *impossible* that everything I suspected is true. We may never find the answer. All we have right now is a theory that happens to fit the facts, and unfortunately, it will likely never be anything more than that—just a theory.

Whatever it was, Little Man recovered anyway.

Thanks be to God.

Little Man certainly has no problem with his hind legs now!

Little Man in his other favorite chair—feelin' no pain, that's for sure.

When Mommy isn't looking ...

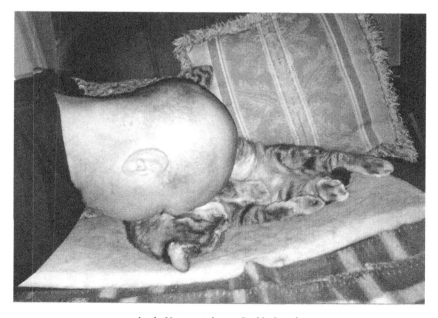

Little Man gettin' some Daddy-lovin'.

More cuddle time with Daddy in our recliner.

Mighty Little Man.

SOME FINAL THOUGHTS

I know I am very fortunate in that Little Man's story ends on a happy note. But I also know there are many people whose pets' stories end differently—and very painfully. While my purpose here is to share some thoughts with all pet owners and animal lovers, this last chapter and the short story told within it are intended particularly for those people who have lost a beloved pet.

Little Man had one other bout with seizures a few months after we started him on the Zonisamide. I was unable to control them with his emergency medication, so back to the ER he went. He was there for only a little while, and as before, we had to wait for additional medication to build up in his system. He wound up back on the Phenobarbital, and the good news is that he has had no seizures since then.

Before I brought Little Man home again, I arrived at the emergency vet clinic one evening to feed him and give him his meds. As soon as I walked in, I realized what was happening. An older couple was there saying goodbye to their beloved pet, a dog.

Almost immediately, I felt as though I had intruded upon a very tender, private moment, but I simply could not bring myself to leave. Rather than stare, I turned my attention to Little Man. I opened the door to his kennel and sat on the floor with my back to the painful scene, but I could hear every word. The veterinarian in charge of the dog's care explained to the couple that there was simply nothing more that could be done and that the only option was to put the dog to sleep.

As I sat there listening and petting Little Man, I could hear the wails and sobs of both of them as they earnestly and repeatedly said over and over again, "We're so sorry," and, "We love you." They hugged and cried all over their fur-baby.

I found myself wondering, *Why do people do that?*

I knew, of course, that they are not alone. I did the very same thing when Buttercup was put down. But why?

Suddenly, from my unique perspective of being able to observe the event without feeling quite the same level of emotion, I realized the answer; it's because we all desperately want to know that our pets know just how much they are loved. It's also because we hate the thought of even the slightest possibility that creatures so loved could pass into oblivion as though they never existed.

After it was over and the dog was finally at peace, the couple stepped outside. I followed. I knew what had to be said.

Once we were outside, the man walked away while the woman waited behind. I asked if I could share something with her, and she nodded. After I spoke, she looked at me for a moment, and then with tears streaming down her face, she reached up, wrapped both arms around my neck, and said, "Thank you so much."

Afterward, I turned and walked back into the clinic to feed Little Man while the ER staff prepared the dog's body for burial. Later as I walked to my truck to leave, I saw the couple sitting in their truck. The dog's body had been wrapped in a box and was lying in the truck's bed. The man motioned me over.

With tears in his eyes and a quivering voice, he asked only one question, softly, "How do you know?"

The simple truth is that the Bible provides no direct answer to this question. Attempts to answer this question through research reveal opinions of various scholars, religious leaders, and commentators that are as varied as the number of articles found. The best answer I can find from these articles is no better than a definite "maybe." The number of articles with opposing conclusions leads only to more confusion. Because of this, we are left with our own devices in our efforts to answer this question for ourselves.

Fortunately, I had already researched this for myself.

For my research, I used two sources: the King James Version of the Holy Bible and *The New Strong's Exhaustive Concordance of the Bible*[2]. Strong's concordance

---

2 Strong, James, LL.D., S.T.D. *The New Strong's Exhaustive Concordance of the Bible*. Nashville, Tennessee: Thomas Nelson, 1996.

includes every English word in the Bible and the corresponding Old Testament Hebrew or New Testament Greek word from which it was translated.

The difficulty in answering this question is due partly to the confusion resulting from attempts to define the words *soul* and *spirit*, among others. Even modern dictionaries provide definitions in terms of each other, and in many cases of modern usage, they are used interchangeably. However, a study of Scripture with regard to the soul and spirit of man and beast and an understanding of how these terms are used in Scripture are more important than any definitions conceived by man.

Consider the following verses from the King James Version of the Holy Bible in reference to the word *spirit*:

> And the earth was without form, and void; and darkness was upon the face of the deep. And the **Spirit** of God moved upon the face of the waters. (Gen. 1:2)

> For that which befalleth the sons of men befalleth beasts; even one thing befalleth them: as the one dieth, so dieth the other; yea, they have all one **breath**; so that a man hath no pre-eminence above a beast: for all is vanity. (Eccl. 3:19)

In the first verse above, Moses refers to "the **Spirit** of God." In the second verse, King Solomon refers to both man and animals and states, "they have all one **breath**." The words in bold font, *Spirit* from the first verse and **breath** from the second, were both translated into English from the same Hebrew word, **ruwach**. Therefore, the Bible provides clear evidence that both man and animals have a spirit.

Now consider these verses in reference to the word *soul*:

> And the Lord God formed man of the dust of the ground, and breathed into his nostrils the breath of life; and man became a living **soul**. (Gen. 2:7)

> And out of the ground the Lord God formed every beast of the field, and every fowl of the air; and brought them unto Adam to see what he would call them: and whatsoever Adam called every living **creature**, that was the name thereof. (Gen. 2:19)

In the first verse above, Moses states, "and man became a living **soul**." In the second verse, he refers to animals as "every living **creature**." However, the words in bold font, **soul** from the first verse and **creature** from the second, were both translated from the same Hebrew word, **nephesh**. Therefore, the Bible provides clear evidence that both man and animals were created from the dust of the earth and are souls.

God tells us more through the Bible, however. Consider the following verse from Ecclesiastes:

> *Then shall the dust return to the earth as it was: and the **spirit** shall return unto God who gave it.* (Eccl. 12:7)

In this verse, King Solomon tells us that the *spirit*, or **ruwach**, "shall return unto God who gave it" after the death of the body. No distinction is made between the spirit of man and the spirit of an animal.

In yet another verse regarding the Great Flood, God said something very interesting:

> *And I will remember my **covenant**, which is **between me and you and every living creature of all flesh**; and the waters shall no more become a flood to destroy all flesh.* (Gen. 9:15)

Note that God made no such promise to the earth, to the trees, or to the grass. He made this promise only to every living **creature** (soul), or in Hebrew once again, **nephesh**, and lumped both man and the animals into the same category as worthy of such a promise.

Based upon this brief word study of the use of these words in Scripture, no matter how we define the terms *soul* and *spirit* with regard to man or beast, it is apparent that whatever man is, the animals are also.

But in other ways, there are differences, of course. Some would correctly point out that man was created "in the image of God" and given "dominion" over the animals. While there has been much debate over the true meaning of these concepts, to me they point to one simple truth: only man was given a moral choice.

Unfortunately, man chose the sinful path. But with no such choice available to them, animals are therefore completely blameless—without sin.

Why then would God seem to put aside his concern for sinless animals in favor of sinful man? Jesus Himself gave us the answer with the parable of the lost sheep:

> *4What man of you, having a hundred sheep, if he lose one of them, doth not leave the ninety and nine in the wilderness, and go after that which is lost, until he find it? 5And when he hath found it, he layeth it on his shoulders, rejoicing. 6And when he cometh home, he calleth together his friends and neighbors, saying unto them, Rejoice with me; for I have found my sheep which was lost. 7I say unto you, that likewise joy shall be in heaven over one sinner that repenteth, more than over ninety and nine just persons, which need no repentance.* (Luke 15: 4-7)

In this parable, the lost sheep represents mankind, and Jesus is the shepherd. Here, the shepherd (Jesus) has put aside his concern for the ninety and nine who were not lost (like the animals) in favor of the one who was lost (all of mankind). To God, mankind is lost and in need of salvation. Animals are not.

But are there really animals in heaven? The prophet Isaiah described the state of the earth during the Millennial Kingdom of Jesus Christ in this way:

> *6The wolf also shall dwell with the lamb, and the leopard shall lie down with the kid; and the calf and the young lion and the fatling together; and a little child shall lead them. 7And the cow and the bear shall feed; their young ones shall lie down together: and the lion shall eat straw like the ox. 8And the sucking child shall play on the hole of the asp, and the weaned child shall put his hand on the cockatrice' den.* (Is. 11:6-8)

But perhaps even more telling is this passage by the Apostle John:

And I saw heaven opened, and behold a white horse; and he that sat upon him was called Faithful and True, and in righteousness he doth judge and make war. (Rev. 19:11)

These are but a few examples, but the evidence seems clear. While I found much evidence to suggest that our pets *will* go to heaven, I found no evidence to suggest that they won't. It was because of this that I was able to speak to that couple at the veterinary ER with confidence—and faith.

The message I shared with that woman when we stepped outside is what I wish to share with anyone and everyone who has ever lost a beloved pet.

My message to her was, "Rest assured, my friends, and have no fear. Your Abby is with God now."

In the Prologue to this book, I made the following statement about animals: "I may never really know why I feel the way I do." I think now, however, I should retract that statement. I think I *do* know why I feel as I do about animals. It's because I realize now that they *are* without sin. They are closer to God's intent for man and beast than any other living creature, save One: the Son of the living God, Jesus Christ. As such, I am confident their fate is secure and that God will accept them all into His loving arms when they experience that of which they are completely unworthy: death.

I have faith that one day I will come face-to-face with Jesus in heaven. I will once again see my family and friends who passed on before me, and all my animal friends will be there also.

Someone else is there, too. Right now in heaven, there is a little, unnamed kitten with wispy, gray fur. Oh, how I look forward to seeing her again! She's been there for quite some time now, but to her it probably seems like no time at all.

I have something for her.

If she could hear and understand me right now, just this once, I would say to her:

"There is nothing I can do,
There is nothing I can say,
To atone for your demise
On that horrid, horrid day.

For I was not strong,
But weak of will,
And could not help
When I saw your blood spill,

As the life given you,
By the power of God,
Stained the ground red,
And wet the soft, green sod.

Your soul and spirit forever lost
To those who cherished and knew
The innocence of your sweet way
And your beauty which never grew?

Of me now you have no need,
Though I hope you stand in wait,
For me to come to you one day,
As I pass through heaven's gate.

Though I have no single, mere thing
That you need me to provide
Over all the things which you now have
From God with whom you reside,

I do have but one small gift:
I've a promise to fulfill.
With one last thing for you I'll come ...

And bring your name I will."

Oh yes, she is there, in His arms … and she is waiting for me.

One day, I will even have the opportunity to introduce her to Little Man. I will walk up to her with Little Man by my side and say, "Hey, baby girl, this is Little Man. Little Man, say hello to …."

Just not yet.

Let everything that hath breath praise the LORD.

Psalm 150:6

In His Arms.

To order your own, full-color print of
In His Arms by Carole Forêt,
or to learn more about Mighty Little Man, visit
www.mightylittleman.com.

ACKNOWLEDGMENTS

As I learned very quickly while writing this book, such an endeavor is not a one-person effort, especially for this work of non-fiction. The people, animals, places, and events are all real. Every person mentioned by name gave me their permission to do so. Several also helped by proof-reading some or all of the manuscript or by talking with me over the telephone, and their constructive criticism is greatly appreciated. I would also like to thank my editor, Judy Beatty, especially for her kind words of encouragement.

I also wish to thank Carole Forêt, the artist who painted *In His Arms*. With only a verbal description of what I wanted, she created nothing less than a masterpiece. She met every little change request with a smile and a positive attitude. And I will never forget the unveiling—on the concrete steps of a car dealership where we met at the last minute for delivery and acceptance of the painting!

But there are some who deserve special thanks for their roles during Little Man's many trials.

I would first like to thank my wife, Caroline. Not only did she take a back seat to Little Man throughout his ordeal, but then again while I wrote this book, and still more as I continue caring for him. I could not have done everything I needed to do without her picking up the slack—for everything.

My mother, Karen, deserves thanks as well. After all, she is to be credited with giving me the intense desire to love and care for animals. In fact, every time I find myself in a quandary over an animal, I always say the same thing to her, and she always responds the same way. I'll say to her, "Mama, it's all your fault," to which she always responds, "I know."

I wish to thank Jennifer Wagner, DVM, and the other veterinarians, technicians, and staff at VCA 80 Dodge Animal Hospital in Omaha, Nebraska, not only for their excellent care of Little Man while he was a patient there, but also for the support they continue to provide. Little Man and I have not been to their clinic for several years, yet they continue to respond to every email and answer every telephone call. Their efforts and cooperation are greatly appreciated.

I wish to thank Andy Shores, DVM, MS, PhD, Diplomate ACVIM (Neurology); Simon Kornberg, BVSc; Jill Manion, DVM, MSC; and the technicians and staff at the Mississippi State University College of Veterinary Medicine in Starkville, Mississippi, for their extraordinary care of Little Man—and his nervous Daddy. They went out of their way to make us *both* comfortable.

I wish to thank Travis Wagner, DVM; Stephanie Vaught, DVM; Katha Kennebrew, DVM; and the many technicians and staff at the Veterinary Regional Referral Hospital in Decatur, Alabama, for their efforts to keep Little Man comfortable while in their care and for allowing me to be with him as I saw fit. Even now, whenever I have an after-hours question about Little Man, they are always there to respond to my call, which certainly puts my mind at ease.

Lastly, I wish to thank Stephanie Gandy Murphy, DVM; her relief veterinarian, Julie Tomlinson, DVM; and the many technicians and staff at Catisfaction Cat Clinic in Madison, Alabama. If there is anything about this story that was left understated, it is that I really did drive them all nuts over Little Man's care. However, there is one thing about which I have no doubt whatsoever: if I had called anyone else on that fateful Labor Day other than Dr. Gandy, Little Man would not have survived. From late night phone calls to (very) early morning text messages, she was there and then some, and always when it counted. I am convinced she was the instrument through whom God worked to save my Little Man. For that, I am eternally grateful.

Made in the USA
Columbia, SC
25 October 2018